The Social Psychology of the Classroom

Routledge Research in Education

The Social Psychology of the Classroom

Elisha Babad

Anna Lazarus Professor of Social
and Educational Psychology

School of Education, Hebrew University of Jerusalem

Routledge
Taylor & Francis Group

New York   London

First published 2009
by Routledge
270 Madison Ave, New York, NY 10016

Simultaneously published in the UK
by Routledge
2 Park Square, Milton Park, Abingdon, Oxon OX14 4RN

Routledge is an imprint of the Taylor & Francis Group, an informa business

© 2009 Taylor & Francis

Typeset in Sabon by IBT Global.
Printed and bound in the United States of America on acid-free paper by IBT Global.

Library of Congress Cataloging in Publication Data
Babad, Elisha.
  The social psychology of the classroom / by Elisha Babad.
    p. cm.
  Includes bibliographical references and index.
  1. Classroom management—Social aspects.   2. Teacher-student relationships—
Psychological aspects.   I. Title.
  LB3013.B23 2009
  371.102'4019—dc22
  2009007146

ISBN10: 0-415-99929-4 (hbk)
ISBN10: 0-203-87247-9 (ebk)

ISBN13: 978-0-415-99929-8 (hbk)
ISBN13: 978-0-203-87247-5 (ebk)

Contents

PART IV:
Classroom Management

PART V:
Nonverbal Behavior in the Classroom

PART VI:
Educating and Changing Students

Preface

This is a book about teachers, about students, and about the social psychology of their life and their interactions in the classroom. The book is intended for teachers, for teacher education students (future teachers), for psychologists, counselors and educators, and for a general readership interested in the meeting point of psychology and education and in the application of social psychology to the complex and vibrant "society" of the classroom. When one sets out to write an academic book and target it for defined audiences, one must make decisions about the book's character and style—what it would be like and what it would *not,* what should be included and what should not, how to present and how not to present the materials.

This book was written as "a practical book." A practical book differs from "scholarly books" (the latter are conceptually-driven, presenting all theory, research and methodological issues on a given domain, and intended for a narrow, specialized readership of scholars and researchers). It differs from "comprehensive textbooks" in educational psychology or in social psychology (that are very long and detailed, covering all knowledge in numerous relevant areas, and designed to shift from one area to another every week or two in introductory courses). It also differs from "how-to books" (that provide popular sets of advice and applied cookbook guidance how exactly one should conduct oneself in order to be successful). A practical book should be concise and focused on a well-defined domain. It should encapsulate the relevant knowledge and access it to readers so that they can process it and draw the applied implications for their own conduct.

Teachers in many institutions complain that their training does not provide them with sufficient working knowledge and understanding of underlying social forces and processes in their classrooms (in the student "society" and in teacher–student interaction). Most textbooks in educational psychology and in social psychology of education are too general and cover many domains and areas, and their treatment of the social psychology of the classroom is very limited. Books on classroom management (CM) are more relevant in their classroom-focus and orientation toward teachers, but most of them have two major drawbacks: First, they tend to be too prescriptive and preachy in advocating one ideological image of effective CM to a negation of alternative potential styles and a tendentious and exclusive coverage of relevant conceptions and research. Second, in their prescriptive focus on teacher-student interaction and teacher-student relationships, these books neglect to treat (or even mention) numerous issues and phenomena that are critical for deep understanding of classroom processes. Topics missing in most CM books include: Nonverbal communication and NV behavior of teachers and students; effects of teacher expectancies and teachers' differential behavior (including the teacher's pet phenomenon); social structure of the "student society" and sociometric measurement; working knowledge in behavioral analysis; the literature on classroom environments and classroom climate (which legitimizes various types of teacher styles); and the social psychology of "educating" and "changing" students.

This book has no ideological ax to grind and it presents as many points of view as possible. Two additional foci were intentionally excluded—the instructional/academic focus and the statistical focus. Having decided to focus on the social psychological aspects of classroom life and teacher's work, I did not include any discussion of teaching methods or instruction, nor did I deal with students' learning and achievement. A "cognitive" view was emphasized whenever it was relevant to a social, affective or behavioral aspect (such as students' motivational goals or the formation of teacher expectancies). With regard to statistics and research methodology, I tried to avoid the presentation of complex statistical results, assuming that many readers did not have any training in statistics. Empirical research was presented in most chapters, but findings were presented in the simplest and least "statistical" language. On the other hand, methodological issues were discussed quite often, such as the difference between "high-inference" and "low-inference" educational research, the differences between "affective" and "cognitive" sociometric measurement, or the nature of thin-slices NV research.

The book is divided into six parts and sixteen chapters: There are two to three chapters in each part. Part I is an overall view of the social psychology of the classroom, of students and of teachers. It introduces the language, the concepts and the frame of reference for the rest of the book.

Chapter 1 deals with the classroom as a social environment and discusses "classroom society." Societal characteristics include norms, rules, conformity, and complementary social roles of teacher and students. The chapter emphasizes the dynamic nature of classroom society and the continuous social struggles within it, among students and between students and teachers.

Chapter 2 is focused on students, their social needs, motivations and self-esteem. A discussion of social needs leads to a review of various "self" states (from self-esteem and Rogerian self-ideal concepts to competence, perceived academic control and self-efficacy). The role of social comparison processes is emphasized as a critical motivator. A second part of the chapter presents and evaluates the various developments in the field of achievement goal theory. An attempt is made to integrate the conceptions of mastery and performance goals on the one hand, and social motivations and social comparison on the other hand.

Chapter 3 is focused on teacher's various social roles as staff member in the school society and as classroom instructor and educator. The chapter emphasizes the variety of school and classroom types and the potential alternatives of CM styles. Issues discussed in the chapter include the bases of social power, leadership and teacher authority, the dilemma concerning the demand for teachers to serve as identification models, and teacher burnout.

Part II centers on social measurement in the classroom and presents two methodologies—sociometric measurement of classroom structure and student types, and measurement of classroom climate (CC).

Chapter 4 provides comprehensive information about sociometric measurement—although free usage by teachers is not recommended due to various drawbacks and ethical constraints. Moreno-type measurement via affective attractions and rejections is followed by discussion of sociograms, social structure, status and social classes, friendships, and various forms of relations among students. The two-dimensional model (of Preference X Impact) is presented next, emphasizing defined "types" such as rejected, neglected and controversial students. Cognitive sociometry and typological research are presented last.

Chapter 5 is focused on the measurement of CC as an area of educational research that has been historically distinct from CM research and from teacher expectancy research. High-inference research is distinguished from the formerly-used low-inference research, and the various factors and dimensions of CC are explicated and demonstrated (including the short version of the My Classroom Inventory which I recommend for teachers' use). Following discussion of methodological, conceptual and ethical issues in CC measurement, potential usages of CC in teachers' action research are described (including the positive characteristics of Hawthorne Effects in school practice).

Part III covers the area of teacher expectancies from its onset in "Pygmalion in the Classroom" in 1968 up to its current state. The main emphasis is on teachers' differential emotional behavior in the classroom and the effects of teacher differentiality on students' morale and CC. Current concern about effects of TDB is not connected any more to self-fulfillment of fabricated prophecies, but rather to teachers' deviation from equitable treatment on the basis of real differences among students.

Chapter 6 introduces the notion of self-fulfilling prophecy (SFP), describes the Pygmalion study and the controversy over the SFP issue that lasted for several decades. It then delineates the various links in the chain of SFP from the formation of an expectancy in a teacher's mind all the way to actual effects in students' performance. The remainder of the chapter discusses stereotypes, prejudice, and phenomena of teachers' bias, with a special emphasis on teachers' susceptibility to biasing information and the effects of biased teachers on their students.

Chapter 7 deals with teachers' differential behavior (TDB) in the class-rooms. Originally, TDB was treated as the behavioral mediator of teacher expectancy effects. Today, it is seen as an issue of deviation from fairness and equity, with potentially negative effects on students in the social/emotional domain. The dilemma stems from the conflicting notions that, on the one hand, identical behavior toward all students is undesirable, but on the other hand, some aspects of TDB (especially expressions of teachers' differential affect) are not legitimate and evoke anger. The chapter describes lists of investigated TDBs and the efforts to formulate a theory that would explain the observed patterns. Several types of research—classroom behavioral observations, students' perceptions of TDB, and research on teachers' NV behavior—lead to clear conclusions about the psychological price of teachers' emotional differentiality.

Chapter 8 deals with the well-known but minimally-studied teacher's per phenomenon, the case of teachers' special attachment to particular students. A cognitive sociometric method was designed to identify pets and teachers who have pets, and the high rate of occurrence of the pet phenomenon in elementary school classrooms was recorded. Several studies examined characteristics of teachers' pets, classroom seating locations, teachers' preferential behavior, and, most importantly, the psychological price of the pet phenomenon—especially when teacher's love for the pet is not shared by the students.

Part IV is dedicated to the discussion of classroom management (CM). An attempt is made to transcend beyond the rivalry between the contemporary student-centered approach and the behavioral approach and to offer readers the widest knowledge base about effective management of all aspects in the classroom.

Chapter 9 examines historical trends in the development of CM conceptions and the paradigm shifts that led to the contemporary student-centered approach. It describes the main types of CM research and the image of effective teachers in students' eyes. The central part of the chapter describes in detail the characteristics of effective CM according to this approach. The chapter concludes with a critical discussion of the contemporary conception, emphasizing the dangers of teachers' free-wheeling emotionality and of the demand to avoid punishing students.

Chapter 10 deals with discipline and punishment as necessary components of CM in contemporary schools. It delineates the behavioral approach to the maintenance of social order and "control" of disruptive behavior. The central part of the chapter presents a list of principles and tactics for effective punishment (when that is absolutely necessary). The list integrates behavioral, affective and cognitive components and gives priority to prevention and to careful and rational planning.

Chapter 11 presents a unique analysis of common pitfalls and typical teacher mistakes in CM, intended to "inoculate" teachers and increase their awareness. The phenomena are presented in the language of behavioral analysis, which can be helpful for teachers in its explicitness and accuracy even if they do not subscribe to behaviorism at all and do not practice behavioral methods. The most frequent pitfalls include doing too much (satiation), doing too little (deprivation), lack of appropriate contingencies, delayed reaction, misuse of teacher's attention and praise, dependence on students' reinforcement, partial reinforcement, etc.

Part V is focused on nonverbal behavior in the classroom. Emotions play a central role in classroom life and in teacher–student interaction. Because the NV is considered "the language of emotion," knowledge about NV communication is critical for effective CM. Unfortunately, most texts and books in educational psychology do not deal at all with NV behavior in the classroom.

Chapter 12 presents basic concepts and issues in NV research and their relevance to the classroom. The discussed topics include the definition of NV behavior and the importance of NV processes; the major types in the repertoire of NV behavior; notions of deception, leakage and detection of lying; and the three basic NV skills: encoding (emotional expressiveness), decoding (emotional sensitivity) and display rules (emotional control).

Chapter 13 deals with students' NV behavior. NV skills are important components of social competence, and problem children are often characterized by deficiencies in NV skills. Subsequent sections are devoted to the discussion of students as encoders (in peer interaction and in student-teacher interaction) and as decoders of teachers' NV behavior, demonstrating students' expertise and keen sensitivity to very subtle NV cues of their teachers.

Chapter 14 deals with teachers' NV behavior and raises several issues in NV communication that carry critical implications for CM. The first sections discuss teachers' NV decoding and encoding behaviors that are parallel and complementary to students' decoding and encoding; describe teachers' usage of all types of behaviors in Ekman and Friesen's NV repertoire; and emphasize teachers' use of display rules and of deception when the need arises. Substantial discussion is then devoted to the role of the teacher as lie detector. The final two sections center on "positive" and "negative" aspects of teachers' NV behavior. The positive aspects involve teachers' expressive style and its effects on CC and students' satisfaction. Parallel research on NV expressivity was reported for overall style in the "teacher immediacy" and "teacher enthusiasm" literatures, and complementary NV research analyzed specific teacher NV behaviors in thin slices research. The negative aspects involve TDB toward high- versus low-achieving students in teachers' NV behavior. Clear findings demonstrate the occurrence of NV TDB and the potential damage it can cause to students' morale. The evidence raises grave doubts about the advisability of free-wheeling teacher emotionality and teachers' emotional relations with students as advocated by some CM ideologists.

Part VI focuses on teachers' role in "educating" and "changing" students. Teachers are supposed to socialize and to educate students, to influence the formation and development of students' values, attitudes, world perspective and good citizenship. But books in educational psychology rarely devote focused attention to the psychological processes involved in educating and changing students and to the role of the teacher as "change agent."

Chapter 15 examines processes of educating students from a social psychological point of view. Six major modes of "education" are presented: (1) Education through instruction and teaching (via overall intellectual development and through the various academic disciplines and different subject matter areas); (2) Education by inculcation and preaching (a process seldom admitted by "enlightened" educators yet is actually very frequent and very important); (3) Education via behavior modification (also an area frequently negated by some CM advocates); (4) Education through cultural/social frameworks and normative influences (the most salient normative framework for students is, of course, the school itself); (5) Education through experiential learning and action learning; (6) Educative influence of models and modeling.

Chapter 16 deals with processes of planned psychological change, after values and attitudes had already been formed. Change might be necessitated by altered environmental conditions, by inefficiency and stress caused by the existing modes, or as part of normal development. Formation and change processes are quite similar to each other, except that psychological change almost inevitably involves resistance to change. The discussion of resistance to change highlights the different phenomena and their intense impact in hindering change. Separate analyses deal with cognitive aspects, emotional aspects and behavioral aspects of resistance to change. Subsequently, four generalized strategies for psychological change (adapted from Chin and Benne) are presented and applied to the school context and to teachers' work as change agents: (1) The rational-empirical strategy (changing through understanding and choice); (2) The behavioral ("power-coercive") strategy (changing through action and behavioral change); (3) The experiential ("re-educative") strategy (changing through emotional experiences); and (4) The normative strategy (changing through accommodation to the social environment).

For me, this book culminates almost forty years of research on various aspects of the social psychology of the classroom. A large proportion of my research over the years was related, directly or indirectly, to teachers, to students, and to what transpires in teacher–student and student–student interaction. I was affiliated for many years with the human relations movement, but I always tried to keep an open mind and not let ideological preferences to influence my research, my empirical inferences, and my teaching. I believe that professional decisions about personal style and mode of conduct must be made in a rational, knowledge-based and data-based manner, and I hope that this book can contribute to such decision-making of some readers.

Many people helped me and contributed to my work over the years, and I cannot even begin to list all of them, because many others would be left out. They were my undergraduate and graduate students, my research assistants and my degree advisees, colleagues at Hebrew University of Jerusalem and in many places worldwide, journal editors and reviewers, research collaborators, various audiences, and sometimes even the research participants themselves. I feel blessed to have gained from so many people.

One person contributed immensely to my professional career as a researcher, and that is Robert Rosenthal. I got excited about teacher expectancies as a young psychology graduate student at Duke University, but I met Bob years later when I taught at Wellesley College. We became friends and research collaborators, and published joint research articles in the 1980s, the 1990s and in the present decade. I learned a lot and I owe a lot to Bob Rosenthal, and he remains a source of inspiration and advice for me.

In Israel, Yaakov Kareev has been my best friend and close colleague ever since our undergraduate days at Hebrew University in the early 1960s. With his office never more than three doors away, Yaakov has been my lifelong counselor in matters of methodology and substance, the bouncing board for new ideas, and the critic when necessary.

In the process of writing this book, Yehonatan Benayoun was extremely helpful, especially during my sabbatical in Buenos Aires. His assistance truly contributed to the book and I am thankful.

Finally, special thanks are extended to my family. To Dinah, who encouraged me to write the book and subsequently needed to enlist tons of patience, to son Itai and grandson Ido, who served as "informers" about students' experiences, and to son Gilad, who contributed his name to my TDB questionnaire.

Part I
The Social Psychology of the Classroom

1 The Classroom as a Social Environment

INTRODUCTORY COMMENTS: VIEWING THE CLASSROOM, TEACHERS AND STUDENTS FROM A SOCIAL PSYCHOLOGICAL PERSPECTIVE

School is a central societal institution. Its major purposes are "to teach" and "to educate" the young generation and to prepare students for good and effective "citizenship." Teachers have a dual role as *instructors* (teaching students, developing their intellectual capacities and leading them to academic achievements) and as *socializers* (developing students' values and social selves, their cultural level and social conduct). This book is focused on the social psychology of the classroom. It is intended to help teachers to better understand social psychological forces operating in the classroom, to be aware of implicit and hidden psychological aspects in teacher–student interaction, and to improve their classroom management. For teachers to be competent managers and effective agents of socialization, they must be attuned to the social forces in the classroom society, to have sufficient knowledge in the relevant domains of social psychology, and to have skills for managing the classroom society and for educating and changing students. In short, the main purpose of this book is to turn its readers (experienced teachers, teacher education students, school administrators and students of education and the social sciences) into budding social/educational psychologists.

Going to school is the child's most central formative experience of living in a society and becoming a "citizen." Beyond the social framework of the family, the school and the classroom are the central "societal experiences" throughout childhood and adolescence. Children learn to understand society and how to live in it, what is required of them as citizens, and what are the difficulties that they must cope with to become effective in the social environment. The social self of the individual child is formed through the social experiences in the classroom society. In school children acquire the basic social insights and modes of social behavior. These experiences influence students' self-concept and self-esteem, motivational patterns and eventually the formation of one's attitudes, values and world perspective. The social processes act as moderating factors which influence the other primary objective of schooling; namely learning and achievement.

The instructional and academic parts of the teacher's job are often over-emphasized at the expense of the social aspects. This characterizes numerous teacher education programs, and many teachers complain that their knowledge in the psychology of the classroom is too limited, especially practical considerations how they could apply psychological knowledge in managing their classrooms. When something goes wrong in the classroom (problems in maintaining discipline, conflicts among sub-groups, inexplicably low achievement, negative classroom climate and especially disruption caused by problematic students) some teachers turn immediately to outside experts (e.g., school psychologists, counselors) for help. Quite frequently, the advice of the outside expert would concentrate on social psychological forces in the classroom and on the teacher's strategy of classroom management. The experts would provide consultation how the teacher could modify her/his own conduct in the classroom.

THE CLASSROOM AS "SOCIETY"

The classroom is a mini-society. It has a defined structure and formal goals, it has a "ruler" of legitimate authority and "citizens" who enact their roles and interact with each other and who must "work" toward attaining given goals. Students' membership in this society is coercive rather than voluntary, and this society is non-democratic. (Some types of collaborative classrooms provide students with more decision-making power, but classrooms are nevertheless non-democratic by their inherent nature). Students are continuously required to invest great efforts in activities that are not necessarily to their liking, to follow a rather strict set of rules and adjust to them. Rebellion is not tolerated and might lead to severe punishment. Students must accommodate to school, and they would achieve positive products only if they work very hard according to the rules. The teacher is the powerful leader who can reward or withhold rewards, and teachers can often be quite arbitrary. For many students, their "citizenship" in the classroom "society" is not a very pleasant experience.

I know that the above description is blunt, and the social nature of the classroom society could have been (and often is) described in a more positive manner. But I think that it is important to recognize from the onset that involuntary participation and continuous coercion are the foundations of school culture. From this basic definition, teachers and school administrators can search for means of creating a positive learning atmosphere and for making the school experience as enjoyable and satisfactory as possible for students.

Beyond the universal pre-determined formal structure, each classroom has an informal structure that unfolds and develops through the interactions between students and teachers: Explicit and implicit norms are formed; complex processes of social influence take place; leadership, social classes and roles emerge; and continuous struggles for popularity, prestige and power take place in every classroom. The group dynamics of the classroom influences each individual student (in status, expectations, self-image, social behavior and eventual achievement) as well as the atmosphere and social-emotional climate of the entire classroom (cohesion, cooperation and competition, conflict, tension, social support, etc.).

NORMS, RULES AND EXPECTATIONS

Social norms are behavioral standards, fixed sets of unwritten rules controlling social behavior of group members in defined circumstances. They are the specific reflections of the group's values, goals, and underlying culture. Norms are formed and maintained through group, rather than individual processes, but they determine and control individuals' behavior, so that social behavior in the group becomes predictable. Norms represent consensual joint expectations concerning appropriate and inappropriate behavior. Although most norms are implicit and hidden, individual members are well aware of them and of the potential consequences of violating them. Psychologically, norms are very functional both for individual members and for the group as an entity. For the individual, norms make it possible to know what is appropriate, reduce ambiguity and increase self-confidence. For the group, norms contribute to the maintenance of group uniformity and social order.

Norms are quite amazing as social mechanisms because they are usually implicit and hidden, and yet all members know the norms with no need to talk about them explicitly at all. An important part of normal social adjustment is the ability to quickly infer about norms of appropriate and inappropriate behavior in every social situation without focused learning. Students with salient social disabilities such as autism and the Asperger Syndrome (see Chapter 13) indeed lack the ability to infer underlying norms, and therefore they very often act inappropriately. I tell my students on their first day in the university that it is amazing how they know exactly how to dress, how to behave, what to do and what not to do in their first class session, although the university experience is totally new to them. Norms differ from rules and procedural directives in that they are implicit and undefined, whereas rules are delivered in explicit and exact terms, and some authority figure inspects that the rules are indeed followed. Norms prescribe differential behavior in different contexts—in the classroom versus the yard at break; during school ceremonies versus regular classroom discussion; in one instructional situation compared to another, etc.

A known activity in group workshops is "the fishbowl exercise," where a random group of participants is asked to discuss a given issue and to reach a consensual decision. Other participants observe the discussants from outside the circle, and the group process is subsequently analyzed by all. It is always amazing to observe how quickly and without any explicit negotiation the norms are formulated—the group "decides" without words whether it would be cooperative or competitive, whether individuals would be allowed to take control, whether the atmosphere would be tense or relaxed, how roles would be divided and how the decision would be reached. Sometimes an implicit struggle over norm-formation might be observed, but it is always amazing how quickly a random group settles on its set of norms without really talking about it at all.

Types of Norms

Types of norms and distinctions between them should be recognized. The most important distinction is between norms reflecting values and norms intended for the management of the routine life in the group. Of course many norms belong concurrently in both categories, such as not to touch another child's property or not to hit another child. The purpose of norms for maintenance of routine life in the classroom is to enable effective academic work and learning. Many of those norms are dictated by the school authorities—often in the form of rules and procedural directives which are subsequently translated into more specific behavioral norms. Other norms derive from the children's group—how to manage interpersonal relations, kinds of speech and forms of violence allowed and disallowed, relationships between boys and girls, and also norms on how to interact with teachers and with school authorities.

Behavioral norms reflecting values are of high educational significance. They "translate" a general value—such as cooperation or respect for other people—into specific behavioral requirements. Examples might include norms such as waiting until the other person has finished speaking and taking turns, or not mocking others publicly—all for the value of respect; or training children to share toys or solve problems together for the value of cooperation. The educational literature on norms emphasizes the importance of value-reflecting norms. However, it must be remembered that the existence of normative behavior is not necessarily proof that the person holds the value and internalized it. For example, many men open doors for women and let them pass first, but they do not necessarily respect women inherently. Sometimes the behavioral expression—especially if enacted in an exaggerated fashion—is a mask hiding the absence of the relevant value!

Beyond these major distinctions: (a) between norms for management of routine life and norms reflecting values, and (b) between norms formed (or influenced) by external authority and norms formed naturally within the group—several other characteristics of norms and distinctions among norms should be mentioned:

- Some norms are formal and explicit, whereas other norms are more informal, implicit and hidden;

- Some norms are fixed, static and consensually accepted, whereas other norms are more dynamic and flexible, often the focus of struggle within the group;
- Some norms are "strong" and others are "weak" in terms of the required conformity and expected sanctions for violation.

Normative Change

Chapter 16 presents several strategies for psychological change, and one of them is the normative strategy. That strategy is based on the idea that, if the normative environment is changed, a deeper change in participants' attitudes and values might follow, because people's views tend to follow their behavior and to be consonant with their conduct. If "our classroom" is (normatively) known to be well behaved, or always punctual, or has a reputation of hard workers, there is a good chance that these norms would be internalized and "owned" by the students. Teachers also know that appointing a disruptive student to an officially responsible role in the classroom often changes the child's conduct and attitude considerably.

Therefore, the educational literature sees norm development and norm changing as important components of the teacher's educational role. An Internet search for "classroom norms" yields hundreds of sites that include lists of specific norms and intervention programs for norm setting and norm changing. In this chapter, the initial concern is that teachers would become aware of their classrooms' norms and would be able to analyze these norms in order to understand the underlying culture of the classroom. Further down the line, teachers might become involved in planned interventions to set and modify classroom norms.

CONFORMITY

The social psychological concept that complements norms is "conformity"— the degree to which norms are kept obediently by group participants. Group members usually vary in the extent to which they follow the norms, but in order to maintain social order, groups must apply pressure for conformity, punishing violators of group norms. Conformity to normative pressure can derive from real conviction in their value (through internalization, identification and attitude change), but might also be caused by the individual's need "to fit" in the group and to avoid social pressure, rejection, punishment and sometimes even excommunication. Thus, to maintain social order norms must be kept, and groups (even democratic and voluntary groups) must demand conformity.

Readers might have felt uneasy reading the above paragraph about the importance of conformity, because conformity is viewed negatively in modern Western society, and non-conformists are appreciated and viewed more positively than conformists. To be labeled "conformist" is quite an insult! To clarify the issue, I must emphasize the conceptual difference between two different varieties of non-conformism: One is "independence," where one's behavior is independent and cannot be predicted at all from the existing norms; the other is "counter-formism," where one's behavior *can* be predicted from the norms, because one always acts exactly in opposite of the norm! Many people who pride themselves as being independent non-conformists are actually quite predictable counter-formists. Many of the rebels and hippies of former generations had been counter-formists. They strongly conformed to the anti-establishment norms and acted in an identical, contrary manner, but they perceived themselves as independent non-conformists. Counter-formists are really conformists in disguise, and classroom rebels are no exception.

A certain level of conformity is necessary for the maintenance of social order. Good citizenship in any society entails some voluntary conformity on the part of the citizens, and people should not feel ashamed about it at all. The ideal state is one of balance and healthy tension between conformity and independence, where social order is maintained, and yet norms can be challenged, tested and changed.

In the classroom, students relate quite differently to norms emerging from outside authority and norms emerging from within the student body. In fact, most classrooms have special norms that prescribe appropriate rebellious behavior against the coercion of norms from above. And yet, it is inherently accepted that the teachers and "school" in general have legitimate authority to set rules and to prescribe norms for students (see Chapter 3).

SOCIAL ROLES

If norms represent the prerequisites and characteristics of group behavior, roles describe the ways in which individuals structure their positions and their conduct in social situations. Every person has numerous social roles, and roles are enacted in a relevant manner in every situation. "Role" represents a set of norms, scripts, behavior patterns, expectations, rights and obligations that people employ in particular positions. The role is also a label, helping people to characterize themselves and others. They know how to act according to role expectations, what others would expect of them and what they could expect from other role holders.

The number of roles that every person plays over time is very large, encompassing all facets of life. For example, a teacher might play in one day the following roles: classroom teacher (see later discussion of teacher's role); junior/senior staff member interacting with the principal; colleague of other teachers (juniors, peers, or seniors); organizer of activities; helper; facilitator; critic. The same teacher has numerous other social roles outside school: husband/wife (newly wed or "old-timer"); parent; sibling (younger, older); grandchild; lover; consumer; driver; spectator (of sports, of cultural events); neighbor; concerned citizen; and so on and so forth, the list is almost endless. Similarly, students perform numerous roles in the classroom in their interactions with their teachers and their peers.

We move flexibly from one role to another, play each role in interaction with others, and rightfully expect that others would enact their compatible roles. Comedies are built on role confusion, when people demonstrate inappropriate role behavior in given situations. Behavior that deviates from role expectations can be very funny to spectators of comedy (imagine mistakenly playing the "wedding guest" at a funeral, or a teacher playing the "young sibling" role in front of her students), but can be very threatening for those who need to play the complementary role in a real-life situation. Indeed, the term "abnormal" means that the person fails to follow "normal" expectations.

In Goffman's (1956) dramaturgical perspective, "the world is a stage and we are all actors." We hold social positions in every social situation, and we have clear expectations about our own role-relevant behavior and that of the others. The dramaturgical image of "a stage" probably carries an implication of phoniness and lack of personal authenticity—if we play roles all the time, we cannot be truly ourselves! To worry about authenticity in social behavior is indeed a genuine and important concern, but I think that its relevance to role behavior is only marginal. A person cannot exist in the social environment without being involved in role behavior. In every social situation we must play a role and we must change our behavior according to role expectations and role demands. Our "real self" can be expressed in every role we play. A person can be real or hypocritical in every role and in every situation, but it is not the role itself that makes the person non-authentic. Therefore, the shift from one role to another is not, in itself, evidence of lack of authenticity. It is true is that people sometimes *exaggerate* the way the play certain roles, making them unreliable and perhaps they are perceived by others as fakes.

Roles can range from being very global and generalized to being very specific and unique. "Teacher," "student," or "parent" are global roles, and can be divided into a spectrum of specific roles that might differ greatly from each other. In fact, a role such as "teacher" is relevant only in comparison to other global roles (such as lawyer or executive), whereas that global label is almost irrelevant within the context of the school staff. A teacher can play the roles of a bureaucrat, instructor, therapist, traffic cop, judge or time keeper, and might be a friendly teacher, a lenient teacher, a strict teacher, a funny teacher, a perfectionist, etc. Similarly, the student role consists of many different specific roles: the classroom "queen," the jester, the good student, the ass licker, the bully, the victim, the teacher's pet (Chapter 8), etc.

Role Conflict

Central concepts used in role theory (Biddle, 1979; Biddle & Thomas, 1966) include: Role expectations; Role demands; Norms and sanctions; Skill in role performance; Role evaluation; Role taking; Consensus; Conformity; Role conflict and Role flexibility. Of these concepts, "Role conflict" is particularly interesting. The conflict can be within a given role, between different roles of the same individual, or role conflict between individuals. The more a given role is global and generalized—such as teacher or parent—the more role conflict (and also greater variance in role performance) can be expected. On the other hand, in more specific and narrowly-defined roles (e.g., friendly teacher or stern parent) chances for variance and role conflict are smaller.

Conflict within a role stems from the fact that the role could be enacted in different ways, some of which are incompatible with each other. Different goals within the role collide with each other (how to be both demanding and friendly as a teacher; how can a parent love a child and be angry at him; how can one evoke trust but still frighten with punishment) and one is not sure how the role should be played most appropriately.

Conflicts between roles within the same individual are very frequent. Because of the complexities of daily life, a given situation often presents more than one possibility of an appropriate role. Each possible role has it benefits and its drawbacks for that situation, and a quick decision-making process is required. Frequently we have to decide whether to play a rational role or an affective-emotional role in a given situation, and whether we should act "positively" or "negatively" toward another person. Should the parent be a stern parent or a loving parent when the child was naughty? What is the best role to play in dealing with an irrational wish of the old grandmother? Role conflicts are resolved cognitively, and people make decisions, selecting what seems to be the best alternative for role behavior. However, because strong emotions might be tied to the different options, individuals often err and choose less effective options (such as losing control, becoming tremendously offensive or the opposite).

Interpersonal role conflicts are also very common. Under ideal conditions, the roles played by two individuals would be compatible with each other, and the interaction would then be harmonious. But frequently the interaction is characterized by conflict; a struggle of who would determine which roles would be enacted and how they would be played. The individual naturally prefers to select the role expected to bring maximal benefits, and that would often be at the expense of the other. The other would then wish to choose a different role than the one expected by the first actor in order to minimize her/his loss or to increase her/his gain. Thus, choosing an incompatible role and creating role conflict can sometimes be a good strategy.

The classroom is the stage for continuous role conflicts between students and teachers. Teachers have clear images of the ways they wish to play their own teacher role and how they expect the students to play their roles. But the students have their own images and expectations, and those are often in conflict with those of their teachers. The two parties struggle to make the other side play their roles as "we" wish. As the legitimate authority in the classroom (Chapter 3), the teacher has more social power to control students' role behavior, but students are tremendously resourceful and creative in finding implicit and subtle ways to influence teachers' role behavior. Hence the view I present in this book of the classroom as the stage of continuous struggle between teachers and students for influence and control. The words "control" and "power" do not necessarily imply aggression or violence. Struggles for control can be very amiable and well mannered! Students often choose particular role behaviors in order to neutralize and modify the effects of teachers' role behavior. Students face another interesting type of role conflict within themselves, between the role they choose to play vis-à-vis the teacher and the role they wish to demonstrate to their peers.

Similar to the description of norms, roles are also characterized as being implicit rather than explicit. The consensus about role expectations is very strong despite the fact that people never talk explicitly about their roles and about their role performance. However, unlike norms, roles allow a wider range of behavioral variations, because as mentioned previously, roles are more personal whereas norms are group-based. Some roles have a more fixed scenario across situations, whereas other roles might be more changeable from one occurrence to the next. From the personal standpoint of the individual, flexibility in role behavior is preferred: One may love to perform certain roles and to avoid other roles; one may be more skilled in playing certain roles than playing other roles; and one may wish to play certain roles but would not be enabled by the other interacting partners to play those roles (the latter is often true for interaction with superiors and with authority, where one's power to choose roles is limited).

Role Play Exercises

One of the most widely-used techniques in training teachers and other professional in human relations workshops is the role play activity. Participants are asked to playact various classroom and school situations, and each participant is assigned a particular role to play. Analysis of the role-play activity highlights role expectations and role performance, and enables participants first to practice how to play certain roles, and further to analyze the behaviors and reactions of other players to particular forms of role enactment. The activity is very illuminating for many teachers, because (in their testimonies) "they have taken too many things for granted" in their daily conduct in the classroom.

To understand the classroom society and the intricate inter-relationships within it, a deep understanding of norms and social roles is required, supplemented by ample observation and interpretation of social behavior in the classroom. Particular behaviors by different students attain their meanings through the unique social contexts within which they are enacted, considering both the unique sets of norms and the division of social roles among all participants in each classroom.

2 Social Motivation, Students' Needs and Self-Esteem

INTRODUCTION

Motivation is a central domain of psychological theory and research. Numerous volumes have been dedicated to the discussion of motivational processes, especially as they relate to children and to students in the course of their development. For this chapter I chose to discuss succinctly several concepts and issues in social motivation that illuminate central aspects in the social psychology of the classroom. As a rule, discussions of instructional issues and students' academic learning are not included in this book. However, this chapter is an exception, because it is not possible to discuss students' achievement motivation without referring to academic goals.

Historically, early formulations of human motivation emerged from a psychodynamic perspective—that is, from dealing with deep-seated drives and needs and their reflections in emotional conflicts within the person and between persons. Like many other areas of psychology, later formulations of motivation became more "cognitive," focusing on information processing, expectations and decision-making. The concepts discussed in this chapter represent both the dynamic perspective and the more contemporary cognitive perspective.

MOTIVATION AS A PSYCHOLOGICAL CONSTRUCT

In Chapter 1, I used social psychological terminology to describe the classroom society. But the more personal perspective of the individual student is also important for the analysis of social processes in the classroom. In that perspective, the central phenomena to be discussed involve students' self-concept and self-esteem and their social needs as they are expressed in the classroom society. Classroom interaction would then be evaluated by the degree it enables the expression and realization of students' social needs, and by the extent to which the largest proportion of students would enjoy high self-esteem in the classroom. The social structure of any specific classroom and its dominant norms would determine whether only a minority of selected students would enjoy high self-esteem and their social needs would be satisfied, or whether the classroom climate (Chapter 5) would contribute to the psychological welfare of many or most students.

"Motivation" is the *fuel* of our mental system, the force and the energy that activates us and leads our behavior to attain particular goals. Motivation is caused by inner needs and by the necessity to satisfy those needs. The "basic needs" of all living organisms are physical (hunger, thirst, sex, avoidance of pain, etc.), but more cognitive and social needs include curiosity, exploration, manipulation and the need to control the environment competently. In animals, the latter needs are most clearly obvious in the natural behavior of puppies, and they are far more developed in human behavior because of the greater brain and lingual capacities. Thus, human motivation is always connected to thought and language.

Any creature (animal or human) without motivation or with very low motivation cannot be active in the social environment, and therefore would not be able to attain control and competence. Such is, for example, the clinical manifestation of depression. The depressed person does not have enough motivational fuel to energize her/himself to action. Most people do have reserves of mental energy to motivate them, and their action is designed to lead to need-satisfaction.

Motivation involves not only the mental fuel but also the *direction* of activity. The needs determine the direction and goals of one's action, driving toward need satisfaction. It is not coincidental that the terms "needs" and "drives" are used interchangeably in the psychological literature on motivation. Although the basic needs are innate, most human needs are acquired throughout the developmental processes, following the interactions between the individual and her/his social environment. The task of education (for parents, teachers, societal authorities, etc.) means: (a) To develop and to enrich children's motivation so that they would always have ample reserves of mental fuel; and (b) To direct this energy toward positive goals of competence and achievement that would be satisfying and invigorating for the individual.

SOCIAL NEEDS AND SELF-ESTEEM

In early theorizing about social needs (Schutz, 1958; Schmuck, 1978), variations of three central social motivations were described:

1. *The need for affection* (the need for warmth, to be liked and loved by others);
2. *The need for inclusion* (the need to be a member of the group and to avoid social rejection);
3. *The need for power* (the need to have control, power and influence in one's social environment).

Group functioning and the group's "life" reflect the needs of the individual members. The group's development and its emerging social structure are the product of the continuous struggle for the satisfaction of these needs among the members of the group.

Every individual possesses all three needs, although their relative intensities vary. Some children are high on all three needs, some are high on one need (say, the need for affection) but low on another (say, the need for power), and probably some children are low on all needs. The "self-image" of each individual represents the gap between the person's desired level of satisfaction (of which the person is usually not consciously aware) and the actual level of satisfaction. The more any or all social needs are subjectively perceived by the person as being satisfied, the more the person would feel fulfillment and a sense of competence. "Competence" is the extent of achieving what one set out to achieve and the sense of having a sufficient standing in society as being loved, included and/or powerful.

The idea that mental health and psychological adjustment must be understood through the magnitude of the gap (incongruity) between the "ideal self" and the "actual self" was put forward by Carl Rogers (1951, 1959, 1961). The contribution of this conception is the idea that it is the subjective ideal end-state and its congruity or incongruity with the real or actual self that really matters. There is no universal end-state or ideal that determines "success." Instead, the individual sets (with or without awareness) the personal ideal state for her/himself, and good adjustment is indicated by a small gap (that is, relative congruity) between this ideal and the actual attainment in one's social environment. Goals that are set too high might probably lead to disappointment and frustration, and the best goal-setting is always for a little more than what one can actually achieve. The same actual position in the group might be more satisfying or less satisfying to different individuals depending on their imagined ideal state. Aspirations that are too high (say, to be the charismatic leader of the classroom) are bound to remain unfulfilled and more likely to hinder one's well-being.

Sometimes loving parents encourage an over-blown and exaggerated self-image (or rather, ideal-image) of their child's abilities and competencies. That might cause incongruity between that cultivated image and the actual reality of the child's status in the classroom. Despite the good intentions, such inflated expectations might hinder rather than help the child, and the potential tension and frustration might cause a vicious cycle that might further reduce actual attainments. Rogers (1951, 1961) argued that growing incongruity can cause neurosis, up to the point of psychosis (shattered personality) in extreme cases. On the other hand, the ideal-self should always be above the actual-self in a reasonable measure, because in the absence of any gap, one is not motivated to act at all. The distinction between healthy ambitions and hindering ambitions is very fine, and realistic goal-setting is an important part of psychological adjustment.

Because of the duality of the classroom society, students' self-esteem must be attained in two worlds, one relating to school and its objectives of academic achievement, the other relating to the children's society. The two worlds are not always compatible with each other, and sometimes their norms are contradictory of each other. Therefore, "self-esteem" is divided in the relevant literature into "academic self-esteem" and "social self-esteem," and the two phenomena are measured separately. Some students have high (or low) self-esteem in both academic and social domains, but many students experience gaps between their self-image in the two domains. For some students, attaining high scholastic status and academic success comes at the expense of their social status, and quite often the attainment of social success might hamper academic success.

COMPETENCE MOTIVATION AND SELF-EFFICACY

The concept "competence motivation" was introduced by Robert White (White, 1959) and remained a salient concept in motivation, mostly due to Albert Bandura's decades-long work on self-efficacy (Bandura, 1982, 1986). Self-efficacy is the belief that one is capable of performing at a certain level in order to attain certain goals. A person with high self-efficacy believes that s/he is capable of achieving certain goals and to manage various obstacles. Self-efficacy must be distinguished from self-esteem. Self-esteem is related to a person's sense of self-worth, whereas self-efficacy is founded on people's perception that they are capable of achieving their goals.

Students' sense of competence and efficacy is derived from their capabilities, traits and self-resources as these are reflected in their behavior on the one hand, and from their perceived status in the classroom society on the other hand. "Perceived status" includes self-perception as well as perceptions by students' peers and by their teachers. Various definitions of self-efficacy emphasize students' judgments of their own capability for a specific learning or social outcome and their conscious awareness of their ability to be effective in controlling action and outcomes.

PERCEIVED ACADEMIC CONTROL

In attempts to deal with the issue of academic failure in college (and, of course, its opposite—academic success), Raymond Perry (1991, 2003; Perry, Hall, & Ruthig, 2007) developed the concept of "academic control" and studied it for over two decades. The concept is quite similar to cognitive-motivational concepts such as self-efficacy mentioned above, but it is specifically focused on students' motivation and classroom conduct in an attempt to predict academic success or failure. According to Perry, perceived control attracted widespread interest in the social sciences over the five last decades. Alternative terms and concepts in the classroom management (hence CM) literature (Chapter 9) involve students' autonomy, independence and self-reliance.

Perceived academic control is a student's subjective estimate of her/his capacity to deal with the demands of the academic environment, to manipulate, influence and predict scholastic success. The sense of control includes both stable, trait-like attributes and transient, state-like components. Stable perceived control is more enduring and generalized across academic situations, the product of the student's intellectual abilities and additional personality traits such as optimism, self-confidence and a sense of successfulness. In contrast, transient perceived control is less enduring, a product of situational aspects in the context of the classroom. These aspects might include classroom norms and rules, teachers' academic and CM style, and comparative factors involving the student body (see next discussion of social comparison). Perceived control is particularly important in the context of academic failure and in cases of low-control students.

An important aspect in this line of research is the fact that Perry and his associates also investigated remedies for correcting students' motivation and improving their perceived academic control through "attributional retraining." Perry et al. (2007) demonstrated that attributional retraining can indeed be effective in raising perceived control. Teachers can influence students' sense of academic control through their teaching style and their conduct in CM.

A major drawback of Perry's work for the present book is the fact that all theorizing and research work on perceived academic control were conducted in higher education contexts. The ideas are certainly applicable to elementary and high school classrooms, but no research on lower levels of education has been published. The conception of perceived academic control views academic achievements as the direct product of students' high sense of control. Although academic aspects are not in the focus of this book, the concept of academic control is important as a generalized motivational concept that is related to the ways classrooms are managed and to teacher–student relations.

THE MOTIVATING POWER OF SOCIAL COMPARISON

The discussion of social needs, self-esteem, self-efficacy and perceived control is not complete without the introduction of social comparison processes. People evaluate themselves and their achievements through their subjective perceptions of their status compared to others. Self-evaluation is almost never conducted without comparison to others. In the original theory of social comparison, Leon Festinger (1954) thought that we use other people to fulfill our informational needs to evaluate ourselves only in the absence of objective standards. Later writers (e.g. Goethals &

Darley, 1987; Kruglanski & Mayseless, 1990) thought that social comparison processes are so pervasive and powerful that they become habitual–people almost automatically compare themselves to others for any kind of self-evaluation.

I ask my students sometimes if they would have been satisfied with a grade of 93 (out of 100). The automatic answer is always: "it depends." If an individual student compares the potential 93 to her personal average, the 93 might cause a sense of competence if her average is lower than 93. But that is not sufficient in itself, and she must know the grades received by the other students (or by particular students.) If the class average was 96, then 93 would be quite disappointing; but if the class average was below 93, then 93 might be satisfying. Even the perfect grade of 100 does not guarantee satisfaction in the social comparison process, because if all students (including "stupid Joe") would have received that grade, it would not really be such a big deal. Our situation is almost always a relative term, compared to the situation of others in the relevant group of reference.

We usually compare ourselves with our peers or with those who are similar to us. However, social comparison can take an upward or a downward direction. Upward social comparison occurs when we compare ourselves to those with higher status and higher standing than us. That is bound to lead to frustration and disappointment in many instances. Unfortunately, mediocre students conduct upward social comparison quite often. Many teachers encourage it (presumably to increase the students' motivation), inadvertently hindering rather than facilitating their students' progress. Downward social comparison occurs when we compare ourselves with those who are worse off than ourselves. That comparison is likely to lead to a sense of superiority. It seems that people use downward social comparison when their self-esteem is threatened. Students can be quite flexible in the choice of reference others for social comparison, and to set goals that are realistic and attainable. The conscious awareness of the realistic level of goal-setting and the choice of the appropriate social comparison are critical components in attaining a sense of self-esteem and competence. Thus, in the social psychological view of the classroom, social comparison is a powerful motivator, providing both the fuel and the direction that can drive students toward achievements and toward attaining a sense of control, competence and self-efficacy.

STUDENT MOTIVATIONS IN THE
ACHIEVEMENT GOALS THEORY

In addition to the theories and conceptualizations described before, a parallel line of educational-psychological theorizing and research on achievement motivation has developed in recent decades. This line of cognitive research–known as "achievements goal theory"—has become a strong domain in educational psychology. The main characteristic of achievement goals theory is that, unlike the unitary concept of previous theories (such as self-efficacy), this theory presents a typology of motivations: Researchers investigate alternative motivations that can characterize students, and each alternative is associated with different educational outcomes. Therefore, the research on achievement goals seeks to trace *differences* between (or among) various types of motivation. Unfortunately, researchers begin to express ideological preferences that accompany their findings, so that one type of motivation becomes preferred over other types.

Theorizing on achievement motivation is traced back to the seminal work of David McClelland (1953). He distinguished between two independent types of achievement motivation, one directed at attaining success, the other directed at avoiding failure. Julian Rotter (1966) won acclaim for distinguishing between internal and external locus of control. Locus of control refers to persons' perception about the underlying main causes of events in their life, beliefs about causes of good or bad results either in general or in specific areas such as health or academics. People with high internal locus of control believe that they control their own fate, that their successes and failures are guided by their personal abilities, decisions and investment of effort. In contrast, people with high external locus of control believe that their behavior is guided by fate, luck or other external characteristics of the environment, perhaps even by some higher power, other people or chance. Rotter's conception elicited a lot of interest and led to decades-long research. Generally, internal control was considered to be more desirable than external control because of its numerous psychological advantages—more self-determination, more inner-directedness, and ultimately more achievements.

The more general terms that were relevant to subsequent theorizing on achievement motivation were "intrinsic- and extrinsic-motivation." Intrinsic motivation is an innate and natural inclination that enables mental capacities to develop through learning, which is not driven by external reinforcements. The person who is intrinsically motivated does not cling to external goals, such as a reward, a good grade, acknowledgement or recognition, but is driven by internal incentives like curiosity, excitement, enthusiasm and a positive self-image. The goal of the activity is the activity itself, and the learning process is more important than its result. (This type of motivation is seen in contemporary achievement goals theory as characterizing "mastery goal motivation").

Extrinsic motivation is influenced by external reinforcements and circumstances, controlled from outside, and the person acts for possible consequences such as a reward, recognition, status, or good grades, or in order to avoid punishment. The activity itself is of no interest to the extrinsically motivated person.

Achievement goals theory was formulated and published in the 1980s (Deci & Ryan, 1985; Dweck & Elliott, 1983; Elliott & Dweck, 1988;

Nicholls, 1984), and a lively stream of theorizing and research work has been published since then. Achievement goal is the purpose for students' competence-related activities, the motivation that drives them to pursue their learning and leads them to academic achievements. Two types of achievement goals were initially formulated, parallel to the intrinsic and extrinsic motivation discussed above. The intrinsic goal had been labeled "learning goal" or "task goal," and more recently the widely-used term is: "mastery goal." The extrinsic goal had been labeled "ego goal," but the common term used today is "performance goal."

The description of mastery goals and performance goals must be quite familiar to the reader at this point. Mastery goals promote intrinsic motivation, foster perceptions of challenge, encourage learning- and task-involvement, generate excitement and task-enjoyment, and increase self-determination and persistence in the face of failure. Performance goals represent extrinsic motivation by focusing on external success and recognition through ego-involvement and competition. Innate ability, rather than effort, is seen as the cornerstone for successful performance, and one is more concerned about success than interested in the actual learning task.

Because this book is focused on the social psychology of students, teachers and classrooms, it is interesting to distinguish between mastery and performance goals from a social psychological perspective. It seems quite clear that performance goals are basically social motivations and are influenced by social needs and social comparison processes, whereas mastery goals seem to be non-social (perhaps "personal" or "individual") as they are intrinsically motivated and not given to the influence of social factors in the classroom society. Self-efficacy, then, can have both social and non-social roots.

In the 1990s (see Elliott & Harackiewicz, 1996) the dichotomy of mastery versus performance goals was replaced by a trichotomy. Performance goals were divided into independent "performance-approach" and "performance-avoidance" goals. The performance-approach goal represents a success motivation, a striving for respect, recognition and high status, and is a demonstration of superior ability. In contrast, performance-avoidance goals aim at avoiding failure, attempts to hide inferior ability and prevent low status. Elliott and Harackiewicz (1996) demonstrated the independence of the three achievement goals, and argued that only performance-avoidance goals lead to negative results and undermine intrinsic motivation, whereas both mastery and performance-approach goals yield positive educational outcomes.

A fourth type can be added to the three achievement goals, and that is "work-avoidance," represented by a type student who lacks achievement goals altogether. In the absence of any achievement goals that would drive this student to action, her/his purpose is simply to pass the day (or the week, or the year) in peace. This type was not in the focus of much investigation, but it stands to reason that s/he can be frequently found in most classrooms. This type presents a particularly nagging problem for teachers, because a preferred cognitive mode that might push this student to action does not exist at all!

The literature on achievement goals does not give equal value to all types of goals, and the ideological preference is quite salient. Mastery goals are consensually considered as representing the highest quality of motivation, and the various authors could unanimously recommend that teachers should develop and promote mastery goals in their students. Performance goals are seen as inferior to mastery goals, perhaps necessitated by the social shortcomings of human beings, but not promoted as educational ideals. (The positive views of Harackiewicz and her colleagues about performance goals are probably the exception.) At the bottom of the classification of achievement goals, the performance-avoidance goal, and certainly the work-avoidance situation are perceived as negative motivations.

STUDENTS' ACHIEVEMENT GOALS AND CLASSROOM MANAGEMENT

The relationship between CM (Chapter 9) and students' achievements is directly mediated by students' achievement motivation. Of course the major determinants of any student's achievements would include her/his innate intellectual abilities, home background and early education. But classroom atmosphere and the teacher's CM can have the most significant influence on students' learning and educational outcomes (at both the individual level and the collective level). Students bring to the classroom the fruits of their socialization and of their long history of personal development, but school has a central role in continued socialization and education, and it can modify and change students' motivational patterns and develop attributes and motivations that would lead students to the best educational outcomes.

Individual students can be characterized by their salient achievement goal, and researchers distinguished between students with mastery, performance-approach and performance-avoidance orientation (as well as the fourth work-avoidance orientation). In the same manner, entire social entities such as the classroom (or even the school) can be characterized by the salience of particular achievement goals, and classrooms can be mastery-oriented, performance-approach-oriented, etc. The students try to decipher what is appreciated in their classroom, what is the teacher's premier value and what the teacher really wants, and they try to accommodate themselves to adjust to the system and to fit well in it. Therefore, the achievement goals of the students are influenced by the achievement orientation of the teacher and of the school. If the drive to understand and make progress (relative to yourself, not to others), to develop learning skills and self-reliance, and to *enjoy* the learning process are all appreciated in the classroom—then students would indeed intensify their mastery goals. On the other hand, if the atmosphere is more competitive and excellence compared to one's peers is valued—then the performance-approach goal would be intensified.

Students derive the information concerning the relative importance of particular achievement goals in their classroom in both direct and indirect ways. The direct way is through teachers' explicit statements and explanations about goals and values, norms and rules, and processes of inculcation and preaching that are part of "educating students" (see Chapter 15). The indirect (and probably the more significant) way is through the methods of instruction, the learning contents and the assignments, through the methods used for evaluating students, and through various characteristics of instruction and CM. Mastery goals would be developed through making educational materials more challenging, affording students more choice, and promoting creativity, autonomy and self-determination. Performance goals would be developed through the encouragement of competitiveness, provision of rewards, and in the giving recognition and respect for academic excellence.

As previously mentioned, most researchers and educators have a strong, almost exclusive preference for mastery goals, and therefore the recommended teachers' conduct and instructional methods are structured to promote mastery goals. As will be seen in Chapter 9, the leading contemporary ideology of CM is indeed structured to maximize the development and maintenance of mastery goals in the classroom. Carol Ames, a leading figure in the study of achievement motivation in school, wrote in her seminal work in: "Classrooms: Goals, Structures, and Student Motivation" (Ames, 1992) that "central to the thesis of this article is a perspective that argues for an identification of classroom structures that can contribute to a mastery orientation."

A CRITICAL LOOK AT THE APPLICATION OF ACHIEVEMENT GOALS THEORY IN THE CLASSROOM

I must admit that I feel uncomfortable about some dominant assertions in the achievement goal theory literature. I feel apprehension when it seems that researchers' ideology gets mixed with their research; when dichotomies (or trichotomies) are presented in a fashion where one option is initially considered better than another; and when two psychological literatures lead to very different, almost contrasting conclusions. And I am worried by the thought that perhaps classroom reality concerning students' achievement goals is different than the "reality" of goals as investigated by the researchers, a thought that might cast doubt about the applicability of research findings to actual classrooms. More specifically, I believe that the objective of promoting students' mastery goals and intrinsic motivation is wonderful and should be applied in all classrooms—but I feel uneasy about the exclusion of social motivations and social comparison processes (in the form of performance goals) from the suggested treatments for improving students' achievement motivation.

Psychological dichotomies are very appealing, because they present two options as opposites. I remember how, as a young graduate student, my peers and I were excited about Rotter's (1954, 1966) dichotomy of internal versus external locus of control, and about the dichotomy of extraversion versus introversion in personality research. The distinction between mastery and performance goals in the present achievement goals theory is intellectually inspiring in the same way. But when I filled out the locus of control questionnaires (Crandall, Katkovsky, & Crandall, 1965; Rotter, 1966) I discovered that I fell smack in the middle of the continuum, which meant either that I was neither internal nor external, or that I was both internal and external. My experience with an extraversion–introversion scale was similar, and I concluded that I am both an extravert and an introvert, probably depending on the social circumstances involved in given situations.

Decades later, I had a similar experience when I began to read the literature on mastery and performance goals. I think that I have strong mastery goals and intrinsic motivation in my scientific work, but I am as strongly motivated by performance-approach goals (to prove my intellectual ability and to gain status and recognition). I often also experience performance-avoidance goals, trying to hide my insecurities and my incompetence. Thus, I am motivated by all achievement goals, and all of them together drive me to work hard and to reach a high level of self-efficacy. Any one of the separate achievement goals would not *alone* be sufficient to produce in me a high level of motivation. This conclusion is certainly true about the long and extended effort involved in writing this book.

I believe that I am not an exception, and that most of us are motivated by all three achievement goals. Therefore, it should be possible to increase students' achievement motivation by concurrently promoting all achievement goals. In this way the social needs and the driving force of social comparison would be integrated with the intellectual power of mastery goals. In the research it is necessary to isolate the concepts and to trace the psychological correlates and potential outcomes of each achievement goal separately, but application should integrate the concepts so as to fit the psychological realities of students' motivation.

These ideas resonate in the (lone) voice of Hidi and Harackiewicz in their seminal article (2000) entitled: "Motivating the academically unmotivated: A critical issue for the 21st century." They argued that the polarization of extrinsic and intrinsic motivation and of performance and mastery goals must be reconsidered. They wrote: "We urge educators and researchers to recognize the potential additional benefits of externally triggered situational interest, extrinsic motivation, and performance goals. Only by dealing with the multidimensional nature of motivational forces will we be able to help our academically unmotivated children" (Hidi & Harackiewcz, 2000, p. 151). This argument complements the claim made by Elliott and Harackiewicz

(1996) and by Harackiewicz et al. (2002) that performance-approach goals represent a positive success motivation and should not be dismissed as inferior to mastery goals in promoting students' achievement motivation.

Another problematic issue concerns individual differences in achievement goals. All studies show variance among students in their salient achievement goal—some students prefer mastery goals, for other students the salient goal is either the performance-approach or performance-avoidance goal, and still others demonstrate work-avoidance. How should teachers deal with students whose salient mode does not consist of mastery goals? Should teachers try to increase achievement motivation differentially according to the salience of each type for relevant students, or should only mastery goals be promoted for all students? Chapters 15 and 16 discuss the differences between strengthening existing attitudes and modes of action on the one hand, and changing attitudes and behavior on the other hand. Change is more difficult to attain, because of students' natural resistance to change.

Current research (Butler, 2007) demonstrates that much as the four achievement goals are distributed among students, teachers also differ in their salient achievement orientations. Some teachers are motivated by mastery goals (striving to improve their teaching and to develop themselves as effective teachers); other teachers are motivated by performance-approach goals (to be recognized as better than other teachers); others are driven by performance-avoidance goals (to avoid being less successful than other teachers and to conceal their inefficacy); and still others suffer from work-avoidance (just hoping to reach the end of the day peacefully). It would seem reasonable that each teacher (especially those salient in mastery goals and performance-approach goals) might be most effective in motivating students using the mode that is more salient and more natural for her personally.

The last issue concerns the conceptual possibility that achievement goals might be hierarchical. In his famous theory of motivation, Maslow (1943, 1954) posited several levels in a hierarchical model of human motivation, where higher-level needs (such as self-actualization or esteem needs) are evoked only if lower-level motivations (such as physiological needs, safety needs or social needs) are met and satisfied. In the same way, it is quite conceivable that performance-avoidance, performance-approach and mastery goals also form a hierarchy of achievement motivations. In that case, mastery goals could more likely become salient for students whose lower-level performance needs had been satisfied. That would mean that mastery goals would be more salient among excellent students, those whose initial intellectual abilities and their past academic achievements are high, so that they enjoy high academic and social status and do not have reasons to be concerned about their status in the social comparison process. On the other hand, mediocre students and under-achievers would have more reason to be concerned about their academic abilities and status, and would therefore show greater salience of performance goals (performance-avoidance, and then performance-approach). I believe that the literature on achievement goals indeed confirms the unequal distribution of the types of goals among excellent, mediocre and academically weak students. It might be justifiably argued that appropriate mastery goals can be tailored for weak students and under-achievers to strengthen their mastery orientation, but their social concerns cannot be ignored and must be entered into the equation for effective motivational training.

3 The Teacher's Role(s)

INTRODUCTION

This chapter presents a social-psychological perspective of the teacher's role, or rather, teacher's roles. Teachers experience a duality between their role as authority figure, leader and manager in their classroom society, and their role as a staff member under the management and influence of others in the school society. In their classrooms, teachers actually play a whole spectrum of distinguishable roles, depending upon the nature and demands of each situation. In this chapter, central terms and concepts in the social-psychological perspective are presented and applied to the role of the teacher, such as leadership and its various manifestations, authority and the bases of social power, classroom management (CM) and the view of the teacher as an executive manager. Concurrently with the presentation of basic concepts, issues concerning educational ideology and demands made on teachers are raised, and will be discussed at length in subsequent chapters. The last section introduces the phenomenon of teacher burnout.

THE DUAL ROLES OF THE TEACHER

Teachers live and work in a dual world in school. Every day, they continuously alternate between two roles—classroom teacher and member of the teaching staff. In the classroom, the teacher works alone with the students, carrying a high status of authority and a heavy burden of responsibility. As a member of the teaching staff, the teacher is part of the school society with peers, superiors, administrative staff and an assortment of specialized professionals. The continuous shifts from the teacher role to the staff member role are part of the daily routine, and they really require teachers to have mental flexibility in shifting perspectives. Within the classroom, the teacher's role is further divided into separate roles, most notably instructor and educator, and a common view holds classroom manager as a third role, distinguished from the roles involving teaching and educating.

TEACHER AS STAFF MEMBER IN THE SCHOOL SOCIETY

All concepts and characteristics discussed earlier with regard to the classroom society (Chapter 1) are relevant to the discussion of the school staff society, including norms, roles, expectations and self-esteem as well as struggles for status, leadership and influence. Compared to the classroom society, the school staff society is more complex and hierarchical, with implicit and hidden facets. Teachers' central professional tasks—teaching end educating students—are carried out in the privacy of their classrooms, and other staff members have no direct access to that closed context. Therefore, the evidence for assessing the performance of the teacher is hidden and inaccessible. The evidence can be inferred indirectly through students' achievements, rates of absence or gross violations of discipline, but teachers' professional status among their peers is largely determined by rumors and gossip.

Because of the solitude of the teacher's work in the classroom, the school culture is very important, especially the extent to which peers within the school society can provide a support system for the individual teacher. The literature on the organizational culture of the school indeed emphasizes the significance of teamwork and of the collaboration among staff members in planning their work and retrospectively reflecting on it. In-service training for teachers is always recommended and often required, with a high premium given to in-school training, together with teachers' immediate peers. In most schools, disciplinary and/or inter-disciplinary collaborative teams work on selected topics to plan together their educational interventions and their teaching. Beyond such planned, intentional "institutional" collaboration, the informal support system to help the individual teacher is no less important. Some schools formalize the role of big brother to novice teachers, and most individual teachers seek among their peers those who could be helpful to them in their work. Therefore, the overall atmosphere of the school and its social/emotional climate play a central role in determining the effectiveness of each teacher's work.

Teachers' trials and tribulations, especially those experienced by novice teachers, can be quite stressful. Unlike managers in other types of organizations, their work is carried out alone in their classroom; they are required to carry out many different tasks concurrently, some of them contradictory (controlling the classroom and at the same time teaching, educating, and "producing" achievements); they must cope with tremendous challenges (differences in ability and learning styles among students, individuals with special needs and special problems, disruptive students, etc.); they must be capable of dealing with discipline problems; and they are constantly inspected from above and must demonstrate excellence in divergent directions.

A brand of popular movies and novels about teachers dramatize their professional struggles in their classrooms and in their school staff society. The heroes of those dramas are usually extremely dedicated, stubborn and driven, and they introduce innovative approaches that run counter to the school ethos. Their classrooms are also quite resistant to their style, so that they must cope with tremendous cross-pressures (usually all the way to the happy end of the drama). The situation of most real teachers is probably not as dramatic, but the motives of searching for your way as a teacher; fitting in the school society; coping with difficulties in the absence of a sufficient support system; and dealing with explicit and/or implicit conflicts are very common and frequently experienced in every school.

Schools can be of many kinds in their overall characterization and culture: Achievement-oriented schools, competitive schools, socially-oriented schools, democratic or cooperative schools, exclusive schools, innovative schools, schools with a particular or ideological mission (e.g., religious practice), and schools fighting for survival. The problem is that there is often a gap between the declarative level and the actual reality in the self-characterization of schools, caused by the normative pressure and competition among schools. Some schools are democratic only by declared title and might actually be quite authoritarian; sometimes the stated social goals of a school are phony and the pressure for achievements takes premium; and often schools are geared toward the high-SES population despite statements about deep concern about the underprivileged population.

To navigate themselves most effectively in the school environment, teachers (especially novice teachers) must learn to understand the implicit scenarios of their school, to distinguish between myth and reality, to know the real demands and the unspoken order of priorities, and to be able to diagnose the power structure and the informal status hierarchy of the staff. Awareness of one's own strengths and weaknesses in social settings on the one hand, and understanding of the hidden scenarios of the school society on the other hand, are the keys for effective functioning and success in the school society.

TEACHER AS CLASSROOM INSTRUCTOR AND EDUCATOR

In the classroom, the teacher's work environment is relatively well-defined. The teacher usually works in the classroom for scheduled sessions of fixed length (in the past, the teacher worked with the same classroom almost all hours of the week, and the number of hours is still high today in the lower grades). The teacher is usually alone with the students, managing the classroom and directing the students' learning in a passive or an active mode. The teacher sets the agenda and the timing of activities, controls the classroom, assigns tasks and evaluates the students for their performance. The agenda—particularly in the instructional domain—is explicit and well-defined, so that learning activities can be carried out according to a structured plan.

On principle, the teacher is responsible for both cognitive processes and socio-emotional processes in the classroom—for students' learning and achievements, but no less for their well-being and satisfaction. How-ever, over the last decades the scope of teacher's responsibility to students' learning and education has been diffused by school realities. In the past, the classroom was a permanent group with unchanging membership, and each classroom had a teacher whose entire teaching time was devoted to that classroom. In that situation, teacher's responsibility to all instructional and social aspects in the management of the classroom was immense. But today classroom compositions and teacher–classroom combinations keep changing in every teaching day.

Today, the only permanent composition is that of the home classroom, but the students keep diverging into other compositions for various activi-ties and class sessions. The most permanent teacher is the home room teacher who is responsible for the students in the home classroom in most aspects. In high school, the permanent composition is almost nonexistent, and classes are specialized by divergent topics, different levels of study ("groupings") and other divisions. In elementary school, where the concept of the generalist teacher still exists, teachers continue to spend more hours with the same classrooms. When my grandson, Ido, was in second grade, he told me that he had sessions with seventeen different teachers in a typical week! Thus, we must talk about the teacher and her/his various classrooms, and about the classroom and its various teachers. This situation hinders the exercise of teachers' responsibility to students' development, especially in the educational, socio-emotional domain. As far as the pure instructional aspects are concerned, teachers are fully responsible to advance students' learning in the particular content domains in their limited hours of expo-sure to every classroom.

From a social-psychological point of view, the role of the teacher changes considerably along the developmental continuum from kindergarten and preschool to higher education. New teachers should be aware of the expected role demands when they make their professional choice at what level they wish to teach. In the pre-elementary school level, the teacher has almost total responsibility for the children, for their well-being and for their "education" in every respect. At the extreme other end of the continuum, in university teaching, the responsibility of the teacher for the students' devel-opment is very limited. A university instructor teaches a given subject for a limited number of hours and a limited period to a "random" collection of students. Except for instruction and academic duties, the instructor has no responsibility for the students. Between the preschool and the university, teacher responsibility becomes more limited to the instructional domain with the growing age of the students. Furthermore, the responsibility is divided among more and more teachers who, unfortunately, are not coor-dinated with each other in many cases.

In a similar fashion, the differences between role demands and expec-tations for home-room teachers and specialized content discipline teach-ers in elementary and high-school classrooms must be emphasized. The home-room teachers are the "educators" in charge of their classroom, whereas the responsibility of specialized content teachers is limited to the instructional domain in their specific disciplines. In fact, in Israel the home-room teachers are called "classroom educators." Home-room teachers are responsible for the well-being of their students, for handling the life of the classroom and solving students' personal problems. They are supposed to be coordinated with all other teachers who enter the classroom, and perceived as the referent authorities in eyes of the students in all maters. This responsibility is not decreased even if the home-room teacher does not spend many hours in the classroom. In short, home-room teacher is a formal role in school! Because of this formal role, specialized teachers in the various disciplines (math, language, etc.) often take the freedom to absolve themselves of any responsibility to the classroom beyond the boundaries of their specific disciplines, and that might cause severe problems for students.

TEACHER AS CLASSROOM MANAGER

The attainment of the central objectives in the academic and the social domains is mediated by the effectiveness of teachers' CM. The teacher is the general manager of the classroom society, and her/his task is to lead the entire classroom and all individual students to reach academic success and to reach positive levels of satisfaction and self-esteem. Much has been written in recent decades about CM. In the educational literature for teachers it takes second place only to writings about didactics and teaching technologies in various content disciplines. In this book, Part IV is dedicated to CM, with a chapter about historical developments in CM and the contemporary salient approach, a chapter on discipline problems and punishment, and a chapter on typical and frequent pitfalls that might hinder effective CM. Therefore, the present discussion of CM is only preliminary, intended to introduce some elementary terms.

One of the simple and popular old models in organizational psychology was The Managerial Grid Model, developed by Blake and Mouton (1964). The model identified five different managerial styles based on combinations of two dimensions: *Concern for people* and *Concern for production*. The grid consisted of the graphical representation of the two dimensions on a 9 x 9 matrix, and the five styles were identified by the coordinates: 1.1 ("impoverished style"); 1.9 ("country club style"); 9.1 ("produce or perish style"); 5.5 ("middle of the road style"); and 9.9. ("team style").

In the impoverished style (1.1), these bad managers have low concern for both production and people. Like the work avoidance motivation described in the previous chapter, they want to avoid trouble, protect themselves, and hope to finish their work time in peace. The country club style managers (1.9) have high concern for people but low concern for production. The atmosphere in their work environment is usually warm and friendly, but they are not very productive (say, in the academic achievements of their students). The produce or perish style (9.1) is high with concern for production but low in concern for people. With production and competition above all, these managers often tend to be quite dictatorial, and while production (e.g., academic achievements) might be high, their work environment is unpleasant and stressful for the participants. In the desirable team style (9.9) managers are very high in both their concern for production and concern for people. Success in both domains is achieved through teamwork and collaboration, autonomy and self-regulation. However, this ideal combination is often unattainable, because the concern for production and the concern for people may clash with each other, leading to different behavioral options. Therefore, the middle of the road style (5,5) is a pale but nevertheless more realistic option for effective management.

The Managerial Grid Model cannot be automatically applied to education, because, in the organizational perspective, "production" refers to some product that workers produce which is external to them. In education, the "production" is internal, consisting of students' own personal development, self-esteem, learning gains, etc. But the model *is* applicable to education in its emphasis on the distinction between two basic attitudes that teachers might hold in managing their classrooms. Concern for production is expressed by an achievement-oriented approach, perhaps in the sense of the performance-approach goal and extrinsic motivation described in Chapter 2, whereas the concern for people might be represented by mastery goals.

Like every good manager in any organizational context, a good teacher should be expected to be a 9.9 type, integrating and maximizing the advantages of both approaches. However, emerging situations and problems in the classroom might increase the necessity to emphasize one attitude or the other. In addition, educational ideologists may well have an initial preference for one attitude (see Chapter 9) and they would advocate its advantages over the other attitude.

TEACHER AS AUTHORITY—THE BASES OF SOCIAL POWER

French and Raven (1959) analyzed bases for success in management and formulated a theory that identifies five (actually six) bases of social power. The theory is as applicable today as it had been when it was formulated, and most bases are relevant for teachers as authority figures and as managers of their classrooms. The bases of social power are:

1. *Reward power.* The perceived ability to provide positive consequences or to remove negative consequences, the power to reinforce.
2. *Coercive power.* The power to punish those who do not conform with your ideas or demands.
3. *Legitimate power* (organizational authority). The perception that someone has the right to prescribe behavior and to control others due

to appointment or election to a position of responsibility. (Also called *normative power*).

4. *Referent power.* Power attained through the association to those who have power.

5. *Expert power.* Power resulting from having distinctive knowledge, expertness, ability or skills that are needed by others.

6. *Information power* (similar to No. 5). Controlling the information needed by others in order to reach an important goal.

All (or almost all) of these bases of social power can characterize teachers' position in the classroom and constitute their potential power base for CM. Conversely, lacking one or another of these bases might hinder teachers' conduct and limit their managerial possibilities. Teachers indeed have reward power and coercive power, and can (and must) reward, reinforce and sometimes punish students; teachers have legitimate power and are recognized by students as the organizational power figures with a legitimate right to put on normative pressure; and teachers certainly have expert power and information power, and their main task is to develop students and to make them learn and grow through their knowledge and information. I believe that referent power, through the association with others who have power, perhaps is somewhat less relevant to the classroom (unless association with the principal might be a source of teacher's referent power in students' perceptions).

Each of the bases of social power has distinctive and characteristic behaviors associated with it, and teachers exercise the different bases as they find appropriate and desirable. Each type also has different consequences for the students. I think that teachers and students have shared expectations of the type of teacher behavior appropriate for particular situations. In addition, individual teachers have an order of priorities among the different bases of power, and they prefer to manage the classroom through particular bases. For example, some teachers are perfectionists and punitive by nature, whereas other teachers prefer to avoid using their coercive power. Some teachers might be successful in leading their classrooms through their expert power, whereas others may need to use their legitimate organizational power more frequently. In situations of conflict, difficulty, or of a problem in CM that requires a solution (say, about truancy or homework assignments), it is most interesting to find out which of the power bases (or which combination of power bases) a teacher would select to deal with the problem (when, as mentioned previously, each choice has different consequences for the students).

TEACHER AS LEADER

By any role definition and according to all bases of social power, the teacher is the unquestionable leader of the classroom. Teachers' leadership qualities and their exercise of leadership determine to a large extent the educational outcomes and the emotional climate of their classrooms. The study of leadership in educational and organizational settings dates back to the 1930s. Lewin, Lippitt, and White's (1939) study of the impact of three types of leadership, which was conducted in an educational setting, is one of the classical, most-widely quoted experiments in social psychology. Decades later, it still carries immensely important implications for the classroom teacher.

Lewin and his colleagues arranged for ten- and eleven-year-old boys to meet after school to partake in various hobbies. They met in small groups and were led by an adult male. Three types of leadership behavior were examined:

1. *The authoritarian (or autocratic) leader* told the boys what to do without much explanation; took no input from the members in making decisions about group activities; often criticized the boys, arbitrarily paired boys with work partners; and emphasized his authority.
2. *The democratic (or participatory) leader* made sure that all activities were first discussed by the entire group; let the group make decisions while he provided advice and guidance; encouraged the development of an egalitarian atmosphere; and rarely criticized the boys or gave them orders.
3. *The laissez-faire (let do) leader* allowed the boys to work in whichever way they wished and rarely intervened in the group activities; the group worked without any supervision and the adult functioned primarily as a source of technical information when necessary. The leader did not offer information, criticism or guidance.

The effectiveness of leadership styles was measured by two types of outcomes: Productivity and group's emotional climate. The laissez-faire leadership was least effective by both counts: The boys spent much time working at cross-purposes, their production was very low, and they did not enjoy the experience and demonstrated negative emotional reactions. Thus, "let do" leadership is considered in the literature as non-effective leadership.

The comparison of democratic and autocratic leadership demonstrated greater productivity under the autocratic leader and a more positive emotional climate under the democratic leader. The autocratic-led groups spent more time working on the task and were more efficient than the democratic-led groups (but spent less time working when the leader was absent). The democratic-led boys enjoyed the experience more than the autocratic-led boys, liked each other more and showed less aggression and tension.

Over the years, numerous writers (educators, human relations specialists, etc.) interpreted the findings—with more than a trace of ideological wishful thinking—as demonstrating the superiority of democratic leadership over autocratic leadership. Subsequently, the democratic leadership style is most often advocated and recommended for educational and organizational management.

In studies of childrearing and parental styles, Baumrind (1971) replaced the term democratic by authoritative (as distinct from authoritarian leadership). The shift in terms was justified by the fact that the so-called democratic leadership is not really democratic at all, because decisions are not made by majority vote. Authoritative leaders take responsibility and retain decision-making authority, but solicit input, seek consensus and voluntary participation, and encourage members' autonomy. Authoritative leadership is the founding cornerstone of the contemporary salient ideology of CM (see Chapter 9), and Brophy (2006) argues that it is most effective for developing in students the desirable cognitive structures and behavioral control mechanisms that would lead them toward autonomy, self-determination and self-efficacy.

This trait-approach to leadership (meaning that the style of leadership is a fixed personal attribute of the leader and is systematically enacted by the leader in all situations) was dominant for several decades. Eventually it was substituted by more situational approaches that sought to determine the effectiveness of leadership behavior as a combination of leader's trait and the characteristics of the specific situations involved. In his Contingency Theory of Leadership, Fiedler (1978, 1981) argued that different leadership styles work better in different situations. He tried to predict differential effectiveness of styles considering three factors: leader/worker relations; degree of task structure; and leader's power to reward or punish group members. According to Fiedler, effectiveness also varies between favorable and unfavorable situations. Similar ideas were salient in Hersey and Blanchard's (1982) Situational Model of Leadership.

The implication for teachers' leadership in their CM is that, different styles and combinations of styles of leadership might be effective in particular classroom situations. Even if one style of leadership (namely, the democratic/participative/person-oriented style) is thought to be more preferable on ideological grounds, an alternative style is more likely to yield the best outcomes in certain classroom situations, especially in crises.

Two additional leadership styles must be mentioned—transformational leadership and charismatic leadership—although these styles are less likely to be frequently demonstrated in classrooms. Transformational leadership is a concept that has become a focus of investigation in recent years (Bass, 1998). It is a supreme leadership style where the leader and the followers collaborate and raise one another to higher levels of motivation, morality and performance. The group and the leader become fused together and elevate themselves.

Charismatic leaders are admirable and most influential leaders who serve as models and cause followers to identify with them. Charisma is a rare combination of attractive personality attributes which appeal to group members on an emotional level, and they would admire and idealize the leader and accept her/his convictions and values. The following of charismatic leaders is usually very intense and extremely loyal, and the charismatic leader is idolized and becomes a strong identification model.

TEACHER AS MODEL

Most of us carry fond old memories of one or two exemplary teachers who became fixed forever in our memory as those who influenced us immensely in the course of our early development. Indeed charismatic teachers do exist, but charisma is a rare quality that could characterize only very few teachers. Of course a charismatic teacher can have a profound educative effect on students.

In the educational literature, one can frequently find the demand that the teacher should serve as a model and as a personal example for students. As a model, the teacher should facilitate students' imitation, internalization, and identification. In my opinion, it would have been wonderful if all teachers would be able to become ideal models for their students, but that demand is unrealistic and might hinder, rather than facilitate teachers' conduct. Such a demand would probably maximize the ideal-self/actual-self gap for teachers, and cause tension, frustration and anxiety. Teachers are normal human beings with strengths and weaknesses, advantages and pitfalls, and it is not fair to pose a demand for perfection and ideal example.

Young children view their parents as ideal persons, and identification with parents as models is part of normal development. Similarly, preschoolers and early elementary school students may hold their teachers as identification models. But as they grow up, children become more realistic and skeptic, they realize that their parents and their teachers cannot be perfect and that even the best idols have clay feet. In adolescence, the course of human development predicts rebelliousness and suspicion of adults, and almost no normal adolescent would hold a parent or a teacher as an identification idol. Probably only charismatic leaders are forever idolized by their young and old followers, but that is the exception rather than the rule, and outsiders are critical of the "stupidity" of the followers' idolism.

Thus, the notion of teacher as model has some relevance in the classroom society in early education due to students' expectations. But as far as the teachers themselves and their personality attributes are concerned, the demand to serve as identification model is unfair and unrealistic at any level of education. Students can, and should appreciate their parents and their teachers, but not idolize them. In my opinion, two aspects are important with regard to the issue of teacher as model:

1. That every teacher would possess some special attributes and characteristics that would make the teacher unique and special in students' eyes; and

2. That teachers would not have salient weaknesses or attributes that would make them "negative models" in students' eyes.

Students often characterize good teachers and bad teachers. Good teachers are typically perceived as being challenging, firm but fair, and knowledgeable. They encourage student participation, take time to talk to students, give constructive criticism, and work to build students up. Bad teachers give no feedback, are too strict, unprepared, patronizing and condescending, and not open to students' input. I believe that, in fact, students are quite forgiving about the human weaknesses of their teachers. However, one type of failure is *not* acceptable in students' eyes, and that is lack of fairness and equity in teachers' behavior toward different students. Unfair treatment is perceived by students as a basic violation and is unforgivable. Chapters 7 and 8 expand the discussion of this issue in the analysis of teacher–student interaction.

TEACHER BURNOUT

This chapter demonstrates the complexity of the teacher's role (even when the discussion was limited to social psychological aspects only, leaving out the major challenges of instruction). Teaching is an extremely difficult and challenging occupation. Teachers do not enjoy sufficiently high financial and social status, and the pressures on the classroom teacher can be immense. Therefore, we must discuss the issue of teacher burnout at the completion of this chapter on the teacher's role(s).

Burnout is a phenomenon of mental and physical exhaustion (Pines & Aronson, 1988), deflation of energies and coping strategies, decrease in self-efficacy (Bandura, 1997) and a diminished sense of accomplishment, caused by overwork and by expectations and needs that cannot be met (Friedman, 1993, 1995, 2006; Maslach & Leiter, 1999). In recent years, teacher burnout has come to occupy center stage in the burnout literature. Compared to other occupations, teachers are in very high risk for burnout. The huge number of hours they spend in their classrooms and the accumulating daily pressures and stress make teachers prone to burnout, and the proportions of teachers demonstrating symptoms of being worn-out and burned-out are staggering. (Worn-out is a milder form of burnout). Numerous reports (see Friedman, 2000, 2006) show especially high rates of burnout in the first few years of new teachers.

Burnout is expressed in reduced self-esteem, external locus of control, decrease in self-efficacy, and symptoms of anxiety, depression, nervousness, apathy and exhaustion. The burnout might be focused on a particular classroom, a particular school or principal, class level, or more global burnout of teaching in general. Many burned-out teachers simply leave the teaching profession altogether. That might be better than a situation where worn-out or burned-out teachers continue to teach their classrooms in apathy, just waiting eagerly for each day to end ASAP.

In the extensive literature on teacher burnout, many factors that contribute to burnout are discussed and investigated. On the overall organizational level, the factors discussed in the literature include insufficient rewards (in terms of both financial status and social status); occupational overload; absence of decision-making power; lack of opportunity for promotion within the occupation (teachers can be promoted out of teaching by becoming principals, superintendents, counselors, etc.); and gaps between the time pressures and whatever is needed in order to attain educational objectives.

Most researchers (e.g., Friedman, 2000, 2006; Wood & McCarthy, 2000) agree that the major predictors of teacher burnout can be found in teacher-students relations in the classroom. Classrooms are overloaded with students; the curricula are demanding and it is difficult to bring heterogeneous classrooms to high achievements; teachers must deal with continuous disturbances, threats and discipline problems; student motivation is often very low; and teachers frequently experience failure with many of their students. Teachers do not receive enough appreciation from their students and from their superiors, and they often become punching bags for frustrated parents and/or the entire community (particularly following some unpleasant incidents involving their students). Many students learn from their parents to disrespect their teachers.

On the conceptual level, a state of a large gap between initial expectations and ideological goals on the one hand, and the realities of the classroom on the other hand (an Ideal-Actual Gap, see Chapter 2) creates the potential for burnout. This explains why rates of teacher burnout are particularly high in the first few years of teaching. Other gaps also contribute their share: Gaps between teachers' self-expectations and those of others in the social environment; gaps between statements on the declarative level and classroom reality; and also wide gaps among the students in the classroom.

Unfortunately, I think that much of the literature in teacher training also contributes to potential teacher burnout. A very rosy and idyllic picture of the teaching profession is often presented (see, for example, Everston & Weinstein, 2006a), without giving a proportional (or even minimal) consideration to the severe problems teachers are likely to experience in contemporary classrooms. Thus, unrealistic expectations are built up for an ideal teacher conduct that very often cannot be implemented in the classroom (see Chapter 9).

Despite the bleak picture that has been described, our outlook about teacher burnout can be more positive. School systems are keenly aware of the burnout issue today, and efforts can be taken to cope with this phenomenon and reduce its intensity. In recent years, an extensive literature (in published works such as Wood & McCarthy, 2000, and on the Internet) offers various means, strategies and workshops for reducing teacher burnout. Much depends on the conduct of school principals and how the teaching staff is managed. Teamwork and mutual responsibility; job enrichment and the creation of an atmosphere of changeability and innovation; encouragement of continuous self-reflection; and especially the creation and maintenance of a support system for the individual teacher—all of these can contribute to reduce teacher burnout and increase teachers' satisfaction and sense of self-efficacy.

Part II

Social Measurement in the Classroom

4 Social Structure and Sociometric Measurement in the Classroom

CHARACTERISTICS OF CLASSROOM SOCIETY

Students' life in the classroom society is very intensive. Beyond norms and roles, every classroom is characterized by social classes and leadership, sets of friendships among individuals and relationships among subgroups, struggles for status and influence, and continuous (open or hidden) competition side-by-side with patterns of support and cooperation. For the students, the classroom society is their central social experience outside the protected framework of their family. Students' satisfactions, achievements, rewards and self-esteem are derived from their life in the classroom society. For young children, the classroom is their first experience of having to navigate oneself in a social/organizational structure. They have to learn what to do and how to do in order to become competent and successful. Of course children have no abstract understanding of social processes and no conscious awareness for analyzing what they experience. Therefore, the processes are not explicitly verbalized, and their intensity for the classroom participants is very high. For some children the experience is fantastic and rewarding, but for many, if not most children, the struggle is difficult and demanding, and its fruits are not always satisfactory. To understand the intensity of these processes, the reader should stop for a moment to imagine the daily classroom experiences of being a mediocre student or being a rejected student. For many children, these are their continuous and central classroom experiences.

In psychological or sociological analysis, the classroom society is quite complex. Above all, it is complex because of the duality of two co-existing life systems—the formal and the informal systems. The formal life of the classroom in the educational context centers on learning and instruction, with well-defined student roles. In this context, formal authority figures (adults) control the events during most hours of the day and dictate most students' activities. Parallel to the formal system, the informal life of the classroom flows all the time, and numerous events and interactions occur all the time. The two systems flow concurrently and influence each other. Students' academic achievements and status in the eyes of the teachers influence their status in the classroom society, and students' status among their peers influences teachers' view of them.

Classroom society is complex because of the great variation among students in all factors that might be involved in the attainment of social status, power, and prestige. In sociological analysis, classrooms are defined as homogeneous or heterogeneous through characteristics of family socioeconomic status, parents' education, occupation, income, and IQ levels. These levels of homogeneity or heterogeneity are important for the planning of instruction. Greater heterogeneity is more desirable from a societal and ideological point of view, but heterogeneous classrooms are harder to teach and they pose greater challenges for teachers. But even if a classroom is homogeneous from a sociological perspective, it always is extremely heterogeneous in personal, personality and social terms. The classroom society is founded on the multitude of subtle differences among members in social competencies, motivations, and personality attributes.

STATUS AND SOCIAL CLASSES

The central terms for characterizing classroom society are presented next, and the explanation is expanded in the subsequent discussion of sociometric measurement. The classroom society is stratified into social classes and characterized by status differences. Hargreaves (1975) defined three main dimensions of social status:

1. *Popularity.* Expressing levels of attraction and rejection among members.
2. *Social power.* The distribution of leadership and influence potential among members.
3. *Prestige.* Related to special roles or special competencies or attributes.

The upper class consists of a few leaders and prestigious members; every classroom has a middle class; and the lower class consists of rejected and neglected children and often also low-achievers. The classroom society also consists of subgroups and cliques who are often competing with each other, and struggles for power and for leadership are quite common. In most classrooms, the "boys society" and the "girls society" are segregated from each other with boundaries of varying intensity. The picture of the inter-gender social relations becomes, of course, more complicated at adolescence! Classrooms differ in their social-emotional climate; in levels of cooperation and competition; in cohesiveness; in open or hidden manifestations of tension and conflict; and in types and levels of violence enacted in the classroom. A central issue concerns the level of disengagement of the upper class from the lower classes. Educators are always concerned about the psychological state of rejected and neglected children in the classroom.

FRIENDSHIPS

Parallel to the group processes I've described, classroom society is also characterized by an important interpersonal phenomenon—namely friendship between children (Pellegrini & Blatchford, 2000). It is very important for every normal child to have a close friend (almost always of the same gender), and pairs of friends are an important part of the classroom society. On average, about one half of the students are paired in dyads, where both children would consensually identify the other as their best friend. Dyadic friendship is a major source of satisfaction and social adjustment, constituting most often the central support system for the individual child. Again, in adolescence interpersonal friendship comes to be influenced by glandular processes and hormonal development, complicating the social perspective of friendships as part of social structure. However, most adolescents try to maintain their same-gender friendships even when they become interested in members of the other gender.

CLASSROOM NARRATIVE

Every classroom is a unique mini-society and has its particular history, scenarios and unique unfolding of social processes. It is very important that teachers will know the particular narratives of the classroom and their particular roles in those narratives. As mentioned in Chapter 3, the teacher's responsibility for the classroom is all-inclusive in the lower grades, and therefore a deep understanding of the classroom society and classroom narrative is critical. In higher grades, teachers' responsibility becomes more diffused, because most teachers are responsible only for the limited segment of teaching their own content discipline. Only the home-room teacher is then more involved in the classroom society, and even that can take place through a limited presence in the classroom. In higher education, teachers are not involved at all in the social life of the classroom, and in many cases a true classroom society does not even exist.

Knowing the narrative of the classroom can enable teachers to lead the classroom to a more peaceful and productive life and to solve many problems. Unfortunately, a great effort is required to uncover the narrative, because many aspects are implicit and hidden from teachers' eyes. Students are not eager to share social information with teachers, and the viewpoint of the teachers is quite limited (see later discussion). The common reality is that principals and school administrations are not interested in the hidden lives of classrooms, as long as instruction, learning and achievement are OK, and as long as no particular issues or problem children are heard about. A good classroom is, in a way, an anonymous classroom.

Classroom teachers are, of course, better informed about their classrooms, but they perceive the students from their role perspective as teachers.

Usually teachers know more about the salient students—the outstanding students and, more often, the problem students—whereas the silent majority remains quite invisible to them. When a special event creates a new experience and novel teacher-student interactions (such as a 3-day trip or intensive preparations for a special end-of-semester event), teachers suddenly discover a rich social world and they learn to know many of their students in a new and different light.

In my course on the social psychology of the classroom, one assignment requires teachers to investigate and to write up the unique narrative of their classroom via observations and interviews with their students. For some teachers, this becomes an exciting learning experience, because they discover hidden aspects that were out of their knowledge although all the information was there to be seen.

SOCIOMETRIC MEASUREMENT AND SOCIOMETRIC STRUCTURE OF THE CLASSROOM

Over seventy years ago, Moreno (1934) coined the term "sociometry" and developed measurement instruments to probe the implicit social processes in groups, especially classrooms. The basic idea was that, in order to know about classrooms, you must ask the students themselves and reconstruct the social structure from their reports. This idea gained momentum and has remained valid in psychological measurement over the years. Moreno believed that the single most important index should be children's emotional reactions to each other, as reflected in attractions and rejections. Various indexes of social information could be derived from the distributions of attractions and rejections. And indeed sociometric measurement was exclusively based for several decades on the statistical classroom summaries of children's liking and disliking nominations (Moreno, 1943, 1960).

Sociometry had many followers over the years, and generations of teachers used sociometric measurement to deepen their understanding of the classroom society. Today, several newer models of sociometric measurement are available, and there is also greater awareness of some of the ethical problems in Moreno-type measurement of students' emotional reactions toward each other.

In the conventional sociometric questionnaire, students are asked to write the names of three students in the classroom whom they like most and find most attractive, and the names of three other students whom they dislike and do not want to be with (rejections). Different sociometric criteria can be used: Who do you like best/or dislike; whom would you choose to move/not move with you to another classroom; play with outside school; want as a close friend; sit next to, etc. All students must fill out the questionnaire and each completes the same number of nominations. Refusal to nominate peers (which is justified from an ethical point of view), or absence from school when the measurement is conducted, create a serious methodological problem of missing data, which might change the sociometric picture of the classroom.

When all nominations are summed up for the entire classroom, matrices of attractions and rejections are constructed. I shall discuss mostly the positive nominations in the following discussion, because they are more important for the analysis of social structure, and because rejection ratings are more objectionable. The number of nominations that a student can potentially receive ranges from zero (nobody nominated her/him as best liked) to N-1 (liked by everybody, a phenomenon that is almost never found). In a classroom with twenty-five to thirty students, sociometric stars might typically receive nine to twelve nominations. When close to half of all classroom peers find a given child as most attractive and wish to be friends with her/him, that child would be considered as having very high status. At the other end of the liking continuum, a few students do not get any liking nominations, and several others receive only one or two nominations. That would indicate low sociometric status. In a totally random distribution, every child would receive three liking nominations by chance alone.

The distribution of the liking nominations in the classroom teaches us about the implicit social structure, and one can think of several potential patterns: In some classrooms a single or a few sociometric stars receive numerous nominations, whereas in other classrooms no salient stars can be observed and the distribution of attractive students is more even and balanced. In some classrooms some, or many students received no nominations at all, whereas in other classrooms each student had been chosen at least once or twice. In some classrooms the middle class is very large, whereas in other classrooms the extreme social classes are more heavily populated. Another important analysis is the comparison of the distributions among boys and among girls, in an effort to detect similarities or differences in patterns.

It is particularly important to note that when teachers are asked to guess the sociometric nominations of their students, they seem to know very little about their students' choices. In fact, on average teachers can identify only about one half of the sociometric stars in their classrooms. When they miss, they fail to identify children who are actually liked by many of their peers, and they think that other children are the sociometric stars. The most common mistake is for teachers to think that the academically excellent students are also best-liked by their peers.

SOCIOGRAM: ANALYSIS OF CLASSROOM STRUCTURE

The next step in the sociometric analysis is to draw graphically the "map" of the liking nominations. The map—called "sociogram"—has the form of a circle, with boys on one side and girls on the other side of the circle. The children are located on the sociogram so that the sociometric stars are in the middle and the children selected least are on the outskirts. Every liking nomination is marked by an arrowed-line, and a mutual selection, by a thicker, double-arrowed line. Therefore, most arrows on the sociogram point inside, toward the center of the circle. A sociogram takes some training and skill to make, but it is an interesting tool for inferring about hidden social forces in the classroom. Even without actually conducting sociometric measurement in their classrooms, teachers can gain an understanding of the social structure of the classroom by being familiar with the sociometric terms.

Mutual selections are very telling about dyadic friendships in the classroom. A mutual selection, where both parties identify each other as the most liked peer, indicates friendship and mutual support. The proportion of mutual selections in the classroom tells us about the atmosphere and the harmony in the classroom. The examination of mutual selections is most important in the margins of the classroom, where children receive few liking selections. If those children have at least one mutual selection, it means that they do have a close friend, and their psychological state might well be expected to be better than what it night have been had they not had any mutual selection. If a marginal child selects only peers who do not reciprocate the choice, the situation is more problematic. Of course those who are not selected at all by anybody are in the worst social situation (see later discussion of neglected students).

Cross-gender selections are also an important indicator of classroom atmosphere. Harmonious classes would have more cross-gender selections, but many classrooms demonstrate a rigid gender boundary, where all selections are made within gender, boys do not like girls and vice versa. Of course gender boundaries change developmentally as children approach adolescence, but within a grade level (that is, at a certain developmental stage) one can find substantial variations in cross-gender selections.

The central analyses of a sociometric map are focused on social networks, chains, and inferred processes of leadership and social influence. Social influence can be deduced from links connecting from one child to another in a continuous fashion. For example, it is important whether the sociometric star was selected mostly by students occupying the middle class or by marginal students as well. A chain with more systematic links can indicate the level of connectivity among students in the classroom. Some classrooms are chaotic, with maps that seem to be random drawings with no systematic relations, whereas other classrooms show a flow of relations and connections. A "leader" is a sociometric star who is connected through chains to many directions in the classroom society.

A closed triangle of three students connected by three mutual selections indicates a clique, a close-knit group of strong friends. A closed triangle located in the center of the sociogram (meaning that many more students select the three members of the triangle) can indicate a leadership group. If the triangle is located far from the center (i.e., with fewer selections by other children) it might indicate an opposition group. Classrooms characterized by more tension and struggles would demonstrate more boundaries between groups that are intra-connected with each other. Thus, whereas triangles (or closed squares, which are quite rare) represent positive friendship, boundaries between inter-connected groups represent tension in the classroom.

Finally, the social situation of any given student can be analyzed through his/her "social atom," which isolates all the arrows leading to and from that particular student. The position of that student in the classroom society can then be examined, together with her/his network of connections (selections and non-selections) with significant other figures in the classroom.

DRAWBACKS OF SOCIOMETRIC MEASUREMENT

Sociometric measurement had been extremely popular for several decades, and generations of teachers had undergone training and used sociometric methods to understand classroom society. The common feeling was that sociometry provides a wealth of (data-based) information that is not easily accessible to the teacher through other means. Teachers also felt that it enables them to plan various interventions in their classrooms to remedy problems uncovered by the sociometric measurement. But certain drawbacks, including ethical ones, must be considered as well. Sociometric measurement (especially in the Moreno tradition which is focused on emotional attractions and rejections) is quite obtrusive. It excites the children very much and creates an atmosphere of dealing with gossip, of giving legitimacy to gossip with no respect to students' privacy. The measurement can upset many children in the classroom, especially those expected to be of marginal status, neglected or rejected. It can also cause unwanted "political" processes, where children campaign for votes.

Therefore, educational authorities have begun in recent decades to control sociometric measurement and limit its free use. In Israel, for example, an investigator who requests permission to administer sociometric measures in classrooms would have to convince the Ministry of Education that the measurement would actually benefit the field *and* would benefit the specific classrooms where data is to be collected. Another danger is that of playing psychologist—where untrained teachers reach hasty conclusions out of sociometric data with no proper professional controls. Still, on the positive side, sociometric measurement represents an impressive case of data-based diagnosis and decision making that can benefit teachers and provide them with rich information about their classrooms.

TYPOLOGY OF SOCIOMETRIC "STUDENT TYPES"

In the 1980s, the "two-dimensional model" of sociometric measurement was developed (Coie, Dodge, & Coppoletti, 1982). The two dimensions are (a) Social attraction (liking minus disliking nominations, that is, "pure" positive attraction); and (b) Social impact (liking plus disliking nominations, because nominations of dislike are also manifestations of social impact in the classroom). From the 2 x 2 combinations of the liking and disliking nominations, the investigators constructed a typology and defined four distinct types of students:

1. *Popular student* who receives many liking nominations and no (or very few) disliking ones.
2. *Rejected student* who receives many disliking nominations and no liking ones.
3. *Neglected student* who receives no nominations of any type at all and is virtually "lost" in the classroom.
4. *Controversial student* who receives many nominations, both positive and negative, that is, a student who is liked intensely by some peers but at the same time is disliked intensely by other peers. The controversial student is the focus of much attention in the classroom and evokes polar reactions. S/he is sometimes considered "a negative leader" in the classroom.

Beyond these types, the majority of the students are labeled "average student." This is not really a distinct type like the previous four types, and these students really remain unclassified. The statistical definition selected by the investigator determines what proportion of students would be classified into each type. For examples, "popular" can be arbitrarily defined to include students in the upper 20% of the nominations in their class or a wider category including 30% of the nominations.

A typology has great advantages in personality research and in clinical psychology and it can also contribute to the understanding of classroom society. Much research since the early 1980s examined these types, their personality profiles, their social and family contexts, and their academic and social conduct. I see two major contributions of this conceptual model to the social psychology of the classroom—one in the definition of controversial children and the distinction between popular and controversial students, the other in focusing attention on rejected and neglected children at the negative pole. The controversial child, the leader who is not simply accepted by everybody but evokes both positive and negative reactions that might be equally intense, is an interesting addition to our understanding of the complexity of leadership processes in the classroom. Controversial students contribute to an atmosphere of tension and un-rest, and probably require much teacher attention to reduce tensions in the classroom.

REJECTED AND NEGLECTED STUDENTS

Focusing attention on neglected children is also very important. Rejected students, who receive many nominations as disliked peers, are usually quite salient in the classroom as problem students, and much attention is required to deal with them. Much of the current emphasis and attention given in recent years to bullying and to manifestations of violence in school is naturally concentrated on the sociometrically rejected students, and a huge literature on the etiology and treatment of bullying and school violence is available today (see, for example, Hyman et al., 2006). But the neglected students are invisible and lost in the classroom, remote from the attention of their peers and their teachers. Attempts to examine teachers' guesses of their students' sociometric choices consistently reveal that teachers are not aware of the unique status of these children, sometimes considering them shy or reserved, but with no understanding that these children are totally ignored, nobody likes them and nobody dislikes them in the classroom. Because they are not problem children and do not draw any attention, the teachers and the school authorities, who must dedicate their time to problem-solving, are ignorant of their state. I think that the definition of this type and the attention drawn to their state of being invisible in the classroom helped to change the situation, forcing teachers and educators to seek out neglected children and to deal with their unique situation.

"ATTRACTIVENESS" VERSUS "POPULARITY"

Experienced researchers can sometimes fall into the pitfall of coining terms carelessly on the basis of their data, inadvertently misleading their readership. In the two-dimensional model described above (Coie et al., 1982) and the multitude of subsequent research based on that model, the "popular student" has been defined by having received a high number of nominations as best liked peer (or rather, "best liked" minus "most disliked peer"). The choice of the term "popular" for this type was intuitively appealing and was generally accepted without dispute. However, this term might be misleading, because popularity as a social phenomenon implies a certain social status that is directly related to leadership, but this student received many nominations for being personally liked by peers who want to be her/his friend. A child who is highly liked personally might not necessarily hold a leadership position in the classroom. To examine this question (Babad, 2001), I asked thousands of students in hundreds of classrooms in which we administered sociometric questionnaires to name not only the three students they best liked personally, but also the names of the students they considered as "most popular" in their classrooms. No explanation was provided at all as to what "popular" means, relying on students' own subjective understanding of the term. The results showed that "best liked" and "popular" types were quite distinct from each other, and the numbers of nominations received for personal liking and for popularity were not strongly related to each other at all. Many children were highly popular but not best liked, and many other children who received a lot of liking nominations were not named as most popular. Only a very small percentage of children were nominated as both best liked and popular. Therefore, I concluded that the term "popular student" proposed in the two-dimensional model to characterize those receiving many personal liking nominations is misleading, and that type should be labeled "attractive student."

Thus, we might think of three types at the top of the sociometric distribution in the classroom structure—personally attractive students, socially popular students, and controversial students. To these, a fourth high-status student type who exists in every classroom should be added—the academically excellent student. The academically excellent students are often also the most popular or most attractive students, but their academic status does not guarantee personal attractiveness or leadership. The impact of academic excellence on the classroom structure might be immense because of the weight of academic work in the life of the classroom society. Teachers often bestow special status on their excellent students (see Chapter 8 for more information about teachers' pets). However, sociometric theorizing and writings focused quite exclusively on socio-emotional aspects and neglected to deal with the social impact of academic excellence.

COGNITIVE SOCIOMETRY

In recent years, application of sociometric techniques (that is, of asking group members about other group members and using their summed responses as the data for analysis) moved from the study of personal attractions and rejections to the cognitive domain, using students as judges of social situations. Whereas the Moreno-type sociometric question always asked respondents for their personal feelings towards their peers, current cognitive sociometry engages students cognitively as judges and asks them to name and to evaluate different role holders in the classroom. They are asked to use their observation and judgment rather than to express their inner feelings. The nomination of popular students mentioned above (Babad, 2001) is an example of this approach. Similarly, students can be asked to identify classroom jokers, rejected students (without having to reject them personally by nominating them as "liked least by me") and many other types.

Chapter 8 focuses on the teacher's pet phenomenon, and teachers' pets were identified through sociometric nominations of all classroom students, who were asked to identify particular students who were best liked by the teachers. A teacher was defined as a "teacher who has a pet student" when there was a consensus in peers' judgments that a particular student was best liked (or loved) by the teacher. These cognitive sociometric nominations were supported by another judgment students were asked to make— whether there was one (un-named) student in their classroom who was most loved by their teacher. Here, too, the status of the teacher was a function of the intensity of the consensus among all students in her classroom.

The cognitive sociometric approach has a great advantage in steering away from students' emotions and in employing them as objective judges of the classroom situation. We know that students are "experts" and they possess invaluable knowledge about the classroom society and its underlying social processes, knowledge that is usually not accessible to the teachers. The issue of students' expertise is discussed in several subsequent chapters. I enjoy my conversations with my grandson, Ido, about his classroom, and I am amazed at the sophistication of his intuitive social psychological knowledge about his classroom society. Once the ethical problem of steering unwanted excitement among the students by Moreno-type measurement of attractions and rejections has been removed, classroom teachers and school management have significant sociometric research instruments that can be employed in school-based research. Such research can be meaningful in data-based diagnoses of social problems and in planning of corrective interventions. Students can be asked directly about social processes in the classroom (see the following chapter for information about the measurement of classroom climate) as well as about the status and roles of their peers in cognitive sociometry, as long as they are not asked about their personal feelings, especially their personal rejections.

5 Measurement of Classroom Climate

CLASSROOM CLIMATE: A SALIENT RESEARCH DOMAIN IN EDUCATIONAL PSYCHOLOGY

Classroom climate (CC)—also referred to in the literature as "classroom environment," "learning environment," or "classroom culture"—is today one of the flourishing areas of research in educational psychology. Extensive research on CC has been conducted and published since the 1980s in Australia, in several countries in the Far East, and in the USA and Europe. A new scientific journal ("Learning Environment Research") was established in 1998, and a new Special Interest Group of the American Educational Research Association is focused on CC (both headed by Barry Fraser of Australia). A large number of questionnaires and instruments for the measurement of CC have been constructed, validated, and published for public use (see Fraser, 1998; Dorman, 2002).

This book covers three central domains in the psychology of the classroom that provide teachers with important applied knowledge for dealing with their classrooms:

1. Classroom climate and learning environment (the topic of the present chapter);
2. Teacher expectancies, self-fulfilling prophecies and teachers' differential behavior in their interactions with students (Part III, Chapters 6–8);
3. Classroom management (Part IV, Chapters 9–11).

It would have been most advantageous if these domains would have been integrated with each other, but unfortunately they have remained distinct and the three literatures are separate from each other. To put these domains in perspective and to understand their origins, a brief historical background is provided next:

1. *Classroom climate (CC)*. This domain grew from methodological developments in the measurement of various social environments such

as hospitals, prisons and different types of workplaces by Rudolf Moos (1974, 1978). The growing emphasis on high-inference measurement in educational research in the 1970s and 1980s (see later discussion) gave a push to extensive measurement of classroom environment as well. Work was conducted concurrently by Moos & Trickett (1987), by Herbert Walberg (in examination of innovative projects in science teaching in the USA), and by Barry Fraser in Australia. This field emphasizes methodological and measurement issues and remains strongly (though not exclusively) connected to science teaching and to measurement of the outcomes of educational innovations. However, the concept of CC is highly relevant to *all* classrooms and all educational environments, regardless of age level, content discipline or any other dimension.

2. *Classroom Management (CM)*. This domain grew within the field of teacher education out of efforts to define ways for teachers to effectively manage their classrooms. The historical roots of the contemporary approach to CM (see Brophy, 2006) can be found in the human relations movement and in early attempts to create collaborative and "democratic" classrooms (Schmuck & Schmuck, 1975). The field of CM tends to be quite ideological. The ideas and techniques for CM are strongly influenced by particular images of the ideal classroom held by the influential leaders of the field (see Chapter 9). Thus, CM tends to be process-oriented whereas the CC literature is more measurement-oriented. Scrutiny of the CM research literature shows that CM researchers usually do not tend to employ CC instruments, preferring instead to construct their own ad-hoc questionnaires.

3. *Teacher expectancies and self-fulfilling prophecies*. The origin of this domain is clearly traced to the phenomenon of "Teachers' Self-Fulfilling Prophecy," first exposed in the dramatic study "Pygmalion in the Classroom" (Rosenthal & Jacobson, 1968). Teachers' expectations might facilitate or hinder the academic performance and/or the self-image of particular groups of high- or low-expectancy students through teachers' differential treatment of those students. This possibility raises a grave concern that must be considered and dealt with (see Chapters 6 & 7). And indeed, a multitude of research on teacher expectancies has been published in the last forty years. This domain is also more process-oriented, but it is not connected with any specific educational ideology and this topic was actually de-emphasized in the CM literature

Given the distinct circumstances of the development of these three domains, it is easy to understand why they flourished as independent fields of research. And yet, the classroom teacher is necessarily involved in classroom phenomena representing all three domains. Expectancy effects, CM and CC are intertwined in the daily realities of the classroom society.

WHAT IS CLASSROOM CLIMATE?

The concept CC is a global summary of the psycho/social/emotional and organizational/managerial state of the classroom. It is measured via numerous questionnaires and instruments, and constitutes an important construct in educational research on classrooms and schools. CC can serve both as a predictor or independent variable (for example, to predict academic achievements from CC) and as a criterion or dependent variable (for example, to examine the success of educational interventions in changing CC, or for investigating the influence of class size or level of heterogeneity on CC). CC reflects students' overall satisfaction, their degree of contentedness and the classroom atmosphere and harmony. Classrooms with high positive climate are characterized by mutual support and fair division of social influence, by much interpersonal attraction and little friction, by open communication and norms supportive of everybody's success, and by the best academic achievements given students' abilities. Some authors might have added to this description a collective division of authority and responsibility among the teacher and the students or even collective decision-making, but the latter characteristics are not consensually held.

Walberg (1981) theorized about global "educational productivity" and saw school learning as a function of three clusters of components: (a) Students' age, given abilities and motivations; (b) The quality and quantity of instruction; and (c) The psycho-social environment of the classroom, of the school and the peer group. As a global concept, CC is understood intuitively very clearly by students and teachers. However, CC is not as easy to define operationally because it involves decisions which specific phenomena should be included and what should be their relative weights in the global index. But somehow all potential components and sub-structures seem to be encapsulated into one global concept of CC, and everybody understands that global concept. Some of the methodological issues and their implications for teachers are discussed later in this chapter.

"LOW INFERENCE" VERSUS "HIGH INFERENCE" CLASSROOM CLIMATE RESEARCH

Three general approaches were used over the years to assess classroom environment:

1. Conducting classroom observations by trained observers to code specific behaviors and events. This approach is known as low-inference measurement (Chavez, 1984), or alpha press (Murray, 1938), and is also known as the teacher-centered approach.
2. Collecting students' perceptions of CC through self-report questionnaires. This approach is known as high-inference measurement, or beta press, and also known as the student-centered approach.

3. Using ethnographic and qualitative methods, including participant-observations and interviews. (Because of the strong methodological and quantitative nature of the field, qualitative methods were used quite infrequently in CC research).

In low-inference research (or alpha press in its former formulation), CC is measured objectively through systematic behavioral observations by trained adult observers, by tests and by manipulations of experimental conditions. The theoretical assumption in the early low-inference research was that teachers' behavior is the critical factor in the formation of classroom environment (Fraser, 1991, 1994).

The most salient study in this tradition was published in 1939 by Lewin et al. (see Chapter 3). They manipulated experimentally teachers' leadership styles (autocratic, democratic and laissez-faire leadership styles) and examined their effects on students' behavior and educational outcomes. As could be expected, democratic leadership yielded the most positive outcomes, whereas laissez-faire leadership was inferior to democratic and autocratic leadership in almost every respect. That study became a classic, a landmark in behavioral research on leadership. In that research tradition, various observational instruments for the assessment of group and classroom processes were developed. The instruments by Bales (1965, for interactions in groups) and Flanders (1970, for analysis of classroom interaction) have been used for decades, and Good and Brophy's book "Looking in Classrooms" is today in its 9th edition (2003).

Because low-inference measurement involves direct observations with valid instruments, it was considered highly objective. In contrast, beta press (high-inference measurement) represented the classroom environment as perceived and subjectively experienced by the students. Even early on, Murray (1938) speculated that beta press might exert greater influence on students' behavior because it is what they feel, interpret and respond to. In fact, both practical and theoretical considerations led to the historical transition from teacher-centered, objective, low-inference measurement to the student-centered, more subjective high-inference measurement of CC that is dominant today.

The practical consideration is very simple. The less expensive the research and the more it can be conducted with limited resources, the higher the chances for more research to be conducted in schools. Research based on systematic behavioral observations in classrooms is very expensive and requires considerable investment of resources. In addition, the measurement process itself—especially the presence of observers or a camera—interferes with the routine flow of classroom life. Research on classroom environments began to bloom when researchers turned to use inexpensive and easy-to-administer high-inference student questionnaires. Furthermore, high-inference measurement via students' questionnaires can be conducted by the schools (and by the teachers), whereas low-inference measurement requires professional experts from outside. Thus, the shift made it possible to conduct in-house action research and to utilize the measurement of CC for applied purposes.

The conceptual consideration stemmed from a certain doubt about the theoretical assumption that teacher's conduct is the major factor determining CC. Today, researchers prefer to view CC as a student phenomenon, and put the emphasis on their subjective reactions to particular contingencies in the classroom. In the past, typical behaviors (such as: "acts as a democratic leader," or "uses punishment," or "praises a lot") were interpreted in a uniform and static manner. But the growing trend in social psychology has been to think that particular behaviors acquire their meanings only in the unique situations within which they are enacted. This is salient in the study of leadership, which has shifted from s static conception (with assertions such as: "democratic leadership contributes to social climate" or "autocratic leadership hinders group harmony") to a contextual and situational view of transformational leadership (see Bass & Riggio, 2006) where particular leadership behaviors have no fixed meanings. In certain classrooms, teacher's autocratic leadership might contribute to positive CC, whereas democratic leaders might sometimes hinder CC and be ineffective in particular situations. The current conceptualization, based on high-inference measurement, maintains that students' self-reports best capture the uniqueness of every classroom, and students' subjective experience reflects all social processes in the classroom, including the effects of teacher's conduct.

Therefore, the measurement of CC is conducted today almost exclusively via self-report questionnaires administered to the students. In those questionnaires student express their opinions and make judgments about the various characteristics of CC. These judgments are presumably objective (e.g., opinions about friction or satisfaction in the classroom), but they are based on the subjective experience of the responding student. Readers are reminded of the discussion of the differences between affective sociometry and cognitive sociometry in the previous chapter. In CC measurement, students are employed in a cognitive capacity as judges of social aspects in their classroom society, basing their judgments on their subjective experiences within the classroom.

In the same way as in sociometric research, an unresolved conceptual question still remains open—whether the averaged summary judgments of the entire classroom can be considered as representing its objective reality. One student's report is probably very subjective, but the averaged ratings of all students might be considered a more objective reflection of classroom reality. On the other hand, perhaps even the classroom average represents a subjective experience of the collective that might deviate from objectively-measured reality. Let's assume, for example, that the students in a given classroom show consensus in their (averaged) ratings that their teacher is very strict and uses much punishment, but an objective measurement through behavioral observations shows that the teacher is not particularly strict and does not use much punishment compared to other teachers. The objective finding does not reduce the need to find out why the students in that classroom feel the way they feel, and what events led to their consensual judgment.

SPECIFIC COMPONENTS IN CLASSROOM CLIMATE QUESTIONNAIRES

CC is measured through students' self-report questionnaires. Fraser (1998) described nine major questionnaires that have been widely used, and many more instruments are readily accessible today. The purpose of this section is to provide readers with a comprehensive list of the different CC components and factors appearing in the various published instruments. Each instrument emphasizes particular components and fits defined populations. Potential users—researchers and practitioners alike—can pick up among the multitude of available instruments and make up combinations that best fit their specific purposes. They can choose to use an existing questionnaire (often in long or short form); they can combine sub-scales from different questionnaires; and they can add new self-report items to assess a particular aspect or phenomenon.

Every questionnaire is divided into several factors which represent different components of classroom environment. Each factor is represented in the questionnaire by several items, usually randomized in their order of appearance. The total score summing all items (reversing items that are presented negatively, such as "there is a lot of tension in this classroom") represents overall CC, but separate scores for each factor are usually examined as well, because they represent defined components. Regardless of the particular questionnaire or combination of sub-scales used, the overall CC summary score is generally accepted as representing the global concept of CC or classroom environment, with higher scores reflecting a more positive and desirable CC. To increase the diagnostic capacity, especially in action research in school, attention can be given to particular individual items in the questionnaire.

Following Moos (1974), the components of social climate in the various questionnaires are divided into three dimensions:

(I) *The relationships dimension*: Students' judgments about social processes in the classroom, support, personal involvement, competition, friction, etc.

(II) *The personal development dimension*: Students' reports about opportunities for personal growth and self-enhancement in the classroom, particularly in terms of opportunities for learning and for other school objectives.

(III) *The system management and system change dimension*: Students' judgment about classroom organization, order, clarity, conflict management and teachers' behavior.

The following list presents the major components and factors within each of these dimensions, with sample items as examples. The description is quite lengthy and rather detailed, because this classification illuminates many important items and aspects in the social psychology of the classroom. Readers may find this detailed list and the examples helpful even if they do not intend to become involved in actual measurement of CC.

I. *The relationships dimension.* This dimension describes the classroom society as experienced by the students in terms of interpersonal relations. The various components characterize the atmosphere in the classroom and document student satisfaction and contentedness—the extent to which the classroom is a likable, enjoyable environment. Within this dimension, the components used in the different questionnaires can be further sub-divided into: (A) Those focusing on the individual (scores averaging all students' judgments as to how "the student" in this class feels); (B) Those focusing on interpersonal relations among students in the classroom; and (C) Those focusing on relevant teacher behaviors.

I.A. *Factors focusing on the experiences of the individual student in the classroom:*

1. *Satisfaction*—the overall sense of well-being in the classroom (sample items: Students seem to like this classroom; children like to come to school to this classroom).
2. *Participation*—(sample items: Students like to participate in classroom activities; in our classroom everybody participates with others).
3. *Involvement*—the sense that most students feel involved in the classroom and partake willingly in its various academic and social activities.
4. *Personal relevance*—the degree to which students feel that whatever takes place in the classroom is relevant and meaningful for them (and, one might add, the degree to which they feel that *they* are "relevant" in the classroom).
5. *Apathy*—a negative component describing students' lack of interest and lack of participation in the classroom, actually the absence of all characteristics that have been described in this list.

I.B. *Factors focusing on interpersonal relations in the classroom:*

1. *Cohesiveness*—the overall sense of unity and cohesion of the classroom society, a kind of bonding which is manifested by a collective classroom identity (sample items: We all feel united in school; "all for one, one for all").

2. *Affiliation*—feeling emotionally connected to other students and to the group.
3. *Cliqueness*—division of the class into separate groups (sample items: The classroom has several groups that don't talk to each other; some students keep together and have nothing to do with the other students).
4. *Competition/Cooperation*—this factor appears in both the relationships dimension (as related to social factors in the classroom) and in the personal development dimension (as related to the learning atmosphere and the academic environment). As a social dimension, a competitive atmosphere means that one always has to compete with others or that subgroups (cliques) compete with each other for position of power and influence.
5. *Friction*—an atmosphere of tension (sample items: In this classroom, children are always fighting each other).

I.C. *Factors focusing on teacher's behavior (within the relationships dimension)*:

1. *Teacher personal support*—the degree to which the teacher is perceived by the students as taking personal interest in (all) individual students, as considerate and understanding of students' feelings, and as attentive to students' needs and supportive in crises.
2. *Favoritism*—the degree to which students are treated equitably or diffenrentially in the classroom. Later chapters deal extensively with the issue of teachers' differential behavior in interaction with students (Chapter 7), and with the teacher's pet phenomenon (Chapter 8) which describes instances of extreme emotional favoritism in the classroom. Perceptions of teacher favoritism can seriously damage students' satisfaction and hinder CC.

II. The personal development dimension. This dimension focuses on the academic aspects of classroom climate as related to teaching and learning. The students characterize the academic atmosphere, the teaching style and the kinds of demands they face in the classroom. The next paragraph contains a list of six main factors of the personal development dimension appearing in various questionnaires. These dimensions are general (e.g., difficulty, task-orientation) and therefore important for the analysis of the climate of every classroom. Researchers add more specific components (e.g., investigation, open-endedness) when they want to examine specific teaching methods or particular interventions.

The main factors in the personal development dimension are:

1. *Difficulty*—students' assessment of the overall level of difficulty of studies in that class. Level of difficulty is an important dimension

of CC—and the atmosphere in difficult classes might be radically different from the atmosphere in easy classes. However, students may find it difficult to assess overall difficulty of studies for the entire classroom and to distinguish it from their personal experience of level of difficulty.

2. *Competitiveness*—some schools and some classrooms are designed to be competitive and to encourage academic competition, whereas other schools and teachers try to dull the competitive edge and to emphasize a more cooperative learning style.

3. *Speed*—another dimension of the academic style, whether the pace in the classroom is rushed or relaxed, and whether pressure is put on students to quickly move on from one task to the other.

4. *Task-orientation*—the extent to which the academic tasks are performed with minimal interference, and teachers spend less time in non-academic activity (sample items: Activities in this class are clearly and carefully planned; in this class we learn and study almost all the time).

5. *Involvement*—the extent to which all or most of the students are personally involved in the academic activities (sample item: Most students in this class really pay attention to what the teacher is saying).

6. *Responsibility*—the shared feeling of responsibility and commitment to learning among students, the sense that the class and the teacher are working together.

III. *The system management dimension.* Moos defined this dimension as including "system change," and some questionnaires indeed included openness to change as a characteristic of CC. Because many classroom environment studies were initially designed to examine the effects of various educational interventions, researchers felt that the questionnaires should include factors such as innovation, individualization, and openness to change. Other researchers were keen on advocating a particular ideology about CM, and therefore emphasized climate factors such as democracy, student freedom, and formality. In the following list, I included only the factors directly related to CM.

The main reason for teacher failure and attrition is their difficulty in handling discipline problems and being effective in CM (see Chapter 3). Clearly one of the first prerequisites for being a good teacher is the ability to control the classroom, to prevent and subsequently to solve problems. For the students, too, the system management characteristics are critical factors in determining CC.

The factors in the system management dimension:

1. *Teacher control*—the extent to which the teacher is successful in controlling the classroom effectively (sample items: The teacher is well in control of this classroom; the teacher can successfully solve every problem).

2. *Order and organization*—(sample item: Students know how to keep order in this classroom; our classroom is very well organized).
3. *Rule clarity*—(sample item: In this class we have a clear set of rules to follow).
4. *Strictness*—teacher's style in controlling the classroom and maintaining order (sample items: Students know that every infraction will be punished; our teacher is very strict; our teacher gets angry very easily).

ITEMS OF THE SHORT FORM OF MY CLASS INVENTORY (MCI)

The specific items of the short version of the MCI are presented next for practical purposes of potential users. The long list of factors in the system management dimension was presented to illuminate dimensions and aspects of the social psychology of the classroom. In contrast, the following instrument *is* intended for readers who are interested in actual measurement of CC. The MCI (Fraser, Anderson, & Walberg, 1982; Fraser & O'Brien, 1985) is widely used in elementary school classrooms by both researchers and practitioners involved in action research. The short form consists of five factors: Satisfaction; Friction; Competitiveness; Difficulty; and Cohesiveness. Each item is answered by "yes" or "no"; negatively worded items are reversed in the scoring; and scores are added up for each factor.

Item #	Item	Direction
Factor 1: Satisfaction		
1	The pupils enjoy their schoolwork in my class	+
6	Some pupils are not happy in class	-
11	Children seem to like the class	+
16	Some of the pupils don't like the class	-
21	The class is fun	+
Factor 2: Friction		
2	Children are always fighting with each other	+
7	Some of the children in our class are mean	+
12	Many children in our class like to fight	+
17	Certain pupils always want to have their own way	+
22	Children in our class fight a lot	+
Factor 3: Competitiveness		
3	Children often race to see who can finish first	+
8	Most children want their work to be better than their friend's work	+
13	Some pupils feel bad when they don't do as well as the others	+
18	Some pupils always try to do their work better than the others	+
23	A few children in my class want to be first all of the time	+

Factor 4: Difficulty

4	In our class the work is hard to do	+
9	Most children can do their schoolwork without help	-
14	Only the smart pupils can do their work	+
19	Schoolwork is hard to do	+
24	Most of the pupils in my class know how to do their work	-

Factor 5: Cohesiveness

5	In my class everybody is my friend	+
10	Some people in my class are not my friends	-
15	All pupils in my class are close friends	+
20	All of the pupils in my class like one another	+
25	Children in our class like each other as friends	+

CONCEPTUAL ISSUES AND METHODOLOGICAL PROBLEMS IN MEASUREMENT OF CLASSROOM CLIMATE

In the past few decades we witness heavy measurement of CC in educational research and in action research within schools. As previously shown, numerous factors and dimensions of CC have been defined, and many different questionnaires have been constructed. The questions (items) in climate questionnaires are simple and straightforward, designed to enable even young students to form and express opinions and to judge classroom processes. As mentioned, it is also quite possible to invent new items and to add new factors when the need arises. Thus, we have a rich field of meaningful investigation open to teachers, schools, and practitioners no less then to educational researchers. However, some conceptual, methodological *and* ethical problems must be discussed, because they might influence potential application.

The Issue of "Climate" as a Global Concept

Intuitively, it is very easy and meaningful to discuss "CC" as a global, monolithic concept with a relatively uniform meaning. Researchers indeed discuss overall high or low CC interchangeably among various questionnaires and the generalization is accepted. Thus, like IQ, CC is treated as an all-inclusive term—much as IQ sums up cognitive ability, the climate score sums up a social reality. But the global score in climate questionnaires is problematic, and the overall score averaging all factors is not readily interpretable. Some factors (for instance satisfaction, friction, apathy, or discipline problems) can be consistently determined as representing positive or negative climate, but numerous other factors (such as speed, difficulty, or even academic competition) cannot be divided dichotomously, and one cannot be sure whether to assign a positive or negative climate sign to them. Therefore, an overall score averaging all factors should be treated very carefully, and distinct factors and dimensions should be examined separately.

Classroom Climate as a Continuum

The two ends of the CC continuum are easy to understand, when a classroom has a distinct highly positive or highly negative climate. But for the majority of classrooms in the middle of the continuum, it is more difficult to understand the nature of their affective status. Unlike IQ or achievement scores, the absolute score (the actual number representing the classroom mean) does not have a clear consensual meaning. Many of the factors included in the measurement of CC are not linear, and the positive meaning might be found in the middle of the continuum rather than at the upper end. For example, for speed, or difficulty, or pressure put on students, too much and too little are negative, whereas the desired level is the middle, moderate intensity.

Within-Classroom Variation

In typical analyses of CC data, researchers use classroom means as the datum for analysis and comparison. The mean is the best statistical indicator of central tendency in a given distribution, and the use of classroom means in educational research is certainly justified. But every mean always has some distribution of scores around it, and the magnitude of the variance is quite important, especially in action research within the school. The larger the variance, the more the students disagree with each other in their judgments of classroom reality, whereas small variances indicate greater consensus. For big time researchers, variance is a nuisance, and they prefer to stick to means and ignore the variance. But in order to understand more deeply a given classroom, the intensity of consensus or disagreement among students is an important indication, and it is doubly important if the variation is systematic rather than random. If boys and girls assess a given factor differently, or if low-achievers report certain judgments in a systematically different manner than high-achievers, those differences should be diagnostic in making inferences from the data.

How Can We Know What is "True" in Subjective Judgments?

High-inference questionnaires trace students' judgments based on their subjective experience in the classroom, but researchers would like to give students' judgments a cloak of objectivity. As discussed earlier, the use of classroom means is a partial solution, but still, even a classroom mean only averages a collection of subjective reports, and the question of the true objective nature of what characterizes a given classroom is still nagging. As mentioned earlier, some researchers argue that subjective reality, even if biased, is the truth in children's eyes, and is therefore valid. Other researchers would wish to anchor means of subjective reports with at least some evidence of more objective data.

In any event, a common myth must be explicitly ruled out, and that is the belief that teachers' reports about classroom reality are more accurate and objective than the averaged student judgments. Teachers' judgments seem to be as biased as those of their students—although not necessarily for the same reasons and not in the same directions. In fact, teachers are less informed than their students about the social life of the classroom society and their perceptions tend to be more glowing and positive than those of their students.

Ethical Considerations

When sociometric measurement was discussed in the previous chapter, I emphasized the ethical problems involved (a) in the violation of students' privacy, and (b) in the excitement that the sociometric measurement evokes in the classroom. I mentioned that education authorities are wary of sociometric measurement. They try to minimize its use by withholding permission to administer sociometric tests unless the potential benefits to the responding students can be indicated. Sociometric measurement presents a more severe ethical problem than CC measurement because children are asked (actually required) to express their innermost feelings of attraction and rejection, and they are required to identify themselves and their peers by name. I also mentioned that "cognitive sociometry," where children report their judgments about "types" and role holders in the classroom without identifying themselves and without expressing their personal feelings, constitutes less of a problem from the ethical point of view.

The anonymous administration of CC questionnaires and its focus on classroom phenomena rather than personal attractions and rejections makes it less problematic, but one should still be aware of ethical pitfalls. The topics raised in the questionnaire evoke much excitement, because they are usually unspoken and unmentioned in the classroom. Therefore, the mere focus on the socio/emotional undercurrents in the life in the classroom society and the fact that students are asked to judge and to express their opinions about the classroom and about the teacher might affect the classroom negatively.

Presumably it is very easy to maintain anonymity, but when teachers examine data of their students' views of the classroom process, it would be quite difficult for them to overcome their curiosity . . . When the data illuminate surprising facts, and especially when insulting or angry judgments are exposed, or when a few students gave responses that differed dramatically from the consensus of the other students—the urge to find out who wrote what or to take some action on the basis of guesses about the identities of particular respondents might be very powerful.

One of the major applications in CC measurement is to provide teachers with feedback data of the averaged responses of their students. Teachers who are flexible and open to feedback can derive great benefits from such feedback data. I think that sometimes feedback data, especially when the data reveals new facts or information that differs from the teachers' own view can be beneficial to the teacher. However, feedback data might sometimes disrupt teachers' work and throw them off-balance. In addition, attempts to remedy the situation by corrective interventions are not always successful—they might lead to excessive correction or to attempts to change aspects that are basically unchangeable (see Chapter 16). Therefore, great care and awareness are required when teachers make use of CC questionnaires in their classrooms. Probably teachers should consult with peers, counselors or school psychologists before the administration, and particularly when they actually examine the data and try to design corrective interventions.

VARIATIONS IN ADMINISTRATION AND ANALYSIS OF CLASSROOM CLIMATE QUESTIONNAIRES

A wide range of published questionnaires (including short forms) is available to practitioners, and it is always possible to construct new items and scales to fit particular objectives. Therefore, the potential for using CC questionnaires in action research within schools as a tool for improving teacher practice is great. Next, several additional variations of CC application are described.

In the conventional CC questionnaire, students report their judgments about the actual, or current situation in their classroom. A known variation (Fraser, 1998) is to ask students to fill out the same questionnaire a second time and to describe the preferred state, how they wish the classroom situation to be. (Minor changes in wording are required, like "there should be" instead of "there is"). Readers probably recall an earlier discussion (Chapter 2) about the ideal self and the actual self, how the size of the gap between them serves as an index of psychological adjustment. Here, too, the gap between the preferred and the actual CC might have the same meaning on a collective level, a statistically-inferred index of classroom well-being.

A second known variation is to ask the teachers themselves to fill out the questionnaire given to their students, and to compare agreement and disagreement between students' and teachers' judgments. That can be quite illuminating, especially if a varied pattern of agreement and disagreement across the various factors and items is discovered. In my own research, I tried two sub-variations in teacher questionnaires—one is to ask teachers to provide their own judgments about the classroom situation, the other to ask teachers to try to guess the averaged ratings of their students. The two options require teachers to access cognitively two different types of information. These variations, combined, provide several very interesting cross-comparisons between actual and preferred states and between students and teachers. One should remember, though, that teachers' view of CC is no less subjective than students' views, and perhaps they have a stronger need to perceive the classroom (and their own conduct in CM) in a particular light!

Returning to student questionnaires, another variation involves the personal questionnaire. Here, instead of being asked to judge the overall classroom situation, the student responds to each item as it applies personally to her/him. Instead of "the teacher is concerned about students' needs" the wording becomes "the teacher is concerned about my needs," and instead of "the work in this class is difficult" the personal item reads: "I find the work in this class difficult." Some differences between the personal and the collective questionnaires are typically found, and students' ratings on class forms tend to be systematically higher than their ratings on the personal forms. It is particularly interesting, however, to diagnostically identify for a specific classroom the unique pattern of gaps between these forms. Fraser (1998) suggested an expedient strategy where the class is randomly divided into two groups, one half is asked to fill out the regular class form, and the other half fills out the personal form.

RESEARCH ON CLASSROOM CLIMATE

Much research on CC and school environment has been published in the last thirty years. The field has become a central domain of educational research, especially with regard to the psychology of the classroom and the analysis of factors contributing to various types of educational outcomes. Much of the research has been focused on the construction of different CC instruments (for various populations and developmental levels, for different research questions and applications, and following different conceptualizations of classroom environment) and the examination of their reliability and validity (see Dorman, 2002; Fraser, 1994, 1998).

Beyond the construction and validation of instruments, there has been a dual usage of the CC phenomenon in research: One direction is to predict CC—to examine factors that can cause negative or positive CC and how CC could be changed. In such research CC is the criterion or dependent variable. The other direction is the methodological opposite, where CC is examined as a predictor, or independent variable, to predict a variety of phenomena and educational outcomes. The prime example of this direction is the research on students' academic achievements and other educational outcomes in classrooms differing in various characteristics of CC (see next). The first direction also includes studies that examine the personality and behavioral attributes of good and effective teachers, where resultant CC is used as the predicted criterion. Of course such studies would not necessarily be labeled "CC research," and they might be also be identified as CM research or good teaching research (see Chapter 9 and Chapter 3). This dual usage of CC enriches the research and widens the possibilities for both research and application.

As mentioned, the central research question focuses on the influence (or association) of CC on students' educational outcomes. It can be summarized very succinctly that *positive CC is good!* Most studies indeed show that positive CC is systematically associated with a multitude of positive educational outcomes both in the academic domain and the social/affective domain. Quality of CC is consistently found to be a significant determinant of students' learning and other outcomes (see, for example, Dorman, 2002; Fraser, 1994, 1998; MacAuley, 1990). To quote Barry Fraser, "better achievement on a variety of outcome measures was found consistently in classes perceived as having greater cohesiveness, satisfaction and goal direction and less disorganization and friction" (1998, p. 20). MacAuley (1990) elaborated that classrooms characterized by high degrees of teacher-direction, structure and order tend to produce most favorable student outcomes. MacAuley focused her attention on students with behavioral deficits (that is, problem students), and argued that the importance of structure, order, rule clarity and organization cannot be underestimated, especially in schools increasingly burdened with students' inability to conform to socially acceptable norms of behavior. A happy, satisfied, content classroom is a good classroom for attaining a wide range of schooling objectives, and it constitutes a productive environment for the students in the classroom society. Other studies emphasized the shift from competitive to cooperative classrooms and the importance of teachers' understanding and empathy in creating a helpful/friendly environment and in developing students' pro-social skills. The latter findings are well in line with the contemporary conceptualization of CM (see Chapter 9).

Some research has focused on the differences between students' ratings of their actual CC and their view of their preferred CC. Differences between the preferred and the actual environment (labeled by Fraser "the person–environment fit") always exist, but educational outcomes improve when that difference is smaller (Fraser & Fisher, 1983). Achievement of a better match between students' preferences for CC and the actual characteristics and instructional settings of the classroom is an important condition for maximizing students' cognitive, social and affective outcomes. In action research, both actual and preferred students' ratings of CC can provide specific data that might enable teachers to plan changes in CM. As mentioned, systematic evidence also shows that teachers' own ratings of their CC are more positive than students' actual ratings in many aspects of classroom environment (Dorman, 2002; Fraser, 1998). Such gaps provide excellent feedback data for the planning of change, where particular, specific differences of opinion are identified and analyzed. In general, all reviews of CC research cite various studies that illustrate the advantages of CC questionnaires and CC data in teacher education and in ongoing teachers' training in the schools.

Finally, CC research continuously accompanied the implementation of educational innovations throughout the past forty years. Ever since Herbert Walberg's involvement in the Harvard Project Physics (Walberg & Anderson, 1968), the assessment of classroom environment became a necessary component in evaluating the contributions of various educational interventions and innovations. This trend has intensified in recent decades, especially in connection with the implementation of technological innovations and various programs in science education. Numerous studies have been conducted in Australia (Fraser, 1994, 1998), in the Far East (e.g., Goh & Fraser, 1998) and in many other countries. Most innovations are associated with (some would simply say "cause") improvements in CC. Classrooms that go through educational innovations tend, in general, to be happy classrooms. However, glowing reports on the success of some educational interventions (especially in influencing CC) might also be due, at least in part, to Hawthorne Effects.

THE PHENOMENON OF "HAWTHORNE EFFECT": AN OBSTACLE TO RESEARCHERS, A POTENTIAL GIFT FOR PRACTITIONERS

The Hawthorne Effect is a classic phenomenon that emerged from experiments designed to increase workers' productivity through changes in the workplace at the Hawthorne Works factory outside Chicago from 1924 to 1932. The initial purpose was to examine whether changes in illumination would influence workers' productivity. Subsequently many other changes (e.g., maintaining cleaner workstations, clearing floors of obstacles, relocating workstations, etc.) were implemented, and their effects on productivity were measured. It turned out that any change that was implemented resulted in increased productivity for a short period of time and later returned to normal levels. Even a change back to a previous state resulted in an increase in productivity.

The unavoidable conclusion was that the mere fact that a change or an innovation is implemented was sufficient in itself to improve workers' performance regardless of the specific nature and content of the particular innovation (Landsberger, 1958; Mayo, 1933). The improvement is probably caused (or mediated) by the increased motivation of the workers who participate in the project, fueled by the intense involvement and investment of the innovators (experimenters). Both contribute to create a positive dynamics of change in the social environment. In folk wisdom "A new broom sweeps better!" and the Hawthorne Effect indicates that, on principle, any new broom might sweep better!

For experimenters and innovators, the Hawthorne Effect is a nightmare—a potential bias that might discredit their successful projects and threaten the validity of their findings. If the implementation of any change would lead to favorable results, how can you prove that your particular idea and particular innovation had been the cause of the improvement? And indeed the proper design for studies evaluating the implementation of innovations requires the inclusion of a control condition (placebo condition) where an alternative treatment—equally invested in resources, involvement and change dynamics but differing in the content of the treatment—is compared to the intended innovation (Rosenthal, 1966). Hawthorne effects can demonstrate dramatic improvements, but these are short-lived and performance returns to the previous normal level once the excitement of the project withers down.

The danger of Hawthorne Effects is very apparent in education. Educational projects and innovations of many types tend to be successful in their initial experimental stages. Their success might be due, at least in part, to Hawthorne Effects. The problem begins when, following successful results of the pilot intervention, wide range implementation of the innovation in an entire educational system is planned. Now the innovation must be applied by a wider population of educators who lack motivation and involvement, and who do not particularly wish to invest extra energies in somebody's innovation. And then, the positive outcomes documented in the earlier stages begin to wither! Therefore, we should always be skeptic about glowing reports on the positive outcomes of evaluation research on new innovative interventions. The inclusion of appropriate placebo control conditions in the evaluation research is required in order to rule out possible Hawthorne Effects.

Many flops of this kind are known in educational research, where wide-range implementation failed to fulfill the expectations based on the success of experimental projects in improving CC and students' performance.

But the lessons to be learned from the Hawthorne Effect phenomenon for practitioners, teachers and action researchers in the schools are quite different and rather positive. If a new broom sweeps better, let's introduce new brooms periodically in the classroom, and let's enjoy their sweeping effects. The classroom teacher is responsible for her/his own classroom, and therefore the improvement that might be caused by any kind of intervention is positive and welcome, even if no more than a Hawthorne Effect had taken its effect. A temporary revival of good spirits and improved atmosphere might trigger a dynamic magic cycle, and positive outcomes tend to increase the probability for additional positive products. Thus, in terms of educational practice, teachers should aspire to introduce different innovations periodically into their classroom life and to maintain the spirit of changeability as a characteristic of the classroom society. Of course the innovations would represent the best ideas for change that the teacher might have for the students in the classroom, and then the content of the innovation, in addition to the dynamics of change, would contribute to the classroom.

Part III

Teacher-Student Interaction and Teacher Expectancy Effects

6 "Pygmalion in the Classroom"
Teacher Expectancies and Teacher Bias

THE NATURE OF "GROUND-BREAKING" RESEARCH

In the history of science, a well-known but rare phenomenon is the publication of a ground-breaking study that can revolutionize an entire field of investigation. In psychology, several ground-breaking studies illuminated new phenomena and put new concepts on the professional agenda. Such studies led to hundreds of subsequent studies and influenced both theoretical research and the practice of psychology. The original study might eventually fade or become qualified by subsequent research that might be superior to the original study in methodology and in advanced conceptual sophistication. However, the ground-breaking impact of the original study remains intact because of its seminal quality.

In social psychology, two classic ground-breaking studies were published before the middle of the 20th century, and both had a tremendous impact on the field. One was Lewin et al.'s (1939) research on democratic and autocratic leadership that revolutionized and shaped the study of leadership for decades to come (see Chapter 3). The other was the study of the authoritarian personality (Adorno et al., 1950) that illuminated and opened up the study of prejudice, fascism and dogmatism as social phenomena and as a personality syndrome.

In educational psychology, Rosenthal and Jacobson's (1968) research *Pygmalion in the Classroom* was a ground-breaking study that had a huge impact in the last three decades of the 20th century. It evoked a bitter controversy and stimulated hundreds of studies. The Pygmalion study is used in this chapter as a pivot for discussing teacher–student interaction in the classroom. It provides a conceptual framework for the various phenomena related to teacher expectancies and to teachers' differential behavior in the classroom.

PYGMALION IN THE CLASSROOM

In the early 1960s, Robert Rosenthal demonstrated in a series of studies that experimenters' beliefs about the expected outcomes of their experiments could act as a self-fulfilling prophecy and influence the findings. In other words, experimenters are likely to obtain ("find") results that fit their expectations, and results might have been very different had the experimenters been led to hold different expectations. Thus, experimenter effects (Rosenthal, 1963, 1966) can bias the results of experimental studies in psychology (with animal subjects and with human subjects alike).

In the mid-1960s, Rosenthal collaborated with Lenore Jacobson, a school principal, to examine the effects of teachers' self-fulfilling prophecies in their classrooms. That ground-breaking research culminated in the book *Pygmalion in the Classroom* (Rosenthal & Jacobson, 1968). The researchers administered a relatively unknown IQ test to all students in the eighteen classrooms (grades 1–6) of Jacobson's school. The teachers were told that the test (renamed: The Harvard Test of Inflected Acquisition) was a recent innovative test that could identify students of high, yet unrealized intellectual potential. The teachers were told that late bloomers, who have not yet shown their potential in the classroom, would be identified from the test results. Rosenthal and Jacobson then selected at random 20% of the students in each classroom (essentially every fifth student), and gave their names to their teachers as those who had presumably been identified as the potential late bloomers in their classrooms. At the end of the year, a parallel form of the original IQ test was administered again in all classrooms, so that a change score from pre- to post-test IQ could be computed for each student. The IQ gain scores of the experimental group (those labeled late bloomers) were compared to those of the control group (the 80% of the students in each classroom who were not labeled in any way).

IQ scores tend to increase a bit from first to second administration of the same test (even in parallel forms), and therefore an increase of about three IQ points meant no change. However, some students labeled late bloomers improved their IQs by a whole standard deviation (fifteen IQ points) or even more, and the differences between the mean improvement of the experimental condition and the control group was statistically significant, with substantial differences found in some classrooms. Rosenthal and Jacobson concluded that teachers' beliefs about student potential could turn into a self-fulfilling prophecy (SFP) and influence students' subsequent intellectual performance. Because the late bloomers were selected randomly and were not different from the control group in any respect but the fabricated label, the effect could be causally attributed to the self-fulfillment of the teachers' expectancies. (It must be pointed out that the IQ increase was not automatic for every student labeled late bloomer nor for every teacher, but there was a better than chance probability that in some classrooms, some children might improve their intellectual performance as a product of their teacher's expectancy).

Controversy Over Pygmalion Effects

From the time it was published, Pygmalion evoked intense reactions and controversy. Many educational and social researchers were excited about the new developing field of research on teachers and classrooms. The possibility that teachers' beliefs about the ability of particular students might influence the academic performance of those students was overwhelming in its implications, and hundreds of teacher expectancy studies were conducted over the next few decades. On the other hand, many others criticized the Pygmalion study, doubted the validity of its results and were concerned about simplistic generalizations about teachers and their effects on students.

Since then, hundreds of replications and expectancy studies were conducted all over the world. Today there is no doubt that the phenomenon of teachers' SFP does indeed exists and can be measured empirically. However, SFP effects do not occur automatically to every teacher and to every student, and not every teacher expectation is self-fulfilled. We know today that teacher expectations might influence students, not that they always do.

The late 1960s were years of turmoil in the U.S.A. in general (largely due to the Vietnam War) and in American education in particular. There was a bitter sense of disappointment that the American school system failed to advance minority and lower socioeconomic groups (that is, poor students); that educational reforms (mostly school desegregation) had not succeeded in meeting their objectives of advancing social integration and academic progress of the weaker groups. Following the publication of *Pygmalion in the Classroom* in 1968, some educators feared that "the teachers" might be blamed for the failure of their weaker students due to their low expectations (see, for example, Weinstein, 2002; Wineburg, 1987). For ethical reasons, Rosenthal and Jacobson refrained from examining negative teacher expectations and manipulated only positive beliefs about late blooming. However, the suspicion lingered on that, if positive teacher expectancies could enhance students' performance, then negative expectations might hinder and reduce students' academic performance, leading them to fail even below their potential.

In the Pygmalion volume, as well as in similar SFP studies, teachers' expectations were created by experimental manipulation of fabricated information about students' potential. Expectancy research eventually moved on to field research, where teachers' real expectations about their students were investigated. The range of differences among students in contemporary heterogeneous classroom is wide, and therefore teachers are likely to hold different expectations for different students. Examination of their expectancy-related differential behavior in interacting with students and its effect on the students moved from the investigation of fabricated self-fulfilling prophecies (SFP) to the naturalistic study of more realistic self-maintaining expectancies (SME).

RESEARCH DIRECTIONS FOLLOWING PYGMALION

Today, four decades after the publication of Pygmalion, we know that the likelihood that bogus teacher expectancies would intensely influence students' academic performance is quite low, and the pure Pygmalion paradigm is not part of the common reality of contemporary classrooms. But several directions of classroom research emerged in the wake of the Pygmalion research, each focusing on one link in the sequential chain of the expectancy confirmation process. Some of these areas of research are extremely important for teachers—especially the phenomena of teachers' bias (extensively discussed in this chapter) and teachers' differential behavior in the classroom (discussed in the next chapter).

The conceptual chain of the expectancy formation and confirmation process includes the following major links:

1. *Formation of teacher expectations and teachers' bias (cognitive research).* Teachers form expectations about individual students through information absorbed from many different sources. In Pygmalion research, the information was intentionally fabricated by the researchers to form the late blooming expectation. In actual classrooms, teachers obtain real life information about each student from a variety of sources and they form sets of individually distinct expectations. Bias is the case when a judgment that should have been reached objectively and rationally (such as grading an exam or a paper) is influenced—and distorted in a positive or a negative direction—by the teacher's expectation toward that particular student.

2. *Personality correlates of teachers' susceptibility to biasing information (personality research).* Not all teachers are influenced in the same manner and to the same extent by their expectations, and some are more capable than others to avoid bias or Pygmalion effects. The question is whether particular demographic characteristics (such as age, gender, cumulative teaching experience) or personality attributes might help identify the teachers who would be more susceptible (or non-susceptible) to biasing information.

3. *Teacher transmission of their differential expectations to students (communication research on teacher–student interaction).* This is probably the central link in teacher expectancy research. For the expectations of the teacher to influence the performance of the students, they must be transmitted somehow to students and be absorbed by them. Expectations (especially negative expectations) are not expressed in explicit verbal terms but transmitted through subtle behavioral and nonverbal nuances. Hundreds of studies examined various aspects of the behavioral mediation of teacher expectancies through differential behavior toward different students in the classroom. Theoretical models were constructed to define the specific aspects and factors involved in such mediation and to assess its role in eventually affecting student performance.

4. *How students notice teacher expectations? (research on social perception).* For students' performance to be influenced by teacher

expectations, they must perceive, absorb and internalize the expectancy-related teacher's behaviors directed at them. The transmission of teacher expectations is very subtle, and as will be demonstrated later, teacher transmission may often be deceptive. Therefore, students must become skilled in social perception and attuned to decipher relevant information in teacher behavior. This area of research deals with student perceptions of teachers' differential behavior on both the individual and the classroom level.

5. *Research on educational outcomes (evaluation research).* The early studies focused on the effects of teacher expectations on intellectual and academic performance, and the evaluation was then based on achievement and intelligence testing. Eventually it became clear that teacher expectancies might influence students in non-cognitive areas, and then the evaluation of outcomes widened to include motivational and emotional aspects. And again, individual outcomes (what happens to a particular student who is subject to positive or negative teacher expectancy?) is distinguished from classroom outcomes (what happens to classrooms of teachers who demonstrate extreme expectancy-related differential behavior?)

RESEARCH ON TEACHER'S BIAS

Deep understanding of the social psychology of bias and stereotyping is extremely important for teachers for two main reasons: (a) Teachers continuously encounter in their classrooms a wide range of differences among students along numerous social and intellectual dimensions; and (b) Teachers are perpetually involved in judgment processes vis-à-vis their students, grading and evaluating them all the time. Bias and stereotypy focus on the links between social characteristics of students and social judgments of teachers.

Stereotypes

We are all rational creatures, and we process social information so that we would be able to solve problems in the most effective ways. Social decisions about other people are based on information, and we seek, and need, information in order to reach good decisions. However, we are often faced with an overload of information and it is impossible to absorb and to process all the available information. Therefore, we need shortcuts that would reduce the required effort without costing us with a loss of accuracy. Stereotypes are such shortcuts. They enable us to know enough about other people to promote effective interaction with them without spending too much effort collecting and processing information about them. Stereotypes are generalizations about the characteristics and attributes of entire groups (for example, "women are intuitive" or "Italians are emotional" or "politicians are ambitious"). The stereotype characterizes the average member of a given group. Stereotypes are biased (a) in the sense that they reflect the average and ignore the variance within the group ("all 'X's' are like that") and (b) in that they emphasize characteristics unique to a given group and neglect characteristics common to many groups. Usually we believe that there is no smoke without fire, and therefore the generalization (stereotype) about the average characteristic of a given group must be reasonably valid and true despite the fact that the variation within the group is ignored. Under such conditions, stereotypes are quite helpful and we all use them daily in our social conduct with others.

However, two major problems might hinder the utility of our use of stereotypes (see Babad, Birnbaum & Benne, 1983). The first problem is that people might be rigid in their thinking and treat their stereotypes as if they represent social reality in an accurate and full meaning. They would forget that stereotypes are inaccurate generalizations designed to reduce mental effort. If we treat our stereotypes as representing totally valid truth and refuse to accept exceptions and variation within given groups, the effectiveness of our information processing might be reduced considerably. Our stereotypes might then hinder rather than help us.

The second problem occurs when stereotypes become prejudicial, when strong negative feelings about particular groups of people influence our thinking and behavior towards those people. Prejudice is a set of negative stereotypes loaded with aggression and strong emotions, carrying the idea that "we" are better than "them." Prejudices are often held in an extreme fashion, leading to discrimination of minority groups or even to violence against them. Because "they" are held to be inferior and bad, discrimination and aggression are righteously justified by those who are prejudiced. Stereotypes are cognitive and might include positive, negative, or neutral generalizations about groups—but prejudices consist of negative attributes only and are accompanied by strong negative emotions.

At times of social, economic or political crisis, prejudices in every society (including the classroom society) become more intense. During a war, the enemy is belittled through prejudice and mockery which seems to righteously justify fighting and even killing them. Numerous historical examples demonstrate that conflict between groups, wars and economic crisis tend to increase the level of prejudice in society. In one of the classic field experiments in the history of social psychology, Muzafer Sherif and his colleagues (Sherif et al., 1961) created conflict between two groups of boys in a summer camp located in Robbers Cave National Park in Oklahoma. As the conflict escalated (through separation, competition over limited resources, pitting the groups one against the other, etc.), prejudices of each group against the other group became more negative and intense. The other side of the coin is that when interventions were subsequently made to reduce inter-group conflict (such as contact, super-ordinate goals and mutual dependence), prejudices decreased.

Prejudice is not only the product of external social circumstances and competition on limited resources. The tendency to be prejudicial is also a personality attribute of individuals, a trait that is distributed in a normal curve in the population. Persons holding prejudices are labeled dogmatic (Rokeach, 1954, 1960) or authoritarian (Adorno et al., 1950), and they tend hold prejudices about numerous groups. Such people are usually characterized as being cognitively rigid and intolerant of ambiguity ("Things always have to be clear—it must be this way or that way, nothing in between"), and they use stereotypes excessively without mental flexibility.

Teachers' Bias

Many teacher expectations are based on commonly held stereotypes derived from available information and generalizations about distinct groups of students. It is enough to know who the student is, and a possible set of expectations is set in motion in the teacher's mind without needing more information about the student. The teacher may develop an opinion of who the student is simply by knowing the student's gender, age, ethnic background, socioeconomic status, IQ, previous achievement, physical appearance, former salient events (such as school violence) and perhaps by recalling the student's sibling who had formerly been a student. Such expectations might be helpful for teachers in managing their own conduct, as long as they are well aware that stereotypes are mental shortcuts rather than valid and accurate realities.

We will talk about teachers' bias when a judgment that was supposed to be made in a totally objective manner becomes influenced by stereotypic information and expectations. The judgment is then bent by the stereotype and stops being objective. In the case of teachers, such bias can be measured through grading and evaluations of student performance.

Hundreds of studies examined various manifestations of bias and teacher bias. The basic design of bias studies is very simple: Respondents are asked to evaluate a piece of work (an essay, a worksheet, an exam or paper) presumably written by a particular person (e.g., student), and they are provided with some bit(s) of information about that person. The judgment or grading is supposed to be conducted objectively, but the information that is provided constitutes the experimental manipulation designed to bias the objective judgment. Unbeknownst to the respondents, different groups (of teachers or teacher education students in educational research on bias) receive the same piece of work or student performance to be judged, but are provided with different biasing information. For instance, the information might consist of the student's presumable name—"John Smith" provided to one group of judges, and "Joan Smith" to another group of judges. If the mean grades given to "John" and "Joan" are different (and the difference is statistically significant and of acceptable effect size), a case of gender-bias had been demonstrated.

In the typical bias study, two groups of judges receive biasing information in the form of opposites: male/female (as mentioned above); gifted versus average (the latter usually created by giving no information at all, thereby indicating an average status rather than giftedness); excellent versus weak student; high-SES versus low-SES status; or handsome/pretty versus ugly or homely (often provided through pictures of alleged students, see Dion, 1972). Indeed many studies reported evidence of bias indicated by differences in grades or other judgments assigned by groups provided with different bits of information (see Babad, 1979). It seems that total objectivity is difficult to maintain when biasing information is available.

A methodological note about the prevalence of the bias phenomenon must be added here. Some critics have argued that the published research on teacher bias is in itself biased, because many studies that failed to demonstrate bias were not accepted for publication in the scientific journals. Perhaps investigators would not even try to publish bias studies that failed to show bias, filing them instead in their drawers. Rosenthal and Rosnow (1991) developed a statistical method—The File Drawer Method—that estimates the number of studies that failed to prove the research hypothesis which might annul the published conclusion, studies stacked away in hidden drawers. According to their calculations, the number of negative results required to annul the published results on teacher bias would be enormous, and not very likely to exist.

The bias domains particularly interesting for teacher and classroom research are stereotypic bias, focused on membership in ethnic or social groups differing in social and school status, and ability bias, based on direct information about students' ability or past achievement. In studies of stereotypic bias it is usually sufficient to provide the name of the hypothetical student, like the John-Joan example above. The name would identify the hypothetical student in a group of high status (a WASP name in the USA or Britain, an Ashkenazi name in Israel) or in a group of low status (Hispanic name in the USA, Arab or Pakistani name in Britain, Sephardi name in Israel). The grades assigned to the hypothetical high-status student would usually be found to be higher than those attributed to the low-status student despite the fact that the very same stimulus material was judged by both groups. In studies of ability bias, direct information about ability or past achievement is provided: excellent student, weak student, gifted student, fast/slow track, special needs student, etc. Here, too, expectations may lead teachers to give the high-achiever a better grade than the low-achiever for the very same performance.

More complex designs yield interesting variations of teacher bias. For example, White students in the USA and Ashkenazi students in Israel tended in various studies to receive higher evaluations than Black or Sephardi students. But what would happen if we would have combined stereotypic and ability labels in a 2 x 2 design? We would then have four groups representing the combinations of hypothetical high/low ethnic status and high/low achievement status: gifted Whites, gifted Blacks, weak Whites, weak Blacks. Would the effect of the two bias labels be additive so that gifted Whites would be assigned the highest evaluations and weak Blacks would be assigned the lowest grades? For this particular combination of bias labels the results were not conclusive: In one American study (Rubovitz & Maehr, 1973) the Black student labeled as gifted was hindered by the biased teachers and received the most negative treatment(!), while the gifted White received the best treatment. Those authors concluded that teachers' racism was demonstrated. In a study in Israel using a similar design (Babad, 1980) the findings showed that low ethnic status polarized results compared to high ethnic status, so that the gifted Sephardi received the highest grades and the weak Sephardi received the lowest grades by the biased teachers.

Another known phenomenon is reversed bias, where low-status students receive higher grades or evaluations than high-status students. Reversed bias is usually ideologically motivated, as if "to compensate" the weaker groups (Babad, 1979). Opponents usually characterize reversed bias as bending over backwards. Although reversed bias is no less a bias than the other sorts already discussed, the educational system is more lenient toward reversed bias, and does not judge it as negatively as it judges stereotypic bias or ability bias in favor of the students from the stronger groups.

Because the existence of the phenomenon of teachers' bias is recognized, educational authorities and school administrations take efforts to develop remedies for reducing bias. These include blind grading or double grading. In many colleges and universities worldwide, students' names are removed from exam booklets, and exams are graded anonymously. Other educational efforts are designed to increase teachers' awareness to potential bias through self-examination and reflection.

PERSONALITY CORRELATES OF
SUSCEPTIBILITY TO BIASING INFORMATION

Bias and SFP studies consistently show that not all people are influenced to the same degree by biasing information, and not all teachers transmit differential expectancies to their students. Because of this range of individual differences, it is important to investigate who is susceptible and who is not susceptible to biasing information, and to identify the personality and the behavioral characteristics of each type. This is particularly important if action is planned to remedy the situation in school.

For this kind of research each investigated teacher should receive a score describing her/his level of susceptibility to biasing information. The best design would be to conduct a teacher bias study in which each teacher would be asked to grade or evaluate two pieces of student performance (of equal quality), but would be told that one piece was presumably written by a high-status student, and the other, by a low-status student. The difference between the two grades assigned by the responding teacher to the high-status and low-status students would constitute that teacher's susceptibility score. In my research (Babad, 1979), I taught the participating teacher education students how to score a Draw-A-Person intelligence test that is typically used with young children. (In such a drawing test, points are awarded for accuracy in drawing and for locating body parts and other details according to a specific manual). Then, as a presumable reliability exercise, I asked the participants to score two drawings presumably made by local school children. The name, address and parents' occupations provided at the top of each drawing clearly labeled one child as being of high-status, and the other, of low-status. The drawings were actually reproduced from the test manual, so that their objective scores were known. Individual susceptibility to bias scores were calculated for every investigated teacher, defined by the difference between the scores s/he assigned to the high-status and low-status student. A variety of personality and attitude questionnaires were also administered to the investigated teachers. It was therefore possible to trace personality and attitude differences between susceptible and non-susceptible teachers.

This procedure for identifying teachers' susceptibility to biasing information was administered to hundreds of teachers (Babad, 1998). That made it possible to assess the dimensions of the susceptibility phenomenon and its spread among teachers. With reservations about generalization from one measurement method used in one country, it was estimated that:

- About one sixth of the teachers scored the two drawings objectively and were uninfluenced by the biasing information (unbiased teachers);
- About one half of the teachers were mildly biased and showed a small score advantage to the high-status student;
- About one quarter of the teachers were highly biased and attributed much higher scores to the high-status student;
- A small proportion of the teachers (3–5%) showed reversed bias, and scored the drawing of the low-status student higher than that of the high-status student.

It is very encouraging to find out that one sixth of the teachers were unbiased and not susceptible at all to the biasing information. The mild bias demonstrated by half of the teachers is also not a source of concern, because their judgment process was not seriously distorted by the biasing information. Given that reversed bias is also quite acceptable and does not evoke serious concern, the situation was quite good for three quarters of the teachers as far as the issue of teachers' bias was concerned. However, the fact that a quarter of the teachers showed high susceptibility to biasing information, and their grading in favor of the high-expectancy student deviated dramatically from objectivity is a serious source of concern. To identify personality and behavioral correlates of teachers' bias in the next stage of the research, extreme groups of highly biased and unbiased teachers were identified and compared to each other. Such an extreme group design is often used in typological research—with the high-bias and unbiased groups representing pure types of teachers as far as bias is concerned.

The Profile of the Biased Teacher: Theoretical Hypothesis

Conceptually, teachers prone to demonstrate bias and expectancy effects would be hypothesized to be rigid and inflexible. The formation of bias is essentially a cognitive process, but a behavioral element would be added, where the teacher's expectations would be transmitted to the students through differential behavior (see next chapter). The rigidity would characterize both the cognitive style and the social behavior of biased teachers. In this conception, stereotypic perception causes the formation of bias, and rigid expectations and subsequent stereotypic behavior transmits those expectations to students in a fixed manner. This description is in line with the personality syndrome of dogmatism (Rokeach, 1954, 1960) or authoritarianism (Adorno et al., 1950). This personality style is characterized by lack of cognitive flexibility, intolerance of ambiguity and resistance to disconfirming information (that is, refusing to accept any new information once one's mind had been made up).

The Profile of the Biased Teacher: Findings

Babad (1998) summarized various research findings which demonstrated systematic characteristics of biased teachers and supported the conceptualization (see also Cooper & Hazelrigg, 1988). Brophy (1983, 1985), a salient researcher of teacher expectancies in the 1970s and 1980s, described teachers of this type as over-reactive teachers who hold rigid expectations. Different attributes related to dogmatism and authoritarianism were reported in various studies as characterizing biased teachers. In the cognitive domain, the findings reported by various researchers included:

- Intolerance of ambiguity;
- Difficulties dealing with cognitive complexity;
- Halo effect (tendency to have the initial general liking influence all other judgments of a person);
- Social desirability (i.e., conforming to social norms and being politically correct);
- Making more dogmatic statements (e.g., "students should respect teacher's authority") in discussing educational events; and
- Expressing various attitudes in a more extreme fashion regardless of their content (that is, they did not hold particular attitudes in terms of their content, but held whatever attitudes they had in a more extreme fashion).

An interesting finding (Babad, Bernieri, & Rosenthal, 1989b) focused on the nonverbal (NV) behavior of biased teachers (see Chapter 14). In their classroom behavior, biased teachers demonstrated more NV leakage than unbiased teachers. That means that they were less capable of hiding from the students their negative feelings, and those negative messages leaked through biased teachers' less controlled NV channels, such as body language and voice. Unbiased teachers, who presumably had less anger to hide from students, did not manifest NV leakage.

Some of the findings previously mentioned were collected through self-report questionnaires, whereas other findings were behavioral, derived from classroom observations. A known problem with self-report questionnaires is that the respondent might guess what is measured by the questionnaire, and might (with or without conscious awareness) fake her/his responses in order to make a good impression. It is also likely that biased persons might be more concerned about hiding negative characteristics and providing an ideal picture of themselves. In that sense, one of the early findings (Babad, 1979) was particularly instructive. A personality questionnaire was administered to extreme groups of biased and unbiased teachers, comprising of 300 adjectives for self-rating. Surprisingly, the biased teachers described themselves as more reasonable, objective, logical and more unbiased than the unbiased teachers. Because their scoring on the draw-a-person test measuring susceptibility to biasing information indicated that they were highly biased, this self-report contradicted their actual behavior. My conclusion was that their self-report reflected their strong need to view themselves in a certain light rather than actually describing their real mode of conduct. Since then I tell my students and various audiences of teachers that extreme self-assurance in one's objectivity and in one's lack of bias might paradoxically be a characteristic of biased teachers, whereas those who doubt their own objectivity and question their fairness are more likely to be unbiased teachers.

Classroom Behavior of Biased Teachers

Probably the most important question about susceptibility to biasing information concerns the connection between teachers' cognitive and personality style (that is, their susceptibility to bias) on the one hand, and their actual behavior in the classroom on the other hand. A more particular question was whether there would be a higher probability of SFP effects to take place in the classrooms of biased teachers. Studies by Babad, Inbar, and Rosenthal (1982a, 1982b; Babad & Inbar, 1981) compared classroom behavior of extreme groups of highly biased and unbiased teachers. In the first study (Babad & Inbar, 1981), behavioral observations of teaching style were conducted in the classrooms of highly biased and unbiased physical education teachers. Those teachers were also evaluated by their immediate supervisors on the same set of behaviors as the classroom observations. In both sets of data, the conclusion was that the unbiased group consisted of better teachers in terms of their classroom behavior, teaching style and overall interaction patterns with students.

The second study (Babad et al., 1982a) examined the effects of teacher expectancies in the classrooms of these highly biased and unbiased physical education teachers in a Pygmalion-type design. The teachers themselves nominated three high-expectancy and three low-expectancy students in their classrooms, and two additional (randomly selected) students were subsequently named as having been identified by a particular novel test as potential late bloomers in physical education. Teachers' behaviors toward those eight students were carefully observed, and the achievements of these particular students in performing tasks for these teachers were measured as well. This design made it possible to examine both Pygmalion-type effects of positive expectancies and effects of negative expectancies (labeled Golem effects). The design also made it possible to investigate not only teachers' expectancy-related differential behavior but also to examine the reflection of those teachers' behaviors in the actual performance of the students for these teachers.

The results were strong and highly consistent: Expectancy effects were found only in the classrooms of the highly biased teachers, and no expectancy effects were found in the classrooms of the unbiased teachers. The highly biased teachers demonstrated both Pygmalion and Golem effects, and the latter was particularly salient—the biased teachers treated their low-expectancy students in a distinctly negative manner, and these students, in turn, responded with particularly low levels of performance for these teachers. In contrast, the unbiased teachers did not treat their low-expectancy students differently than the other students, and the physical education performance of the low-expectancy students was almost equal to that of the high-expectancy students!

Thus, the cognitive tendency to be susceptible to biasing information in forming expectations about students that characterizes a certain fraction of the teacher polulation is associated with a more dogmatic and rigid personality style and behavioral patterns. In turn, the susceptibility to bias is also related to particular behavioral patterns in teacher–student interaction, and carries a higher likelihood for negative expectancy effects in the classroom.

CURRENT THINKING ABOUT TEACHERS' SELF-FULFILLING EXPECTANCIES

The main finding in *Pygmalion in the Classroom* was the increase in students' IQ following bogus information about their potential for late blooming that had been provided to the teachers. But most of the controversy that lasted for several decades was tied to the Golem implication that was not put to test at all in Pygmalion, namely that teachers' negative expectancies might hinder students and damage their academic performance. If it had been only the possibility of performance being improved by positive expectations, nobody would have been too concerned about it (see Eden, 1990).

The shift from experimental studies to application in the real world always presents a complicated issue. Research conclusions should presumably be directly applicable to real-life situations. However, this is usually not the case, and research results demonstrate potential occurrences, but not necessarily the most frequent or most likely occurrences. To investigate psychological phenomena in a clean fashion, various intervening and mediating influences must be controlled. Sometimes a controlled laboratory simulation of the real-life situation must be created, to be sure that only the independent variable that is investigated actually caused the measured effect. The Pygmalion study was indeed conducted in real classrooms, but outside of the research framework, teachers never receive fabricated expectancy information about potential late bloomers. Thus, that research demonstrated what could happen and how teacher expectancies might influence students' intellectual performance.

Differences among students are part of the reality of every classroom, and teacher expectations based on such real differences do indeed exist. Thus, the discussion shifted quite early from "self-fulfilling prophecies" (SFP) to "self-maintaining expectancies" (SME). Brophy emphasized the differences between "teacher effects on students" (SFP) and "student effects on teachers" (SME). After two decades of expectancy research, Brophy (1985) reached the conclusion that, as a classroom phenomenon, teacher expectancies alone have a relatively small influence on students' academic achievement. The influence on achievement is small, he argued, because teacher expectancies are "accurate, reality-based, and open to corrective feedback." Brophy thought that only a particular type of over-reactive teachers (equivalent to the highly biased teachers discussed earlier in this chapter) are prone to demonstrate substantial SFP effects in their classrooms.

Lee Jussim and his colleagues (Jussim et al., 1998) reviewed the field of teacher expectations and highlighted the various methodological issues involved in attempts to determine the pure effects of teacher expectations on students' academic performance. Some of Jussim's own investigations (alone and with various colleagues) involved the collection of longitudinal data in actual classrooms over periods spanning several consecutive years and the employment of sophisticated statistical time-lagged analyses.

In a recent review article, Jussim and Harber (2005) summarized their conclusions from the decades of teacher expectancy research. Their conclusions express the consensus among most researchers about the effects of teacher expectancies on students' academic performance:

1. SFP effects do occur in classrooms, but these effects are typically small and likely to dissipate over time.

2. Powerful SFP effects (Golem effects, as defined earlier) may selectively occur among students from stigmatized social groups.
3. Whether SFP affects intelligence, and whether teacher expectancies in general do more harm than good, remains unclear.
4. Teacher expectancies may predict student outcomes more because these expectations are accurate than because they are self-fulfilling.

In my opinion, the Pygmalion study brought the issue of teacher expectancies to the awareness of educators and teachers, and the issue must remain in focus even if events of creation of SFP by bogus information are very rare. In the reality of the classroom, teachers form differential expectations about all students, and they interact with students according to their expectations and interpretations. The same behavior enacted by different students might be interpreted and reacted to differently by the teacher in accordance with the teacher's expectation. The potential danger is that teachers' judgments would be influenced and biased by their expectations, and their resultant assessment of students (present chapter) and treatment of students (next chapter) would be influenced not only by students' attributes, real potential and actual behavior but by teachers' expectations and interpretations as well. We saw that susceptibility to bias is a very serious problem with some teachers, but all teachers must be influenced to some extent by their expectations. Only sharp awareness and investment of effort can help teachers to maintain their mental flexibility and to avoid cognitive and behavioral fixation which might prevent students' development and change.

From a historical perspective, the problem stems from the extreme fashion in which the teacher expectancy issue has been viewed and dealt with in the educational literature. When it was thought that teacher expectations could be easily manipulated and that students' academic performance might be readily influenced by teacher expectations, both proponents and opponents over-reacted rather intensely. And when it became apparent that SFP is quite limited in its potential impact on students' academic performance, the issue of teacher expectancies almost disappeared from the literature on classroom management. The more appropriate stance is one of proportional concern—teacher expectations certainly exist, and even if they are based on real students' attributes, they might cause fixation in students' status and narrow the flexible flow of students' potential and development. The next chapter is focused on the issue of teachers' differential behavior (TDB) and its potential effects on classroom climate and on students' emotional reactions to their teachers. TDB is discussed as a basic issue in CM independent of SFP and how expectations are formed, because differential behavior based on real attributes of students might be as serious in its classroom implications as TDB based on bogus teacher expectancies.

7 Teachers' Differential Behavior in the Classroom

THE IMPORTANCE OF TDB AS AN INDEPENDENT CLASSROOM PHENOMENON

Today, teachers' differential behavior towards different students is a major issue in the psychology of the heterogeneous classroom. Hundreds of TDB studies were conducted in the 1970s and 1980s following the publication of *Pygmalion in the Classroom* and the intense interest in teacher expectancies. As mentioned in the previous chapter, TDB was considered the major link in the conceptualized chain of the self-fulfillment of teachers' expectations, constituting the behavioral mediation of SFP. For teacher expectations to influence students' performance or behavior, they must me transmitted to students via differential behavior, which is, in turn, perceived by students, and influences their self-image, their self-expectations, and eventually their academic performance as well.

Over the years:

1. Lists of the most frequent differential behaviors enacted by teachers towards their high-expectancy and low-expectancy students were published (Brophy, 1983, 1985).
2. Meta-analyses summarized statistically the relative intensity of TDBs and their impact (Harris & Rosenthal, 1985).
3. Theories about the behavioral mediation of teacher expectancies were formulated—most notably Rosenthal's four-factor (1973) and two-factor (1989) mediation theories.
4. Rhona Weinstein (2002) demonstrated in several studies that the main source of students' knowledge if they are smart and when they are smart comes from their perceptions of their teachers' differential behavior towards them.

TDB must be distinguished from teachers' overall style, because differential treatment of students or groups of students can occur in any teaching style. Individual teachers choose their own style of conduct and their way of dealing with all students. The notion of TDB emerged out of teacher expectancy research and focused on differences in teacher's conduct toward different students because of expectations based on their individual characteristics. One exception within the expectancy literature, in which an expectancy researcher talked about overall style rather than differential behavior is found in work of Dov Eden (1990, 1992) about "Pygmalion management." Eden described an overall management style where managers transmit positive expectations toward all subordinates.

Today, the phenomenon of TDB is detached from teacher expectancy research and stands on its own accord as a problem characterizing many teachers and classrooms. The detachment of the TDB phenomenon from the expectancy domain stemmed from two types of findings discussed in the previous chapter:

1. The influence of teacher expectations alone on students' academic performance was found to be quite limited in real classrooms.
2. Most expectations held by teachers for different students in their classrooms are quite accurate and reality-based, reflecting real differences among students.

TDB can be viewed as a positive and as a negative phenomenon. On the positive side, the ancient Biblical dictum "Train a child according to his way" (Proverbs, 22:6) is an educational value. The wide differences among students in the heterogeneous classroom along a variety of dimensions require teachers to deal differently with them according to their abilities, their motivations, their skills, and also according to their weaknesses. Each student must be taught and treated in the most appropriate manner for her/him, and therefore TDB is educationally justified. On the negative side, TDB potentially violates the important normative values of fairness and equity, because all students are not treated equally. Even if TDB is based on the best intentions and on real differences, it can cause a sense of discrimination, and sometimes even a feeling of victimization among students. TDB might also fixate students and perpetuate their academic performance, preventing opportunities of student change and progress. As will be shown later, there are deep gaps between students and teachers in the ways they perceive and interpret teachers' differential behavior. Thus, to be able to evaluate when, where, and how TDB would be desirable or undesirable we need empirical data on various differential teacher behaviors and their measured effects in the cognitive and non-cognitive domains. We also need a good practical theory that will enable us to assess clusters of behaviors and reach conclusions about the effective practices for teachers.

LISTS AND CLUSTERS OF TDBS

The published works on TDB focused mainly on differences in teacher behavior toward high-expectancy and low-expectancy students, namely, differences in teachers' treatment of high-achievers and low-achievers. It must be emphasized first that many differential behaviors are implicit and subtle, consisting of very fine, almost undetectable nuances. For example, length of eye contact with a student might be measured in fractions of seconds, and differential eye contact might be almost undetectable in natural observation. But such fine nuances accumulate consistently over time and are perceived and interpreted by students.

Summarizing a large number of studies, Brophy (1983, 1985), Good and Weinstein (1986) and Harris and Rosenthal (1985) compiled lists of specific TDBs and of generalized dimensions of TDB. Brophy simply listed behaviors investigated in different studies; Good and Weinstein defined general dimensions of teachers' communication of differential expectations; whereas Harris and Rosenthal conducted meta-analyses on four theoretically-defined factors to assess the rate of occurrence of each type of behavior and its impact on students' performance. Especially instructive in Brophy's (1985) list was the specification of teachers' typical behaviors toward low-expectancy students: not helping enough to improve students' answers; praising incorrect answers or inappropriate behaviors; demanding less of them; shorter and less informative feedback; less intrusive instruction; and less use of time-consuming instructional methods. In Good and Weinstein's (1986) summary, teachers were concluded to provide students believed to be less capable with: less opportunity to perform publicly; less opportunity to think and analyze; less choice on curriculum assignments; less autonomy and more frequent monitoring; and more gratuitous and less contingent feedback.

Rosenthal's (1973) four-factor theory grouped the various TDBs in four clusters:

Climate. Teachers tend to create a warmer social-emotional climate for their high-expectancy students, transmitting more warmth, support and liking through verbal and NV channels.

Feedback. Teachers provide more positive feedback to high-expectancy students and more negative feedback to low-expectancy students. In later formulations, teachers were described as giving more informative and instructive feedback to high-expectancy students.

Input. Providing high-expectancy students with more instruction and with more difficult material.

Output. Giving high-expectancy students more opportunities to respond, maximizing their chances of learning. Behaviors included in differential learning opportunities ranged from explicit teacher acts such as turning to student, asking questions, inviting a student to perform publicly or ignoring a student on the one hand, to very implicit behaviors on the other hand, such as length of eye contact after a faulty response or after failing to respond. If the teacher turns her gaze away from a low-achiever a fraction of a second faster because she does not expect that student to provide the proper response, her expectancy was transmitted to the student.

Harris and Rosenthal (1985) meta-analyzed thirty-one specific differential behaviors (grouped into the four factors listed in the four-factor theory) that had been investigated in 131 studies. Meta-analysis is a statistical method for examining effect sizes across studies for purposes of reaching generalized conclusions. They examined the effect sizes of both the intensity of differentiality in teacher behavior toward high-and low-achievers, and—when such information was available—the effects of teacher differentiality on the academic performance of high- and low-achievers. For the four factors, they found: (a) Stronger effects for affective climate (including behaviors such as physical distance from students, smiling, etc.) and for instructional input (including behaviors such as frequency and length of interaction with students); (b) A smaller effect for output (including behaviors such as ignoring students, asking questions, and length of eye contact); and (c) A practically negligible effect size for differential feedback behaviors (including various forms of praise and criticism).

Thus, contrary to the notions and early findings of the 1970s, teachers in the 1980s demonstrated differentiality in affective behaviors and in direct instructional behaviors, but divided their feedback in an equal manner among students. Rosenthal (1989) later modified the four-factor theory into a two-factor theory: *Affect* (similar to the original emotional climate factor) and *effort* (an instructional dimension combining input and output). In the following discussion, I use these two factors in a broader meaning as *emotional support* (ES) and *learning support* (LS).

What happened to the feedback factor over the decades? If one would try to guess intuitively the relative intensity of teacher differentiality in the four TDB factors, the feedback factor would probably be the first to spring to mind. One would guess intuitively that the strongest TDB would be for teachers to vary the manner in which they provide feedback to high- versus low-expectancy students. But the findings in the 1980s showed that teachers' feedback was distributed quite equally in their classrooms. I believe that teachers' shift into a more equal distribution of feedback reflects the accumulated influence of the teacher expectancy literature. As more and more teachers learned about Pygmalion and SFP, they became more aware that they must reduce their differentiality, and probably made more conscious efforts to dispense their feedback in an equitable fashion in the classroom.

Another shift over the decades involved the component of learning support. The early notion was that high-achievers receive both more instruction and better instruction than low-achievers. That notion became less applicable towards the end of the 20th century, as it became evident that teachers tend to provide more learning support to low-expectancy students. It became important for teachers to deal with differences among students in heterogeneous classrooms. Therefore, teachers began to invest extra instructional effort in low-achieving students in order to compensate them for their weak starting point. Thus, the more recent studies began to demonstrate a reversed trend for the instructional factor, with low-achievers receiving more LS than high-achievers. However, the change was evident in quantity of instruction, whereas the quality of instruction more often continued to show that high-achievers receive instruction of higher quality (e.g., more difficult questions and tasks) reflecting the teachers' higher expectations.

THE NEED FOR A PRACTICAL THEORY OF TDB

The previous comments about TDB can be quite perplexing for the practicing classroom teacher. On the one hand, TDB is positive and desirable because it is responsive to real differences among students, because it fulfills educational ideology by fitting the appropriate instruction to each student according to the student's needs, abilities and personal style. On the other hand, TDB is negative because it violates basic social norms of fairness and equity. Thus, perhaps TDB contributes to attain certain educational goals but hinders the attainment of other important goals. Teachers may well wonder which specific differential behaviors are OK and which are not OK; when differentiality in one direction (that is, giving advantage to the lows) or in the other direction (giving advantage to the highs) would be appropriate or inappropriate?

When facing such a dilemma, a practical theory is needed to sort the issues out. Kurt Lewin, one of the founding fathers of modern social psychology, was considered a practical theorist (Marrow, 1969). Although it is commonly held that the theoretical and the practical are two opposing poles, Lewin used to argue that "there is nothing more practical than a good theory." Rosenthal's previously mentioned four-factor and two-factor theories of TDB are descriptive but not practical. They classify the types of TDBs but do not provide sufficient consideration for teachers' decision-making in this dilemma situation. A practical theory should explicate the relevant underlying factors and their inter-relations to allow clear decision-making in particular situations. It should consider educational goals, norms and sanctions for each potential line of action, take into account teachers' ability to act in each way, and examine potential cognitive and affective outcomes of each alternative.

Some years ago (Babad, 1993a, 1998) I proposed a conceptualization intended to resolve some of the contradictions and to allow teachers to make rational decision-making how to deal with differences among students. The theory (now somewhat revised) is based on several components (or questions):

1. What are the specific types of differential behaviors? The most important distinction is the one between LS and ES.
2. What is the ideological legitimacy and educational desirability of each type of differential behavior?

3. Which group of students receives an advantage by each type of TDB?
4. What is the teachers' natural tendency and how would they wish to deal with particular students and different groups of students?
5. To what extent are teachers able to control their specific verbal and nonverbal behaviors?

The combination between the first component (types of TDB) and the second component (ideological legitimacy) is quite clear. In the instructional domain, teacher differentiality is legitimate and even encouraged. Instruction must be adapted to specific students, and weak students must be provided with more LS. The third component (target of advantage) would clarify that advantages in LS must be given only to low-achievers and underprivileged students, never to the high-achievers. But this clashes with the fourth component (teachers' wish and natural tendency) because teachers wish to provide instruction of the highest quality, and such instruction is usually more effective with high-achievers than with low-achievers.

Thus, the resolution for LS is quite clear. Differential LS is permitted to improve the performance of low-achievers, but no instructional advantage should be provided to high-achievers. Differential LS constitutes of corrective or compensatory discrimination to improve the relative position of the weak students. Of course, the question is whether teachers keep to this resolution or deviate from it? From the empirical findings, it seems that teachers indeed invest more effort and energy in teaching their underprivileged students, but quite often they do give LS advantage to the high-achievers by providing them with instruction of higher quality. And when that is perceived by students, it can affect students' morale and CC negatively.

With regard to feedback behaviors, it seems that teachers would make efforts to exercise self-control (fifth component) and to dispense feedback in a fair and equitable manner to all students. Here, the influence of teacher expectancy research and of the educational dictum about fairness (second component) is clear. Because teachers can reasonably control their verbal feedback and they wish to avoid differentiality in this domain (fourth component), relatively little TDB is found for feedback behaviors.

The problem becomes more complicated in the affective domain, because here the components of the theory clash with each other more strongly. From an ideological viewpoint (second component), any kind of emotional differnetiality is simply not permitted. Teachers and parents are not supposed to demonstrate emotional preference to particular children even if their inner emotions toward children are differential. Total equality in affective displays is demanded, regardless of one's true feelings. It can be presumed that high-expectancy children are usually better liked by their teachers: Their academic performance is high and they give their teachers much satisfaction; they are usually more obedient, behave better and pose fewer problems in regard to the teacher's ability to manage the classroom; and teachers can more readily control their behavior and teach them effectively (Cooper & Good, 1983). On the other side of the spectrum of differences among students, low-achievers and problem students often evoke negative emotions in teachers, because they are less amenable to teachers' instruction and teacher influence. Teachers would then tend to favor the highs and to demonstrate differentiality in their ES of high- versus low-achievers (third and fourth components). In order to treat all students equally in the affective domain, teachers must exercise a great deal of control over their emotional behavior (fifth component) and to conceal their differential affect.

The ability to control affective displays and to conceal negative emotions varies considerably within the person. Some channels (especially words and verbal content) can be readily controlled to demonstrate equal treatment, such as in the case of teachers' verbal feedback to students. But other NV channels (body, voice intonations, and, to a lesser degree, facial expressions) cannot be controlled as easily. Therefore, negative affect cannot be concealed and it leaks through those NV channels. The conception of NV leakage (see Chapter 12) was first introduced by Ekman and Friesen (1969b), and a great deal is known today about the hierarchy of NV channels in terms of leakage potential. With regard to the theory of TDB, the control aspect would imply that teachers would experience difficulty in hiding their negative emotions toward particular students, and therefore would not be able to treat all students equally in their affective behavior.

There is also an added danger that attempts to control emotional displays would lead teachers to demonstrate excessive sweetness toward disliked students, and that might well be perceived by students and interpreted by them as reflecting *negative* affect. Reversal of emotional expression is often more convincing for the person displaying the emotion than for the receiver, and as mentioned earlier, students are experts in deciphering teachers' hidden messages.

Another potential danger arises from the contemporary leading ideology of CM (see extensive discussion in Chapter 9). In this approach (Everston & Weinstein, 2006a), teachers are encouraged to form emotional relationships with their students and to spontaneously express their emotions in the classroom. Unfortunately, this literature largely ignores the accumulated research findings on TDB. Because teachers' feelings towards different students vary a lot, they are likely to demonstrate great differentiality in their free-floating emotional displays, and they would not exercise self-control about their differential ES. The good atmosphere predicted by the CM advocates due to teachers' freely expressed affect might boomerang and hinder students' satisfaction because of that emotional differentiality and the negative affect directed at some students.

More recently, TDB has been investigated via judges' ratings of teachers' nonverbal (NV) behaviors in their interactions with low- and high-expectancy students. Measurement of NV behavior (Chapters 12–14) tends to highlight emotional aspects in teacher behavior, as these are reflected in facial expressions, gestures, body language and tone of voice. Therefore, the study of TDB can be enhanced by investigation of teachers' NV behavior.

In one study (Babad, Bernieri, & Rosenthal, 1989a, see also Babad, 1992, 1993b), differences were found between teachers' NV behaviors when they were just talking about low- versus high-expectancy students to the camera. In another condition, when teachers were talking to individual (low and high) students and interacting with them, expectancy differences were found in judges' ratings of facially communicated expressions and in active teaching behavior, confirming the theory previously presented: Teacher interactions with low-expectancy students were characterized by more vigorous teaching activity (LS compensation), but with more negative affect (ES). Interactions with high-expectancy students showed less instructional effort but more positive teacher affect. In a more recent study (Babad, Avni-Babad, & Rosenthal, 2003), judges viewed ten-second video clips of teachers' NV behavior in interactions with low- and high-achievers and judged how competent, friendly and interesting the teachers appeared to be in these clips. Substantial expectancy-related differences were found, and teacher interactions with high-achievers were systematically rated more positively than interactions with low-achievers.

STUDENTS' PERCEPTIONS OF TDB

The next important link in the expectancy confirmation chain consists of students' perceptions of teachers' TDB. Once it has been demonstrated that teacher expectancies are indeed expressed and transmitted to students via their differential behavior, it becomes necessary to investigate whether students indeed perceive and interpret their teachers' differential behavior. To study students' perceptions, the objective (low-inference) measurement of the previous link must be replaced by high-inference measurement of students' subjective experiences of the classroom behavior of their teachers. Studies on student perceptions of TDB were conducted mainly in three locations: By Weinstein (2002; Weinstein & McKown, 1998) and her associates in Berkeley; By Cooper and Good (1983), then in Missouri; and By Babad (1990a, 1998) in Israel. In general, all investigators found that students (even very young ones) are highly sensitive to TDB and can describe in systematic terms which are quite consistent with the observational findings.

Despite the consistency between findings obtained from low-inference observational studies and high-inference students' perceptions, it must be remembered that students often interpret teacher behavior differently from the automatic interpretations given by adult observers and researchers, or by the behaving teachers themselves. One study can illuminate this gap: Babad (1990b) examined student perceptions about a teacher behavior labeled "calling on students." In the adult perspective, this behavior carries a universal meaning of providing instructional support (LS) in the output category (i.e., providing learning opportunities), and it is viewed as a positive teacher behavior. This behavior was found to have different meanings in student perceptions, depending on who was the target student called on by the teacher: If the teacher called on a high-achiever, students perceived this behavior as reflecting positive LS; but calling on a low-achiever was interpreted by students within the negative cluster of putting pressure. There may well be other behaviors that teachers enact with a positive and helpful intent, but students might consider those behaviors as negative and reflective of low expectations.

My personal experience confirms this point. When I visit the USA, people recognize that I am a foreigner when they hear my Israeli accent. Some will talk to me more slowly in an effort to be helpful, separating their words and selecting "easy" words. They are probably quite smug about their sensitivity and helpfulness, but little do they know how insulting their behavior is for me, as it transmits a negative expectancy!

Weinstein and Babad discovered independently that students' perceptions of their teachers' differential behavior cannot be probed in a direct manner. Direct questions such as "How does your teacher treat you compared to other students" evoke defensive and protective reactions in which students deny teacher differentiality ("She treats me exactly like everyone else" or "She treats everybody here in the same way"). The more effective way is to ask students about their teacher's presumable behavior toward hypothetical low-expectancy and high-expectancy students "that she had taught in the past, in another classroom." In this questionnaire, the responding students rate a list of their teacher's behaviors twice, once for the hypothetical low-achiever and a second time for the hypothetical high-achiever. This method allows students to freely project their current perceptions of their teacher's behavior without feeling constrained.

Weinstein and Middlestadt (1979) found that students' perceptions of their teachers' interactions with high-expectancy students reflected high expectations, academic demand, and special privileges, whereas low-expectancy students were perceived as receiving fewer chances but greater teacher concern and vigilance. In other studies, Weinstein and colleagues (Weinstein et al., 1982; Weinstein et al., 1987) found that low-expectancy students were perceived as receiving more negative feedback, more direction, and more work- and rule-oriented treatment, whereas high-expectancy students were perceived as receiving higher expectations and more opportunity and choice. Weinstein and her colleagues did not put a special emphasis on teachers' affective behaviors, and their lists of teacher behaviors were concentrated on behaviors in the academic-instructional domain.

In Babad's (1990a, 1995) investigations of student perceptions of TDB, the list of behaviors to be rated by students included three factor-based clusters: *Learning support (LS)* (with items like: Teacher approaches to observe student's work; Gives student opportunity to think long enough before answering Explains student's mistakes and how to correct them, etc.); *Emotional support (ES)* (Teacher is warm to student and supportive of her/him; Loves the student; Gives student much attention, etc.); and *Pressure* (Teacher addresses difficult question at student; Is very demanding of student). In large samples of Israeli 5th–7th grade classrooms, students' perceptions of TDB were very clear and consistent: Teachers were systematically perceived as giving low-expectancy students more LS and putting less Pressure on them compared to high-expectancy students; on the other hand, teachers were also systematically perceived as giving more ES to high-expectancy students, being more attentive, warm, supportive and loving towards them. These effects of TDB in students' perceptions supported the theory of TDB presented before. Differences in LS and Pressure are ideologically legitimate and even desirable, but the differences in ES in favor of the highs are not legitimate and quite problematic, potentially spoiling the good intentions in the provision of more instructional support to low-achievers.

COMPARISON OF STUDENTS' AND TEACHERS' PERCEPTIONS OF TDB

In Babad's (1990a, 1995) studies, the investigated teachers also filled out the same questionnaires as their students, and rated their own presumable behavior toward low- and high-expectancy students. Thus, teacher's and students' reports could be compared for each classroom. The patterns of agreement and disagreement between teachers and students followed the reasoning of the proposed theory and reaffirmed the psychological significance of the teacher affect issue. With regard to LS and pressure, there was almost complete agreement between the students and their teachers that teachers give low-expectancy students more LS and put less pressure on them compared to high-expectancy students. But with regard the ES and teacher warmth, the perceptions were diametrically opposed: Whereas the students perceived their teachers as giving more positive ES to high-expectancy students, the teachers themselves reported that they give more positive ES to the low-expectancy students. This pattern characterized almost every classroom in the sample. Thus, the teachers reported a consistent and desirable overall pattern of compensating low-achievers in both the instructional and the emotional domains. The students disagreed, and while they were in consensus with their teachers about the instructional aspects, they clearly perceived the teachers as giving preferential affect, more love and support to the highs.

Both studies (Babad 1990a, 1995) included a feedback intervention in which teachers received empirical feedback on the gaps between their own reports and their students' perceptions. In the early study, each teacher was characterized by the researchers as open or resistant to feedback according to her behavior and reactions in the session in which the feedback was provided. A few months later, both the students and their teachers filled out again the same questionnaires measuring TDB. In the classrooms of teachers characterized earlier as open to feedback, some improvement was observed, and that was evident in both students' and teachers' reports. No improvement was found in the classrooms of the teachers initially classified as resistant to feedback. In the second study, the feedback intervention was not found to have any effects on TDB. (Change interventions in the classroom are discussed in Chapter 16).

TDB IN TEACHERS' NV BEHAVIOR

The studies of teachers' NV behavior provided several opportunities to investigate the validity of students' perceptions of TDB. In the study that examined TDB when teachers talked about highs and lows and then interacted briefly with highs and lows (Babad et al., 1989a), adult judges were used to rate the video clips depicting teacher behavior. Later, we decided to show those teacher interactions with highs and lows to samples of primary school students, as young as fourth-graders (aged nine through ten) in Israel (Babad, Bernieri, & Rosenthal, 1991) and New Zealand (Babad & Taylor, 1992). Because of the young age of the new judges, the judgment task was changed: Instead of rating each teacher on a variety of behavioral scales following each video clip, the children were simply asked to guess the academic status of the unseen student in each video interaction (from weak to excellent student) and the degree to which they thought that student was liked by the teacher. The guesses about the unseen student were based on what they viewed in the teacher's behavior. From these very brief instances of teacher interactions with highs and lows (and in New Zealand, without any comprehension of teacher speech), the young children detected very well the high- or low-achieving status of each unseen student. They also perceived the high-achievers to be better liked by their teachers. Their ratings were well correlated with the ratings of the adult judges of the same thin slices of teacher behavior.

Thus, according to this evidence, exposure of a few seconds to the NV behavior of unknown teachers in interactions with high-and low-achieving students was sufficient for nine- and ten-year-old students to detect TDB. There must be something distinctive (yet very fine and elusive) in the different ways teachers treat their highs and their lows. It must be reiterated again that this differentiation is not simply a matter of being pleasant to those and nasty to those, and sometimes negative affect is inferred from excessive and exaggerated positive affect!

A second opportunity to validate student perceptions of TDB was provided in the more recent study already mentioned (Babad et al., 2003). In that study, high school teachers were videotaped during regular class lessons, and ten-second clips were later isolated from the natural flow to represent several instructional situations, such as disciplinary behavior, lecturing to the entire class, and interactions with students who were later identified as high- and low-achievers. Each of the NV clips was viewed by adult judges (outside Israel) who were not familiar with the teachers and did not comprehend teachers' Hebrew speech. The judges rated each clip on how competent, friendly, and interesting the teacher appeared to be, and a composite score representing their overall impression (negative to positive) was computed from these ratings. Different groups of judges rated teacher behavior toward the high-achievers and the low-achievers. Each teacher's score of differential treatment was derived from the comparison of the judges' mean ratings for the two interaction clips.

At the end of that school year, all students of the videotaped teachers filled out self-report questionnaires about the behavior of their teacher toward a hypothetical high-achiever and low-achiever "that she had taught in the past," and TDB scores were derived from the averaged students' reports for the hypothetical high-achiever and the low-achiever in each classroom. This comparison was interesting because the data on TDB for each teacher were derived from two sources that were very different from each other: Adult judges' ratings following exposure to ten seconds of unknown teachers' NV behavior on the one hand, versus students' judgments based on their accumulated experience with the teacher throughout the school year on the other hand. The results showed (a) that ten-seconds of exposure to teachers' NV behavior was sufficient to reach clear inferences about teacher differentiality; and (b) judges ratings and students' judgments were substantially correlated with each other across the sample of teachers. Thus, students' high-inference judgments based on a year-long experience and judges' low-inference ratings following a brief exposure cross-validated each other in identifying teachers' relative level of differentiality.

The third opportunity to validate students' perceptions of TDB emerged out of a secondary analysis of data in the 2003 study presented previously. An unexpected finding in that study showed that judges' ratings of teachers' NV behavior while addressing their entire classes (i.e., lecturing) were related to teachers' TDB status: Teachers who were judged more positively for their ten seconds of lecturing to the entire classroom were also found to be more differential in their treatment of highs and lows. The same was found for both the judges' ratings of the video clips and for the students' end-of-year perceptions of TDB. I was puzzled by this unexpected association between impressive lecturing and differential behavior, and decided to try a long shot: I showed the lecturing clips (that were directed at the entire body of students and did not single out any individual student) to a sample of eleventh grade students in another city, and asked the students to make guesses about each teacher's level of differentiality "when she would interact with individual low- versus high-achieving students." The results (Babad, 2005b) showed that these eleventh grade students were capable of guessing teacher differentiality quite accurately despite the fact that they viewed only public behavior and no individual treatment at all. Adult judges facing the same guessing task could not predict TDB from the lecturing clips.

It is not intuitively clear why being rated more positively on lecturing to the entire class in high school would be related to higher rates of TDB, and how the students who were not familiar with the videotaped teachers could accurately guess TDB from public behavior. One hypothesis was that good lecturing is like a show, and perhaps teachers who invest more effort in the show are more concerned about their own performance than about students, and then they might also be more differential and preferential in their treatment of students.

Regardless of the explanation of that particular finding, the important lesson in all examples is that students are experts in deciphering and understanding the finest nuances of teacher behavior. Because of students' continuous dependence on their teachers, their sensitivity is highly adaptive and might contribute to their adjustment to school. They are the first to perceive leakage and deception in teachers' behavior, and it is difficult for the teachers to manipulate their students. In terms of the salient conception of information processing in social and cognitive psychology, it might be argued that students have an implicit theory about teacher behavior, consisting of a complex set of relationships and hypothetical correlations between various teacher traits and behaviors. This implicit theory enables students to detect underlying processes even from subtle cues, to predict what might happen, and to deduce one thing from another. The last example demonstrates that students' implicit theories are not limited to their specific teachers and can be generalized to knowledge about teachers in general. Their implicit knowledge enables them to know things that they had not even seen directly.

Many teachers are oblivious of their transparency to students, and unaware of the students' expertise in understanding them. I think that many teachers believe that they can make students see them in the way they wish to appear and that they can be effective in hiding their emotions or displaying false emotions. Perhaps some teachers can also lie to themselves.

THE SOCIAL/EMOTIONAL EFFECTS OF TDB ON CLASSROOMS

The last and perhaps the most important link in the conceptual chain of expectancy confirmation involves the effects of the various expectancy phenomena on the students. As mentioned, the concern over SFP effects had initially been focused on the academic domain. Researchers had been apprehensive about the possibility that negative teacher expectancies might potentially hinder the academic performance and scholastic achievements of low-achieving and minority group students (Wineburg, 1987; Weinstein, 2002). The development of the field has shifted the focus of concern from the academic domain to the social/emotional domain, and from potential consequences to individual students to whole class-room consequences, that is, how TDB might influence the morale of the entire classroom.

From the perspective of a long-time expectancy researcher, it seems to me that after the dust of the controversy over Pygmalion had settled down and actual SFP effects on individual students appeared to be rel-atively minimal, many educators sighed in relief and proceeded to shift their attention to other issues related to teaching, learning and CM. They thought that, indeed, the expectations of a small proportion of teachers might potentially influence their students in a positive or negative direc-tion (biased teachers in Babad's work, or over-reactive teachers in Brophy's, 1985 terms), but this phenomenon is only marginal and does not charac-terize most teachers and most classrooms. As a result of this thinking, the entire field of research dealing with Pygmalion, SFP, teacher expectancies and TDB was dropped from the agenda, and almost disappeared from the literature on CM.

But this approach is faulty, and the issue of TDB cannot be ignored. Over the years I have come to understand that TDB is a generalized issue that concerns teachers' overall conduct in their heterogeneous classrooms irrespective of SFP effects. Even if teachers' differential perceptions of dif-ferent students are accurate and their expectations are reality-based, class-room climate and the morale of *all* students might be affected by their perceptions that their teachers behave in an unfair and inequitable man-ner! Perhaps individual students are not academically hindered by teacher expectations, but excessive teacher differentiality can hinder the morale and satisfaction of the entire classroom because students' basic expectation of fairness and equity is violated.

The significance of students' emotional volatility and their extreme sen-sitivity to the most implicit nuances of teacher's behavior must be remem-bered at all times. Readers are reminded of the description of the classroom as a social environment (Chapter 1); of the discussion of students' social needs, motivations and special sensitivities (Chapter 2); and of the special status of the teacher as the leader of the classroom society, who is responsi-ble for leading students to both academic achievements and social harmony (Chapter 3). Even if differential treatment of different students and groups of students by the teacher in the heterogeneous classroom is necessary and educationally justified, students' awareness of TDB can potentially hinder CC and damage satisfaction and harmony.

Fairness and equity are central and cardinal values of modern human civi-lization. There might probably be only few values equaling them in societal priority. Therefore, violation of equality and unfair or arbitrary action of per-sons in positions of power can have a tremendous impact on individuals and groups under their influence. As mentioned, the social comparison process is extremely powerful, and one's contentment or frustration is determined not only by the objective assessment of one's own product, but also through comparison with others. Differential treatment illuminates and symbolizes differences (in status, in ability, in perceived potential, in likeability, in expectations, etc.) and can therefore trigger a sense of discrimination.

Equity Theory

Adams (1965) formulated his famous Equity Theory to describe personal motivation in the workplace. According to Adams, we seek a fair balance between what we put into our job and what we get out of it. Inputs include effort, loyalty, hard work, commitment, skill, ability, tolerance, determination, trust, support, and sacrifice. Outputs in this theory include pay, salary, benefits and bonuses, plus intangibles such as recognition, status, reputation, respect and thanks. We form perceptions of what would constitute a fair balance or trade of inputs and outputs by comparing our own situation with other reference points or examples. We are influenced by others (friends, peers, etc.) in establishing these benchmarks and our own response to them in relation to our own ratio of inputs and outputs. If we feel that our inputs are fairly rewarded by our outputs, we are happy and motivated to inputting on the same level or a higher level. If our inputs outweigh our outputs, especially by comparison to a referent other, we become de-motivated—we reduce effort and become inwardly disgruntled or outwardly difficult, even disruptive.

Other theories and much philosophical thinking emphasize the importance of the sense of justice, of the elementary expectation in democratic society that authority figures would act in a fair and equitable manner. For classroom students, the teacher is not just a manager in the organizational sense but, more importantly, an educator responsible for their value system. Therefore, teacher's fairness is most important. On principle, every differential behavior involves some form of inequity, but some behaviors or events evoke more students' anger than others. The biblical dictum "train the child according to his way" (Proverbs, 22:6) indeed prescribes differential treatment. Such differentiality is educationally justified because it is supposed to eventually promote equality—unequal treatment would provide equal opportunity. But when differential treatment is condoned, it should be limited as much as possible so as to avoid violating students' sense of equity. TDB in LS might be acceptable because of the real differences among students in their learning needs, skills and capabilities, but differentiality in the emotional domain (ES) is forbidden and cannot be justified. The same holds for parents. Even if they love one of their children more than her/his siblings, it would be considered extremely immoral to explicitly demonstrate their favoritism.

Empirical Evidence on the Psychological Price of TDB in the Classroom

Babad (1995) examined the relationships between TDB (as perceived and reported by classroom students) and indices of classroom climate (CC) and students' reactions to their teachers. The investigation was conducted in eighty fifth- and sixth-grade classrooms. As described earlier, the students filled out questionnaires ratings their perceptions of their teacher's behavior toward a hypothetical high-achieving and a low-achieving student that "she had taught in the past." Each teacher's TDB scores for the LS, ES, and pressure factors were computed by averaging her students' ratings. The students also filled out self-report questionnaires measuring CC, morale and satisfaction, and their emotional reactions to their teacher (including items about their satisfaction when a substitute teacher replaces their teacher, and their wish to continue with the same teacher next year).

The results demonstrated substantial influence of TDB on CC and overall student morale. The pattern of results differed for each of the three TDB clusters:

1. Perceptions of differential pressure were unrelated to any of the CC outcome variables. Thus, the fact that teachers were perceived as putting more pressure on high-achievers than the low-achievers was probably accepted by the students and evoked no criticism or negative reactions.
2. TDB in the instructional domain (LS), where teachers were generally perceived by their students (and by themselves) as providing more LS to low-achieving students, was weakly but positively related to climate outcomes. Students reacted in a mildly positive manner to teachers' efforts to provide more instructional support to low-achievers, and greater intensity of differentiality tended to be accepted rather than criticized by the investigated fifth and sixth grade students.
3. Strong and substantial negative relationships were found for teachers' differentiality in the affective domain (ES). Readers are reminded that virtually all teachers were perceived by their students as giving more emotional support to their high-expectancy students. In comparing the classrooms (i.e., comparing teachers varying in intensities of differential ES), a stronger differential in favor of high-achievers was associated to lower student morale and less satisfaction in the climate questionnaire; to more negative reactions to the teachers; to a stronger wish to not continue with the teacher next year; and to greater satisfaction with a substitute teacher. In short, the students seemed to be angrier at teachers perceived to favor the highs more intensely in their affective displays and more dissatisfied in their classrooms.

In a more recent study described earlier (Babad et al., 2003), relations between TDB and social-affective classroom outcomes were examined in an older age group of high school students (tenth and eleventh grade). In the published literature, expectancy effects and TDB were investigated almost exclusively in the younger context of the elementary school, where one home-room teacher spends most of the classroom time with the same students, and therefore carries considerable influence on the students. The high school context differs from the elementary school in several ways: First, students are exposed to a larger number of teachers in various disciplines. Second, high school adolescents are more critical than younger children and they have more friction with adult authority figures (parents and teachers). Third, achievement pressure in high school is more intense, especially for those intending to compete for acceptance into institutions of higher education. Therefore, high school students have stronger instructional needs and they are more dependent on teachers' time and assistance, and yet they also tend to be more rebellious and more critical of their teachers.

In the 2003 study, teachers in twenty-eight high school classrooms were videotaped in several instructional situations and brief instances of their NV behavior were rated by judges who were unfamiliar with the teachers. The intensity of teachers' differential treatment was assessed from ratings of each teacher's NV behavior in interactions with (unseen) high- and low-achievers. As mentioned earlier, all students in those classrooms also evaluated their teachers' differential behavior in a self-report questionnaire, and the two measures of TDB cross-validated each other.

The students in all twenty-eight classrooms in the 2003 study also filled out questionnaires in which they evaluated their teachers. Students' ratings of teachers (SRT) are very common in almost all colleges and universities, routinely administered at the end of every course. SRT measurement is less common in elementary and high schools. Unlike CC questionnaires (Chapter 5), which are more student-oriented and attempt to capture the classroom atmosphere, SRT (also called SET) questionnaires are more exclusively focused on the teachers, their traits, teaching style, interaction patterns with students, and course organization. What they have in common is that both SRT and CC questionnaires trace students' reactions to their teachers and reflect students' morale and satisfaction.

The findings (Babad et al., 2003) showed strong relationships between TDB and students' evaluations of the teachers. The teachers who demonstrated greater differentiality were evaluated more negatively and criticized more harshly by their students on almost every dimension measured. Similar negative relationships were found for teacher differentiality measured through judges' (low-inference) ratings of ten seconds of teachers' NV behavior and for students'-rated (high-inference) perceptions of TDB. Moreover, whereas in the elementary school classrooms of the previous studies only differentiality in teachers' affective behavior (ES) was associated with negative outcomes, in this high school study, differentiality in both the instructional domain (LS) and the affective domain (ES) was related to students' harsh evaluations of their teachers. Thus, for the older high school students, all forms of TDB were unacceptable and severely criticized.

CONCLUSION

TDB has been discussed in this chapter both as an expectancy-related phenomenon (potentially affecting particular low-expectancy and high-expectancy students) and as a general classroom phenomenon (affecting the morale and satisfaction of the entire student body). The evidence demonstrated the existence of the TDB phenomenon and the relative frequencies of various types of TDB in classrooms, and a theoretical model was proposed to explain the array of TDB effects. Students' keen sensitivity to perceive their teachers' differentiality was discussed next. The differences between students' perceptions and the teachers' own perceptions and interpretations of their differential behavior emphasized the volatile nature of the TDB issue. The dilemma between the necessity to treat students differently and the potential damage that inequitable treatment might cause to the social fabric of the classroom society forces teachers to maneuver and to seek an optimal path for dealing effectively with their classrooms.

With the decline in expectancy research in recent decades, the issue of TDB in the heterogeneous classroom was ignored and not brought saliently enough to the attention of teacher education students. Indeed only a few studies investigated the relationships between teachers' rates of TDB and students' evaluations and satisfaction. However, the findings are clear and strong, demonstrating the damage that can be caused to classrooms by teachers' excessive and more noticeable TDB.

The next chapter deals with the teacher's pet phenomenon—a unique expression of teachers' differential (actually preferential) relationships with a few loved students. Despite the fact that the pet phenomenon is commonly known to every past and present student, the empirical research on pets and on teachers who have pets has been quite limited. But here, too, empirical evidence has accumulated that demonstrates the potential damage that might be caused by teachers' deviation from equity in their CM.

8 The Teacher's Pet Phenomenon

The teacher's pet phenomenon is related to the previous chapter because it also deals with teachers' preferential treatment and their deviation from fairness and equity in classroom behavior. However, the teacher's pet phenomenon is not an expectancy-related concept. Rather, it is a phenomenon of a special emotional relationship (often a love relationship) between the teacher and a particular student (or two) in the classroom. Although the phenomenon is extremely well known, very little research that focused directly on teachers' pets has been published, and we don't even know its rate of occurrence in schools beyond two or three studies. This chapter is based on a series of studies conducted in Israel.

We all know about teachers' pets and remember their existence in the classroom. Some of us might remember (perhaps nostalgically) how we ourselves had been teacher's pets in the foregone past. As teachers, we might remember how we loved a particular student. Doris Day sang many years ago: "I want to be teacher's pet." But many students and most educators probably do not hold this phenomenon in a particularly positive light, and reactions toward teachers who have pets and hold special relationships with favorite students are probably quite negative.

The presumed importance of the teacher's pet phenomenon stems from the fact that it is a classroom phenomenon that touches the entire classroom society, not only the teachers and their particular favorites. The existence of this phenomenon might have an impact on CC, on students' morale and satisfaction, and most importantly, on students' reactions to their teacher. Teacher's status as an influential figure in students' eyes might be hindered by the existence of the teacher's pet phenomenon in the classroom. The special edge of this phenomenon derives from students' extreme sensitivity to the behavior of their teachers and their uncanny ability to perceive, absorb and diagnose hidden and concealed aspects of teacher behavior. In another meaning, students are also sensitive to their teachers in the sense of being vulnerable to teachers' influence.

TEACHERS EMOTIONAL ATTITUDES TOWARD PARTICULAR STUDENTS

Silberman (1969, 1971) came close to defining and measuring the teacher's pet phenomenon, although he did not use this term in his writing. Silberman defined four emotional attitudes that teachers hold for particular students in their classrooms: attachment; concern; indifference; and rejection. Silberman and several subsequent researchers examined teachers' behaviors toward particular students who were the objects of these four attitudes.

Because this chapter focuses on the teacher's pet phenomenon, I discuss here only the attitude of attachment. The attitude of concern is usually directed at children with special needs and disabilities and perhaps also at underprivileged students. The attitudes of indifference and rejection are similar in some aspects to the concepts of neglected students and rejected students in the two-dimensional model of sociometric measurement, discussed in Chapter 4 (Coie et al. 1982). However, the neglect and rejection in Silberman's model stem from the teacher and not from the classroom peers as discussed in the sociometric literature.

In the research on teachers' emotional attitudes (by Silbernman, 1969, 1971; Brophy & Everston, 1981; and Good & Brophy, 1972, 1974), teachers were asked to nominate students who were the objects of these four attitudes, and observational researchers examined the behavior of these students and of the teachers interacting with them. Silberman defined attachment as an affectionate relation to students that is derived from the pleasure they bring to the teacher's work. In Silberman's questionnaire, teachers were asked to "name those students you would like to keep for another year for the sheer joy of it." Given this emotional bond expressed by the teachers, it is quite likely that numerous students nominated as attachment students might have been considered teachers' pets. However, the attachment group could also have included academically excellent students who are not necessarily teachers' pets in terms of the special emotional relationship between teacher and student.

In the various studies, students who were nominated as attachment students were found (in teachers' descriptions and by some independent measures) to be most positive, almost ideal students: They showed good behavior and high conformity, compliance to school norms, participation, and achievement orientation which were most rewarding for their teachers. However, observations of teacher behavior toward attachment students yielded very weak findings of distinctive and differential behavior. In comparison, more distinctive behaviors were identified in teachers' interactions with concern and rejection students. Although the teachers themselves nominated the attachment students, they were not found to treat them differently than other students!

Perhaps teachers do not treat their attachment students in any special way, but another explanation is more plausible, and it might already have occurred to readers who went through the previous chapter on TDB: Having named those particular students to the researchers as objects of their special attachment, and given the ideological concern about fairness and equity, the teachers would probably have monitored their behavior quite carefully in front of the observers in their classroom. They would be cautious to treat all students equally so as not to demonstrate any preferential behavior. It would have made more sense if attachment students had not been nominated by the teachers if those teachers' behavior towards the nominated students was about to be observed. In light of the discussion in the previous chapter, it might be added that demonstrating differential behavior toward concern and rejection students is more permissible. Concern students are the legitimate recipients of extra teacher investment and attention, and rejection students are probably perceived as children who cause their own trouble in the classroom by their disruptive and malicious behavior.

WHAT DO TEACHERS AND STUDENTS THINK ABOUT THE TEACHER'S PET PHENOMENON?

Because no body of research on the teacher's pet phenomenon was available, it seemed logical that the first step should be to conduct an attributional study, intended to investigate students' and teachers' hypothetical notions about the pet phenomenon. Groups of students in varied grade levels in elementary and high school, teacher education students, and experienced teachers participated in this initial investigation (Tal, 1987; Tal & Babad, 1989).

The recognition factor of the pet phenomenon was extremely high, and over 90% of the respondents recognized the phenomenon and could describe the special emotional relationship between teacher and pet and the mutual rewards they provide for each other. In respondents' open-ended accounts, the phenomenon was characterized mostly in negative terms, emphasizing teachers' preferential treatment of their pets. When positive aspects were mentioned, they referred mostly to the positive personality traits and social characteristics of students who become teacher pets. In comparing the groups of respondents, the reactions of the elementary and high school students were more negative than those of the experienced teachers, whereas the attitudes of students in teacher education (still being students, but soon to be teachers) fell between these extremes. Experienced teachers related to the pet phenomenon in a somewhat lenient and tolerant manner, stressing more often the uniquely positive characteristics of teacher pets (worthy of teacher love . . . so to speak). The teachers believed more strongly than students that they can conceal from their students their special attachment to their pets. In fact, whereas the elementary and high school students were happy about our investigation and welcomed it, many teachers in the sample were apprehensive about our prying into this topic.

In another part of this study, three hypothetical student types were presented—Teacher's Pet, Academically Best Student and Student Leader—and respondents rated the presumed social distance between each type and (a) the teacher, and (b) the other students. The findings showed high consensus among all groups of respondents: Academically best students were considered to be close to both the teacher and the other students; leaders were thought as close to the students but remote from the teacher; and teachers' pets were described as being very close to the teachers but remote from the other students. These perceptions confirmed the existence of an implicit, consensual attributional typology in which the teacher's pet is a distinct type. This conclusion was important for subsequent decisions about how to measure this phenomenon and how to identify teachers' pets in the classroom. However, readers should bear in mind that when student types are considered hypothetically, they can be distinguished from each other quite sharply, but in the actual reality of the classroom the types are often less distinguishable from each other. Some salient students in their classrooms might be both teacher's pet and leader, or both teacher's pet and academically best student, and some might be classified as fitting all three labels.

MEASUREMENT OF THE PET PHENOMENON: IDENTIFYING TEACHERS' PETS

In light of the lessons from the measurement of expectancy-related TDB (Chapter 7) and those learned from the measurement of teachers' emotional attitudes , it was clear that seeking teachers' own nominations of their pets would not be a good idea, and pet nominations—if received at all and not denied by the teachers—would not be too credible. A methodology of identifying teachers' pets by behavioral observations in classrooms was also rejected, (a) because of the great expense and effort required to conduct observations in many classrooms; and (b) because teachers might exhibit their best and most equitable behavior when observers (or a camera) are present in the classroom. In deliberating about the best measurement method, it was clear that it must focus on the social reality of the classroom as perceived and experienced by the students themselves.

Tal and Babad (1990) chose a cognitive sociometric method to identify teachers' pets. To remind readers, in the classic affective sociometry, students nominate their best liked and most disliked peers in the classroom, whereas in cognitive sociometry, students serve as judges and report cognitively who are the children who occupy particular roles in the classroom (see Chapter 4). In cognitive sociometry, students are not asked at all about their own feelings and about their own friends and non-friends. This type of measurement is particularly appropriate for measurement of psychological typologies.

A particular type is defined by the consensus of ratings of the classroom peers, when all or most students agree about the identity of the student characterized as occupying that particular role. The idea was that if a particular student would be named by all or almost all peers in the classroom as being leader, academic best, or teacher's pet, it stands to reason that s/he represents that particular type in the classroom life. For teacher's pets, the consensus subsequently designated the teacher as having or not having a pet in her classroom.

In a questionnaire administered to all students in eighty fifth and sixth grade classrooms in Israel, students were asked to nominate two classmates for each type (including naming themselves if appropriate) holding particular roles in the classroom: Academically best students; leaders of the boys or the girls; quiet students, and several other types. Embedded in that list (and in order to dull the edge of asking about teachers' pets) were nominations of two students Best Liked by the home-room teacher, and later a nomination of the student Most Loved by the teacher.

Defining a type by consensus of sociometric peer nominations is a bit tricky statistically, because arbitrary decisions must be taken. If all classmates named X as leader, labeling X as the classroom leader would be quite simple and straight-forward. But what if 90% of the classmates nominated X? Or what if 83% nominated X? Or perhaps 70% nomintated X? The decision where to put the cutoff point is arbitrary, and different decisions might yield different characterizations of the classroom. To increase the reliability of the nomination of teachers' pets, two questions were included, asking about Best Liked and Most Loved, so that a double-consensus would be required.

The designation of pet classrooms was further complicated by the possible existence of two distinct pet situations. One is the commonly held hypothetical image of one salient student who is the teacher's exclusive pet. The other potential situation includes several pets; two or three students who are especially loved and preferred by the teacher. The two situations would yield different patterns of nominations in the sociometric questionnaire, because nominations must be divided among two or three pets in a multiple-pet classroom. Because two names of Best Liked students are sought in the questionnaire, the potential for distributing the choices among two or three pets is created, and 200% of choices are provided. Thus, three students can each receive nominations of 66.6% of their classmates as best liked by the teacher when two students are nominated.

Tal and Babad (1990) characterized each classroom (actually each teacher) in one of the following three categories:

1. Exclusive pet classroom (characterized by extremely high consensus nominations of one student);
2. Non-exclusive pet classroom (high consensus in identifying one, or two, or three students as teacher's pets);
3. No pet classrooms (where no consensus was found in identifying pets, with nominations distributed among many students).

The first two categories were both considered as characterizing pet classrooms, but the non-exclusive category was considered a less extreme case of the pet phenomenon.

In Tal and Babad's 1990 study, only 20% of the classrooms were designated as no-pet classrooms, and 80% were pet classrooms (26% exclusive
pet classrooms and 54% non-exclusive pet classrooms). In a subsequent
sample of another eighty fifth- and sixth-grade classrooms (Babad, 1995)
only half of the classrooms were designated as pet classrooms (13% exclusive and 36% non-exclusive). Given that the consensus criteria that had been
employed were rather strict, it is clear that the extent of the pet phenomenon in elementary school is very substantial (see Babad, 1998). Between
half and three-quarters of the teachers are perceived by their students as
having a special emotional relationship and as demonstrating detectable
preference for particular students who are consensually identified by their
classmates. No data and no empirical knowledge are available about the
pet situation in high school classrooms. It stands to reason that the issue
of love and a special relationship between teacher and student can be more
complex and multi-faceted in older age groups, much as the reactions of
adolescent students to their teachers might be more intense compared to
those of elementary school students.

CAN TEACHERS IDENTIFY THE STUDENT-NOMINATED PETS?

Having pets is a delicate issue for teachers because of the ethical concerns
regarding potential violation of fairness and equity norms. In the initial
field study (Tal & Babad, 1989) teachers were aware of the pet phenomenon as a hypothetical phenomenon no less than school students and teacher
education students. They were more confident than the other groups of
respondents that teachers can conceal from their students their special
attachment to their pets. In the 1990 study, pets were identified by consensus of students' nominations. Subsequently, we asked the teachers to
guess who were consensually nominated by their students as teacher's pets.
Teachers' guesswork was found to be very poor. Some teachers declined to
answer the question, arguing that there could not be any consensus among
their students about a particular pet. Others often named a student who
was not consensually viewed as a pet by their students. Only 19% of the
teachers named the pets correctly. In contrast, half of the teachers were
accurate in guessing the consensually nominated classroom leader, and
68% correctly identified the names of students selected by consensus as
the academically best students in their classrooms. It is well known in the
sociometric literature that teachers are often unaware of their students'
sociometric status. However, the low rate of guessing the identities of the
pets fell far below the rates usually reported for teachers' guesses of sociometric status and popularity.

Readers may have their own ideas about possible interpretation of this
finding. Perhaps the teachers were defensive and were throwing a smoke
screen to divert attention away from their real pets; perhaps teachers are

really not aware of their students' perceptions; and perhaps the teachers were right, and the student consensus was based on wrong and misguided perceptions. In any event, given the high levels of consensus in students' nominations, we must treat the pet data as having at least some validity

CHARACTERISTICS OF TEACHERS' PETS

What are the characteristics of students likely to become teachers' pets? The studies included attributions made by students and teachers about teacher pets they had known, and actual measurement of some characteristics of the children nominated by their peers as teachers' pets in their classrooms. The emerging picture of the teacher's pet in the elementary school was quite clear and coherent. Teachers' pets are very positive, likable and attractive children. They tend to be girls more frequently than boys, perhaps because at this age, girls are less rebellious and more likely than boys to accommodate themselves to school norms. Pets are almost always students of high academic standing, although not necessarily the most excellent students in their classrooms. It seems that their intellectual ability is complemented by charm, beauty and social skills which include good manners, compliance and flattery (although the teacher's pet is clearly distinguishable from the classroom flatterer who obviously is not the teacher's pet). Research on TDB in the previous chapter showed that teachers often demonstrate excessively positive behavior toward low-expectancy and underprivileged students. However, the empirical evidence on nominated pets indicated that low-expectancy and underprivileged students were not consensually held by their classmates to be teachers' pets.

Thus, the pets loved by the teachers seem to be truly lovable and attractive, and in some way it is easy to understand teachers' affections towards them. Following Silberman's thoughts that these students reward the teachers and give them satisfaction in their hard work, perhaps teachers cannot be faulted for their positive feelings. However, the important question concerns potential implications of these relationships on the classrooms, how the other students are affected and how classroom life and atmosphere might be influenced by the pet phenomenon.

CLASSROOM BEHAVIOR OF TEACHERS WHO HAVE PETS

The first question that comes to mind is whether teacher's pets receive preferential treatment from their teachers. According to the familiar myth and the commonly held beliefs about the teacher's pet phenomenon, the answer must be that they do. But the reality of classroom life and of teachers' behavior is more complex, and blatant favoritism is probably quite rare. The research on the pet phenomenon did not include behavioral observations of teachers' behavior toward their pets. In light of the research on Silberman's attachment students that did not uncover any differential treatment, I would suppose that teachers would not demonstrate intense preferential behavior to their pets, nor would they inflate their grades (which the pets don't really need, as they tend to be excellent students anyway). On the contrary, following the Biblical dictum that "Those who are revered, are treated more harshly," teachers might even demonstrate more strictness and demand toward their pets.

I believe that the special treatment of loved pets would be expressed in rare events that would receive a negligible weight in statistical analysis of behavioral observations, or manifested in fine and subtle nuances of teachers' NV behavior. Such nuances are hard to measure, but classroom students are experts in perceiving and diagnosing such clues in their teachers' behavior. Thus, I think that preferential treatment of teachers' pets probably exists, but it cannot readily be measured.

A question that is more amenable to empirical investigation is whether teachers who have pets differ from teachers who do not have pets in their behavior toward other students in the classroom, especially in terms of their TDB toward low- versus high-achieving students. It was possible to examine this question in Babad's (1995) study because measures of both TDB (by students' reports) and teacher's pet status (by students' sociometric nominations) were available for each teacher. For statistical expediency, the previous dichotomous (pet/no pet) or trichotomous (exclusive pet/nonexclusive pet/no pet) categorization of teachers was abandoned. Instead, a continuous measure of the intensity of the pet phenomenon was computed for each teacher. Quite simply, it consisted of the percentage of agreement among the students in each classroom in naming the first, most salient student best liked by the teacher. Thus, using the eighty teachers as a sample, it became possible to compute a simple correlation between the perceived intensity of their overall TDB toward high- versus low-achievers and the intensity of their tendency to have identifiable pets in their classrooms.

The results showed a clear and substantial relationship between the intensity of the pet phenomenon and TDB: The more the classroom students agreed about the identity of the liked/loved student, the more the teacher was perceived in the TDB questionnaire as demonstrating differential behavior toward high- versus low-achievers in the classroom. This relationship was particularly strong for teachers' differential emotional support, where high-expectancy students were reported as receiving proportionally higher rates of teacher's warmth and positive affect.

These findings are quite important to our understanding of the social psychology of the classroom, and I would like to take a moment to explain its credibility from a methodological standpoint. When the students filled out the questionnaires, they were never asked explicitly about teacher's pets nor were they asked directly about TDB. Both phenomena were derived statistically from the accumulation of all students' responses. Moreover, a different method of questioning was used to measure each phenomenon: Students were asked to name one or two best liked / most loved students for identifying pets; and they rated teacher's presumed behaviors toward a hypothetical high- and a low-achieving student "she had taught in the past" for measurement of TDB. The more differently students in a given classroom had rated their teacher's behavior toward the hypothetical high-achieving and the low-achieving students, the more they also tended to name the same real student as best liked by their teacher. Had the students been asked explicitly about the teacher's pet and about her differential behavior, the suspicion would have lingered on that the relationship between these phenomena might have reflected their implicit theory rather than describing the classroom reality.

In terms of the psychology of the teacher, the relationship between the pet phenomenon and TDB toward high/low achievers illuminates a particular type of teacher who freely expresses intense personal feelings toward particular students with little or no concern about fairness and equity in her/his classroom conduct. The findings indicate that this positive and negative differentiality is noticed and perceived by students. Our culture tries to educate parents and teachers to control the expression of their emotions and to refrain from showing preferential affective behavior toward particular children or students. In the case of these particular teachers–who constitute a very substantial proportion of elementary school teachers—the cultural dictum is not followed, and they do manifest differential and preferential behavior. With regard to their conduct towards their pets, perhaps those teachers believe that they can hide their preference from their students. The findings indicate that the students are well aware of the preferential behavior, and they are also acutely aware of these teachers' differential expression of affect toward low- and high-achievers in the classroom. In the same manner, TV anchormen and interviewers on the public media are required to show fair and equitable behavior in broadcasting. A series of studies proved high rates of deviation from equity in the preferential nonverbal behavior of TV interviewers (Babad, 1999, 2005a).

NEGATIVE CONSEQUENCES OF THE TEACHER'S PET PHENOMENON IN THE CLASSROOM

We already know (Chapter 7) that excessive TDB is related to a more negative CC, to less student satisfaction and to angry student reactions to their teachers. In other words, the previous findings showed that the violation of the cultural norm of equity in TDB carries a measurable psychological price in the classroom. It was now time to examine whether the occurrence and the intensity of the teachers' pet phenomenon in the classroom carries a similar psychological price.

Tal (1987) and Tal and Babad (1990) compared CC, students' satisfaction and their emotional reactions to their teachers in no pet classrooms, non-exclusive pet classrooms, and exclusive pet classrooms. They found a clear pattern of significant results that confirmed their hypothesis: Classrooms with no pets showed the most positive climate and positive reactions to their teachers; exclusive pet classrooms showed the most negative climate and negative reactions to their teachers; and the non-exclusive pet classrooms (with two to three pets of lower sociometric intensity) fell between these extremes, with reactions more similar to those of the students in the exclusive pet classrooms. Thus, in that sample of eighty fifth- and sixth-grade classrooms, the occurrence and the intensity of the teacher's pet phenomenon in the classrooms carried a psychological price similar to the negative consequences of TDB.

These findings were not confirmed in the subsequent study (Babad, 1995), conducted on a new sample of eighty fifth- and sixth-grade classrooms. Here the three types of pet classrooms did not significantly differ from each other in CC and the other outcome variables, nor did the intensity of the pet phenomenon (as a continuous variable) correlate significantly with the outcome variables. These surprising findings necessitated more thinking and deeper probing of additional factors that might mediate the effects of the pet phenomenon on elementary school classrooms. A study on the seating locations of various student types in the space of the classroom (Babad & Ezer, 1993) provided a new insight that contributed to an improved conceptualization of the teacher's pet phenomenon. Therefore, the next section is a detour into the area of environmental psychology, probing the systematic seating locations of defined types of students in the classroom.

DETOUR INTO ENVIRONMENTAL PSYCHOLOGY: CLASSROOM SEATING LOCATIONS OF TEACHERS' PETS, LEADERS, AND ACADEMICALLY BEST STUDENTS

Research on seating arrangements has long been recognized as a subdomain in educational research, integrating ideas from environmental psychology and social psychology (see Weinstein, 1979). One direction in seating research has been focused on the symbolic meaning and potential academic and social implications of different ways of arranging the classroom space and of seating the students in it. One example was the comparison between the conventional rows and columns arrangement and an arrangement of separate groups seated around tables (Wheldall & Lam, 1987). Another direction of seating research examined the particular seating locations of defined students or student types, in an attempt to decipher the hidden meanings of particular seating locations.

Researchers in this field recognized that the determination of a seating location is a complex process: Students select their own seating locations according to various considerations and preferences; but elementary and high school teachers often intervene and either pre-determine or change students' seating. The consensus in the literature is that seating arrangements are meaningful and reflect underlying social phenomena in both self-determined and/or teacher-determined variations.

One interesting example of seating location research will be briefly described before I return to teachers' pets. In the conventional arrangement of rows and columns, one area is known as the activity zone. It is located in the center front of the classroom, close (but not too close) to the teacher. Research shows that the activity zone is characterized by more positive student attitudes, better quality of teacher–student interaction, and higher student achievements (see Moore & Glynn, 1984, Sommer, 1967). An environmental explanation of the superior educational products of students seated in the activity zone emphasizes ease of communication, optimal distance, good quality of eye contact and reduced potential for disruption. A self-selection explanation argues that particular types of students choose this location to satisfy their learning needs—plus the possibility of teachers assigning particular students to the activity zone. Both explanations have merit, and probably both contribute to the educational advantages of the activity zone (see Weinstein, 1979; Koneya, 1976; Stires, 1980).

In Tal and Babad's (1990) study of the teacher's pet phenomenon, classroom maps detailing the seating locations of every student in each classroom were collected. Babad and Ezer (1993) examined the seating locations of the various sociometrically-defined student types in the seventy classrooms arranged in conventional rows and columns. The particular students characterized as representing each type were selected on the basis of the consensus in their peers' nominations.

Babad and Ezer (1993) found that classroom leaders tended to sit in the back of the classroom more often, away from the teacher. Flatterers (clearly not teacher's pets) sat most frequently in the front row, very close to the teacher. Among the type of academically best students the pattern was divided—those nominated by the highest consensus showed a tendency to sit in the back of the classroom, whereas those nominated by a weaker (but still high) consensus tended to sit closer to their teachers. We thought that the former subgroup might consist of the more independent thinkers, excellent students who do not need the teacher so much. The latter subgroup probably consisted of more conforming and conventional best students who are well-connected to the teachers, and therefore sat closer to them. As to teacher's pets, in the initial analysis we failed to discover a systematic tendency for a particular seating location.

Scrutiny of the sociometric nominations illuminated a distinction between (a) students receiving consensual nominations as one type only (pure types) and (b) students who received consensual nominations as representing two types (pet and academic best, or pet and leader, or academic best and leader) or even as representing all three types (mixed types). Because nomination for each role definition was independent of the nomination for the other roles, a particular student could be consensually perceived as being leader and academic best and teacher's pet. In fact, more than half of the students nominated for the three types were actually characterized as mixed types with concurrent two or even three designations.

The finding most relevant to the present chapter concerned the distinction between pure and mixed teacher pets. The combination of pet and leader meant that the student most liked/loved by the teacher was also most appreciated by her/his classroom mates. The combination of pet and academic best meant that teacher's special love was given to a student recognized by classmates for her/his superior academic status. In contrast, the pure pet designation meant that the teacher's special love, appreciation and preference were given to a student who was not particularly appreciated or liked by her/his peers. The conceptual implication of this distinction between pure and mixed pets is that teacher's love and special attachment to her pet may not be the only important aspect of the pet phenomenon. Different pet situations with different implications might be created when the attitudes of the other students in the classroom toward that student are considered as well. In the mixed-pet situation—especially in the pet-leader designation—we find consonance between teacher's and students' emotional attitude toward the pet. In contrast, the attitudes of the teacher and the students are dissonant with each other in the pure pet situation because the students do not particularly like or appreciate that student. Perhaps the mental picture of the teacher's pet phenomenon held by most people involves the pure pet situation, where students consider teachers' special attachment and preferential attitude toward their pets as unwarranted, unjustified and unfair.

With this conceptual distinction in mind, we can return to the analysis of the seating locations of teachers' pets in the classroom space. Babad and Ezer (1993) found indeed that pure pets and mixed pets demonstrated different seating location patterns: Pure pets tended to sit more often in the front of the classroom, closer to the teacher; whereas mixed pets were found to be seated more often in the back of the classroom. Thus, pets who were liked only by the teachers without enjoying high sociometric status among their peers sat indeed in the front locations initially predicted for teachers' pets. On the other hand, pets that enjoyed high status amongst their peers were found seated in the location characterizing other leaders (i.e., the back of the classroom). It might be speculated that their classroom leadership position was more important psychologically to pets-leaders than their position vis-à-vis their teachers.

A REVISED CONCEPTION OF THE NEGATIVE CONSEQUENCES OF THE PET PHENOMENON IN THE CLASSROOM

Applying this pure-mixed pet distinction to the eighty classroom of Babad's (1995) sample, the classrooms were re-classified into three new groups, crossing students' sociometric status as pets (that is, best liked and most loved by the teacher) with consensually rated popularity and/or leadership status among their peers. The groups were:

1. *No pet classrooms* (26% of the classrooms).
2. *Popular pet classrooms* (where the same students were consensually nominated as teachers' pets and also held by their peers as most popular and/or leaders; 46% of the classrooms).
3. *Unpopular pet classrooms* (where the consensual teachers' pets were not nominated highly for popularity and/or leadership among their peers; 29% of the classrooms).

These three re-formulated pet groups were next compared to each other on the student-rated outcome variables: CC, students' morale and satisfaction, and emotional reactions to their teachers. The new hypothesis was that teacher's attachment to a popular pet should not anger the other students, because the students share the teacher's feelings, appreciate the teacher's pet, and hold her/him in special status. The results confirmed this hypothesis: More negative climate, lower morale and student satisfaction, more negative affective reactions to the teacher, more happiness about substitute teachers, and a stronger wish to not continue with the same teacher next year were found only in the unpopular pet classrooms. In contrast, all of these educational outcomes were rated higher and more positively in both the no pet classrooms and the popular pet classrooms, with no differences between the latter two groups.

Thus, the negative image of the teacher's pet phenomenon seems to be justified by the empirical data, and the existence of the pet phenomenon in classrooms (that is, teachers showing special love and attachment to selected pets) may indeed carry negative consequences for the psychological well-being of the entire classroom society. However, the negative connotation of the teacher's pet phenomenon and the negative social consequences for the entire classroom are limited in a justifiable manner only to classrooms where the students do not share in the teacher's love and appreciation for her/his pet. When the pet is appreciated by both the students and the teacher, no harm is caused to the classroom society.

Part IV

Classroom Management

9 Classroom Management
Historical Trends and Contemporary Approach

DEFINITIONS OF CLASSROOM MANAGEMENT

CM is the teacher's central mode of conduct and set of activities in the classroom. It integrates teacher's roles and professional objectives as instructor, educator, and manager. Reporting in the journal "Educational Leadership" on a meta-analysis of various studies, Marzano and Marzano concluded that CM is the single factor with the largest impact on student achievement, because effective CM sets the stage for successful student learning. In their analysis, Marzano and Marzano (2003) concluded that teacher–students relationships constituted the keystone to all other aspects of CM, and specifically, that effective teacher–students relationships consisted of exhibiting appropriate levels of dominance, exhibiting appropriate levels of cooperation, and being aware of high needs students.

Carolyn Everston and Carol Weinstein(2006a), long-time researchers of CM, published an influential (1,346-page) handbook on various aspects of CM. In the opening chapter (Everston & Weinstein, 2006b) they defined CM as the action teachers take to create an environment that supports and facilitates both academic and social-emotional student learning. CM is distinguished from other aspects of the teacher's work, such as didactics and academic instruction or measurement and evaluation. It includes the various organizational aspects of the classroom that influence students and eventually lead to positive academic, social and emotional outcomes.

Jere Brophy (1999, 2006) one of the leaders of the CM field, holds the same view, and emphasizes successful instruction as the central product of effective CM. The overall objective is to create the most effective environment with minimal restrictions, an environment that would achieve its goals with no (or minimal) side effects in a cost/benefit analysis. Therefore, teachers' various classroom interventions, students' socialization, and meaningful teacher-students relationships are all included as important components of CM.

This current conception of CM is widely held today. Some authors emphasize students' participation and partnership in maintaining classroom environment (e.g., Elias & Schwab, 2006; Freiberg & Lapointe,

2006), and most writers stress teachers' role in creating and maintaining an effective classroom environment.

Discipline problems and student misbehavior are the major obstacles to effective CM and hinder teachers' work. Havoc in the classroom and management problems constitute the major causes for teacher burnout (Friedman, 2000, 2006), perhaps even preventing prospective candidates from becoming teachers. Contemporary schools are wrought with problems of violence, misbehavior and poor achievements, and teachers' tasks in CM are formidable.

HISTORICAL TRENDS IN CONCEPTUALIZATION AND INVESTIGATION OF CLASSROOM MANAGEMENT

Conceptions of CM have been known for over a century. William Bagley published a book entitled *Classroom Management* in 1907, and much of the impressive common sense in the Bagley (1907) book in terms of strategies and tactics of handling the classroom is still quite modern today. Early writings were based on the intuitive notions of master teachers that had evolved through their accumulated experience as classroom teachers, and organized empirical research came much later. Actual research on CM was published in a substantial measure since the middle of the 20th century.

The major concerns have always been how to deal with the various complexities of the classroom environment, how to control students and minimize disruption and misbehavior, and how to lead students to the best academic achievements and psycho-social development. Beliefs about CM probably had always reflected the current educational thinking of each period. However, the early writings seem to have been more practical than ideological, and conceptions of CM did not reflect an overriding ideology or philosophy of education. Over time, the trend had changed and the literature dealing with CM became more and more ideological—it became a tool of transferring the classroom into an entity reflecting specific and exclusive ideological images, an ideological perspective into which teachers should be socialized. Using a contemporary euphemism, Brophy (1988) and Jones (2006) argued for emphasizing "a simple integrated approach to CM in teacher training" rather than providing brief coverage of different approaches. This probably stems from the bitter controversy over the behavioral approach to CM, and the rejection of behavioristic methods as tools in the hands of the classroom teacher by many writers.

Three types of factors contributed to change the conceptualization of CM over the years:

1. Changing educational ideologies.
2. New theoretical and empirical knowledge on methods for affecting behavioral change.

3. Historically changing realities of the public school in terms of educational policies (e.g., inclusion of special education students in regular classrooms, school desegregation, etc.) and societal trends of change (e.g., influx of immigrant populations, new realities of school violence, drug abuse and sexual behavior among adolescents, etc.).

In the 1960s and 1970s, the ideology of the open school and the open classroom gained momentum and became quite popular. The ideological purpose was to break the authoritarian framework of the conventional classroom and to create a democratic school. In this new school students would share in decision-making and in school governance, be personally accountable for their own curriculum and program of study, and learn to be democratic through their actual participative experience in a democratic school.

This view was compatible with the democratic, equalitarian and participative image of management offered by the human relations movement, which mushroomed and gained tremendous popularity (especially in the USA) during the 1950s and 1960s. In part as a reaction to the rise of racism and fascism during World War II, the movement (under the leadership of Kurt Lewin, Kenneth Benne, Ronald Lippitt and Lleland Bradford) offered a new image of management based on shared responsibility and collaborative leadership. Many thousands of participants from a variety of fields and occupations took part in human relations training workshops. These labs offered sets of experiential group activities to actually train managers how to apply this new cultural image in their workplaces.

This ideology naturally influenced the field of education, and the conception of the open classroom and the open school were reflections of this perspective. A famous book for teachers by Richard and Patricia Schmuck (Schmuck & Schmuck, 1975), entitled *Group Processes in the Classroom* presented this conception to teachers and offered a variety of exercises and classroom activities for training how to actually realize these ideas in the classroom. The authors discussed the notions of shared leadership and flexible leadership, fostered the notion of the collaborative teacher, and suggested experiential activities on classroom norms and expectations, social interaction, peer relationships and teacher-student relationships, teacher behavior, and school organization. This was the forerunner of the contemporary conceptualization of CM.

Concurrent with these developments but in a diametrically opposite direction, the 1960s and 1970s were also characterized by rapid developments in the scientific research and application of behaviorism. The behavioral approach to learning had developed rapidly in the first half of the 20th century. Concepts such as reinforcement (including positive reinforcement, negative reinforcement, partial reinforcement, secondary reinforcement), extinction, drive, stimulus control and the law of association and law of effect (i.e., classical conditioning and operant conditioning) became very well known and occupied necessary chapters in every introductory psychology textbook.

In the late 1950s, 1960s and 1970s, great advances were made in behavior therapy, where these behavioral concepts were applied successfully to the treatment of a great variety of emotional, mental and behavioral problems. Behavior therapies posed a great challenge to the dominant psychodynamic psychotherapies—they offered more expedient, less time consuming, simpler, cheaper, and potentially widely applied remedies. That included help to populations that were not amenable to psychodynamic treatment before, such as young children and the mentally retarded and psychotic populations.

The behavioristic ideas and the behavioral approach to treatment were quite elementary and simple:

1. Every problem and every symptom had to be defined in operationally measurable behavioral terms.
2. A relevant reinforcement and contingency program was designed and carried out to reduce the occurrence of the symptomatic behavior.
3. The changed behavior was put under appropriate environmental control. Applications were developed during those years in a variety of directions: Treatment of various phobias and anxieties (including test anxiety); problems in sexual functioning; aggressive and anti-social behavior; marital and parental problems; and treatment of exceptional and problem children, including mentally retarded and emotionally disturbed children.

Ample evidence has accumulated attesting to the wide-range success of the behavioral approach. But these developments were accompanied by a bitter controversy that has not subsided over the years, with intense mutual contempt and prejudices of proponents and opponents of behaviorism against each other.

Together with the emphasis on individual treatment—that has been and still remains the strongest type of behavioral intervention—group and organizational applications were also developed, aiming to increase managerial effectiveness through collective stimulus control and the systematic application of reinforcements. The group approaches started with token economies to regulate daily life in mental institutions. Later they were widened to other types of institutions, and were eventually implemented in open organizational frameworks such as classrooms as well. The central behavioral influences in education took two directions: One focused on the organization of teaching to improve student learning (learning by objectives, pacing of student progress, cueing, etc.); the other was the use of behavioral methods in CM to help teachers control the potential havoc in the classroom through stimulus control, reinforcement and punishment.

Thus, within the same span of years, two diametrically contrasted visions of teachers and of classrooms were competing with each other, two potential panaceas to solve major educational problems. Each approach had its ardent supporters, rationale and training methods, and accumulated evidence proving its effectiveness. So, side by side with the different editions of the Schmuck and Schmuck (1975) book *Group Processes in the Classroom,* one could purchase and put into practice O'Leary and O'Leary's (1972) book: *Classroom Management: The Successful Use of Behavior Modification.* As mentioned, the open classroom movement was, first and above all, an ideological movement. The behavioral approach grew out of the accumulation of methodological and practical tactics for overcoming behavioral problems, but it also became an ideological approach. Behaviorists believed that a potential remedy was finally found for teachers' seemingly insoluble professional difficulties in maintaining classroom control, that teachers could be provided with simple and practical techniques for dealing effectively with misbehavior and disciplinary problems in the school.

These two visions, of the open classroom and of behavioral control, peaked sometime in the 1970s and early 1980s, and then lost some of their acute appeal. Today one can find rather few democratic schools and fully open classrooms, much as collective token economy and behavioral control classrooms are quite rare as well. But they did not disappear, and their basic notions strongly affected the developing field of CM. The open school lost its attractiveness because it is very difficult to fulfill its objectives; because of poor scholastic attainments; because it seemed to be more effective with advanced and exclusive populations and less practical for weak and more problematic populations; because discipline problems were intensified in the open schools; and because it put intense pressures on teachers and school administrators. But most of its basic ideas permeated, and they can be identified today as central components in the current conceptualization of CM.

Today, the favored form of schooling is to maintain the conventional structure of the classroom, and fully democratic schools and democratic classrooms are quite rare. Readers are reminded (Chapter 3) how Baumrind (1971) replaced the term democratic leadership in the classic Lewin's et al. (1939) study of the three styles of leadership by authoritative leadership— because democratic leadership is not really democratic. Following the same thinking, the classroom is not considered the most appropriate setting for a real democracy. Authoritative leadership with its collaborative aspects represents today the desirable image of effective CM. Authoritarian leadership is more closely identified with behavioral extrinsic control, and represents an undesirable image of CM. The contemporary literature stresses teacher's role in facilitating students' self-control, self-regulation and self-efficacy through the creation and maintenance of a caring and supportive environment and emotional relationships with the students.

Even in its peak years, behaviorism was controversial and heavily criticized. The central arguments against the behavioral approach focused on the mechanistic nature and robot-like quality of the elicited behaviors; on extrinsic teacher control that does not lead to students' self-control; and on the absence of caring, support and softer emotional tones in the rather technical language of behavioral analysis. The leading figures of the contemporary CM movement oppose behaviorism—Brophy (1999, 2006) wrote against behaviorism; Everston and Weinstein (2006a) included a necessary behavioristic chapter in their recent handbook, but the book as a whole pays little attention to behavioral analysis; Freiberg wrote a book entitled *Beyond Behaviorism* (1999); and Landrum and Kauffman (2006), the authors of the behavioristic chapter in the Everston and Weinstein handbook, complained that most teachers learn about the behavioral approach in a negative connotation and not as a viable alternative for effective CM.

But the influence of the behavioral approach on the current conception of CM is quite strong. The controversy and criticism are really focused on the old mechanistic behavioral models of the 1960s and 1970s, and the behaviorism of the 21st century is quite different, having undergone substantial paradigm changes. Today, the more common and acceptable behavioral treatments are cognitive-behavioral. Current behaviorism is less mechanistic, and thoughts and cognitions are considered to be behaviors. Contemporary behavioral researchers emphasize social learning and modeling, and value behavioral techniques that foster self-control, self-regulation, autonomy and self-efficacy. Thus, even if the salient CM researchers criticize the behaviorism of the 1970s, they actually follow many of the ideas of the more enlightened, contemporary behavioral analysis.

It is true, however, that authoritarian, teacher-centered notions of control via punishment and reinforcement and the exclusive use of behavioral control methods are not acceptable. It is also true that whole classroom behavioral interventions such as token economy are no longer used in regular classrooms. On the other hand, behavioral methods are very widely used in dealing with individual students of special disabilities and students who pose severe behavioral and academic problems. Moreover, the behavioral approach cannot be overlooked in consideration of methods for dealing with disciplinary problems in the classroom (see Chapter 10).

PARADIGM SHIFT IN CLASSROOM MANAGEMENT

Freiberg (1999, 2006; Rogers & Freiberg, 1994; and various authors in his 1999 book) wrote extensively about the paradigm shift in CM. The shift was from classic behaviorism to person-centered approaches that are more student-directed than teacher-directed. Freiberg argued that this was not simply a change in strategy but a philosophical shift in the global view of teaching and learning and of teachers' and students' roles in the classroom.

Teaching is not seen any longer as transmission of information from an active teacher to passive students. Students must become active and take responsibility for their learning, and the teachers become facilitators rather than transmitters. The emphasis shifted from obedience and compliance to more self-direction and self-regulation. Finally, CM shifted from intervention to prevention. As Freiberg put it, why solve a problem if you can prevent it in the first place?

In the same spirit, Everston and Weinstein (2006b) summarized the common themes and consensus among most writers in the contemporary conceptualization of CM:

1. Positive teacher–student relationships are at the very core of effective CM.
2. CM is seen as a social and moral curriculum for fostering students' social, emotional and moral development, not only as a method for controlling the classroom.
3. Strategies based on external reward and punishment are not desirable and do not contribute to students' development.
4. Teachers must take into account student' characteristics and consider the differences among students in age, developmental level, race, ethnicity, cultural background, socioeconomic status and abilities. Variations among students must mediate teachers' managerial decisions and influence their actions.

VIGNETTE FROM TEACHERS' RESEARCH

A vignette from our work with teachers in Israel demonstrates quite vividly the paradigm shift in CM. In the past few years, my colleagues at the Hebrew University of Jerusalem and I ran a project intended to facilitate teachers' applied research in the schools. Doctoral students in educational research went regularly to various schools and preschools in the field, and helped teachers to formulate research questions; to design field studies and to actually conduct the studies in school; to analyze the data; to write short scientific reports; and to disseminate the information to other teachers in presentations and through the Internet.

In one elementary school in Modi'in, two teachers (Yael Karp and Keren Fahima) had an argument about the desirable student stance during frontal teaching. One of them believed that students' attention is more focused and their learning is maximized when they are required to sit still, to avoid scribbling and other unnecessary activities, and instructed to listen attentively to the teacher. The other teacher held an opposite view, believing that attention is more acute when students are left alone with no instructions or teacher control. We encouraged the two teachers to investigate the issue, and they designed and conducted several field experiments in second- and sixth-grade classrooms. In one study, one group of students was explicitly instructed to clear their desks and to sit attentively and quietly during the lesson, whereas the other group received no instructions at all. In another study, one group of students was actually provided with crayons and paper (and in another version, with pipe cleaning sticks that can be manipulated and played with) compared to control groups. The teachers taught new teaching units in those lessons, so that student achievement in a subsequent test was a function of their attentiveness during the teaching session.

The results were very clear and consistent in all variations of the experiment and across the two grade levels: Free-wheeling students whose behavior was not restricted performed better and showed higher achievement than the groups instructed to sit still and to pay attention. Thus, the teacher-directed approach was less effective than the student-directed approach. The more traditional teacher in the pair of researchers was quite surprised by these results, and the study caused her to re-think her philosophy of CM. The study was later discussed by the entire body of teachers and it was clear that the data-based conclusions influenced the teachers.

HOW IS CLASSROOM MANAGEMENT INVESTIGATED?

Data-based images and conceptions of effective CM are derived from empirical research. Data can confirm whether the ideological perspective and the theoretically-desired images of effective management are indeed valid in the educational outcomes they can yield in actual practice. To conduct research on CM, measurement must focus on two major aspects:

1. Processes of teachers' actual management in the classroom.
2. Educational outcomes in various classrooms.

When the actual management processes are defined, operationalized in measurable terms and actually measured in large enough samples of classrooms, and when the educational outcomes are equally defined, operationalized and measured, it is possible to analyze the relationships between processes and outcomes. Subsequently, specific elements and aspects of teachers' and students' conduct that would constitute effective CM can be identified and defined.

How can CM be measured? The best and most common method is to conduct observations in classrooms, recording and analyzing defined aspects of teachers' and students' behavior. But because classroom observations require a great investment of time, effort, and financial resources, researchers often substitute for them with (high-inference) reports of the students, of the teachers themselves, or of school administrators and professional staff (who usually know all teachers very well and can differentiate among them).

Educational outcomes can be measured in a variety of methods. The most common measures are actual student achievement data and students' self-reported evaluations of classroom climate and of their teachers' efficacy. Sometimes the teachers themselves are asked to evaluate the educational outcomes of their classrooms, or researchers would seek sociometric data of teachers' reputation among their peers and school administrators. (Measuring through reputation is fine, because longtime professional peers and colleagues have valuable information about each other. However, reputation should not be self-perpetuated, based on what the teachers boast to their colleagues about their success within their classrooms). Another source of data can be found in the institutional records: Frequencies of truancy, of lateness to class, of problems requiring external intervention, of referrals to experts, etc.

Probably the most common design used in CM research is the extreme group comparison design. This type of research works backwards, from the outcomes to the process: Researchers identify groups of excellent and effective classroom managers, and compare them to appropriate control groups (either teachers not identified as excellent, which constitute neutral control groups, or groups of teachers explicitly identified as weak classroom managers). Those extreme groups of teachers are then observed in their classrooms, in attempts to identify what characterizes the behavior, conduct, attributes and attitudes of excellent classroom managers.

THE IMAGE AND ATTRIBUTES OF
EXCELLENT CLASSROOM MANAGERS

From the extensive literature and the multitude of studies, it is possible to delineate in a condensed fashion the desirable image of teachers who are excellent in their CM. Next, students' images of good teacher-manager are presented first, followed by the presentation of researchers' images of excellent CM. Although derived from different types of studies, the two images are quite compatible with each other, although the specific terms characterizing student perceptions are different from the terms used by researchers.

I must apologize to the readers that the emerging picture is too rosy and idealized. Excellent classroom managers must be almost perfect and superhuman, to possess an amazing collection of good traits and attributes. I feel somewhat apologetic because the required perfection might boomerang and act to deter prospective teachers rather than encourage them to become teachers, especially because many of these traits would seem to be innate and not readily trainable.

Students' Image of Excellent Classroom Managers

Based on a variety of sources, including Kounin (1970), Nash (1976) Good and Brophy (1987) Freiberg (1999) and numerous chapters in Everston and Weinstein's (2006a) handbook of CM research, a condensed picture of students' image of the good teacher-manager can be presented in the following manner:

- A good teacher shows caring for students and is friendly and supportive;
- A good teacher is interesting and turns learning into fun;
- A good teacher teaches you well and explains so that you can understand;
- A good teacher is fair;
- A good teacher listens to students and is open to hear their views;
- A good teacher keeps order in the classroom, but does it in a non-threatening way.

On the other hand:

- A good teacher is not mean or condescending;
- A good teacher does not shout;
- A good teacher has no favorite students;
- A good teacher accuses a student only when the situation is fully justified.

Woolfolk Hoy and Weinstein (2006) summarized student expectations of the good teacher-manager in a similar manner. For students:

- Good CM requires a fair and reasonable system of classroom rules and procedures that protects and respects students;
- Teachers are expected to care for students, their learning and personal lives;
- Teachers are expected to maintain order in the classroom without being punitive or mean;
- Students would be willing to accept differential treatment as long as it does not reflect racism, sexism, classism or favoritism.

Researchers' Image of Excellent Classroom Managers

Again, condensing ideas from a variety of sources it can be said that effective classroom managers:

- Should show maturity and ego strength;
- Should be well organized in every aspect of CM, teaching and learning;
- Should be firm but fair, as well as calm during a crisis;
- Should be challenging in appropriate doses and build students' interest and confidence;
- Should encourage participation and enjoy contact with students (within the limits of the teacher's role);
- Should be constructive in their criticism and maintain boundaries without being threatening;
- Should be authoritative and proactive.

CHARACTERISTICS OF EFFECTIVE CLASSROOM MANAGEMENT

The CM literature is very extensive. It covers ideological aspects, theoretical aspects, and an abundance of empirical findings on characteristics of effective management. That literature also includes applied books, materials, lists of guidelines and training programs that can help both teachers and teacher-education students to plan and to improve their CM (e.g., Emmer & Gerwells, 2006; Good & Brophy, 1990; Jones, 2006; and particularly Everston, Emmer & Worsham, 2003). Next, I present a condensed account that integrates characteristics from a variety of sources. By now, all characteristics are more or less known to the reader from the previous sections, and the following list just organizes the different topics involved in CM:

1. *Planning.* Much of the potential effectiveness of CM is dependent on careful and organized planning. Brophy (2006; Good & Brophy, 1990) emphasized that planning includes both advance planning before the start of the school year and ongoing planning throughout the school year. Because ongoing planning is situational and dependent upon specific events in the classroom, more was written about advance planning.

   a. *Planning rules and procedures.* It is very important that teachers would explicitly plan the rules and procedures to be enacted in the classroom, and would consequently communicate these rules and procedures clearly to the students. Advance explication prevents confusion and lays a foundation of mutual understanding (and usually mutual consent) between teachers and students. That enables teachers to enact their authority in a non-threatening manner. Different writers emphasized the need for a minimal number of rules, and preferably, flexible rules. The rules must also include information about consequences of inappropriate student behavior.

   b. *Organizing the physical environment of the classroom.* The physical environment of the classroom can greatly influence teaching, learning, classroom atmosphere and other educational outcomes (Brophy, 2006; Good & Brophy, 1990; Nash, 1981; Pellegrini & Blatchford, 2000; Weinstein, 1979). The classroom must be arranged to facilitate order, listening and effective schoolwork. Brophy distinguished between considerations concerning smooth movement and prevention of lines and time waste, and considerations concerning effective monitoring of the students. The planning of instructional activities also dictates appropriate arrangement of the physical space of the classroom, for example in order to facilitate particular interactions among students or to enable students to work in teams.

   c. *Planning beginning school activities—"getting off to a good start."* Numerous writers (e.g., Emmer & Gerwells, 2006) emphasized the importance of teachers' early behavior at the beginning of the year with a new class. In addition to providing an orientation and communicating clear expectations, rules and procedures, teachers must establish their style and their personality in students' minds. Students then form their impressions about the teacher (and first impressions are known to be resistant to change): Is the teacher pleasant? Tough? Fun to be with? What are her limits? How does she teach? Experts agree that actual teaching must be started as soon as possible in the early sessions, and teachers' should plan for the most attractive and interesting teaching they can provide.

d. *Planning of teaching.* Teaching should be planned in advance and cannot be done haphazardly. Without going into specific considerations concerning instructional materials and didactic methods, it can be said that advance planning includes decisions about the scheduling of activities, how much demand to put on students, how to deal with differences among students, and how to treat students with particular difficulties.

2. *Monitoring.* The literature emphasizes the importance of teacher's continuous follow-up, monitoring the progress of the entire classroom and the behavior and progress of every student, and planning accordingly how to proceed to advance their development. The follow-up is the complementary process to the advance planning. "Teacher withitness" is the relevant term that appears repeatedly in the literature and is an expression of effective CM.

3. *Clarity of communication.* Clarity of communication and lack of ambiguity in teachers' conduct are critical in the formation and maintenance of effectively managed classrooms. Teachers should attempt to communicate with their students and not to leave out any pertinent information. They should be clear and explicit in the transmission of their messages to students, should be consistent in what they transmit, and should ascertain that their communication is received and understood correctly. Double messages, inconsistent behavior in different situations, teacher's own violation of existing rules and procedures, and (intended or unintended) ambiguity, confuse the students and cause uncertainty in the classroom.

4. *Control / maintaining good student behavior.* As mentioned, the major paradigm shift in the contemporary conceptualization of CM was in the dimension of teacher control, punishment and treatment of students' misbehavior. Various writers demonstrated a strong consensus in their objection to the behavioristic approach to classroom control (Brophy, 2006; Freiberg, 1999; Freiberg & Lapointe, 2006; Weinstein, 1999). The shift from a teacher-oriented approach to a student-oriented approach and the emphasis on teachers' task to develop students' self-monitoring and self-regulation requires teachers to give up their authoritarian position and their control of the

classroom through external rewards and, especially by avoiding the use of punishments. The shift of CM from intervention after the fact to advance prevention is meant to reduce the need for punishment by developing students' internal control over their behavior. Clear and explicit rules and procedures that are well known to the students, including the knowledge about potential consequences of misbehavior, help to increase the effectiveness of CM. As mentioned, this topic is probably the core, or the backbone of the contemporary approach to CM. Above all, teachers are tested on their ability to maintain discipline and prevent misbehavior without excessive use of punishment. However, in recent years discipline problems have intensified and have become more and more acute in schools worldwide, and it is often extremely difficult to control problematic classrooms while maintaining this ideological stance. The discipline issue is probably the main single cause of teacher burnout or of individuals avoiding the teaching profession altogether (e.g., Freiberg & Lapointe, 2006; Friedman, 2000, 2006; Chapter 3, this volume). Therefore, a special, more extensive discussion of punishment and disciplinary control is presented in Chapter 9, summarizing various ideas as to how to maintain classroom discipline and how to make punishment effective.

5. *Teacher–student relationships and students' social-emotional development.* If the above approach to classroom control and discipline is one leg of CM, it might be said that the social curriculum and the emphasis on teacher–student relationships is the other leg of effective CM. Almost all recent writers refer to this dimension in one way or another. If teachers could potentially view themselves primarily as instructors or as socializers (Pianta, 2006), the contemporary conceptualization of CM certainly emphasizes the latter, focusing on teacher–student relationships and students' social, personality and moral development through their relationships with their teachers. Pianta argued that, in order to change school climate and classroom climate, intervention programs and teacher training must emphasize changes in the system of relationships. Other writers also stressed the social and emotional elements in teacher conduct in developing students' social-emotional learning (e.g., Elias & Schwab, 2006) and social competence (e.g., Wentzel, 2006). In students' perceptions of teachers' CM (Woolfolk Hoy & Weinstein, 2006), expectations for teachers' personal caring, support, and teacher–student relations were found to be very central.

Teachers should demonstrate warmth, emotional support, and sensitivity to students, in combination with structure, modeling and direct instruction. Brophy (2006, Good & Brophy, 1990) wrote extensively about this dimension, repeatedly emphasizing that the required social-emotional relationships must remain within the limits of teacher and student roles without crossing into the purely personal domain. In students' perceptions (Woolfolk Hoy & Weinstein, 2006), concern about the limits of these relationships is also clear—together with the emotional care in relationships with students, teachers are also expected to exercise their authority and maintain structure and order in the classroom.

To fulfill the combination of organizational management and emotional facilitation, teachers must exhibit positive personality traits and emotional maturity. Brophy (Brophy & Putnam, 1979; Good & Brophy, 1990) summarized the attributes and characteristics of teachers who are good socializers of students. The list includes the following:

- Likability (including various attributes that make people likable, such as pleasantness, amiablity, etc.);
- Realistic perceptions of themselves and of students;
- Enjoyment of students (but within teacher's and student's role);
- Role clarity and comfort about roles;
- Positive attitude toward being challenged and tested;
- Patience and determination;
- Acceptance of students;
- Firm but flexible limits;
- Positive expectations (such expectations might self-fulfill);
- Consistency in rule enforcement; and
- Serving as a model to students.

A CRITICAL LOOK AT THE CONTEMPORARY CONCEPTUALIZATION OF CLASSROOM MANAGEMENT

Frankly, I must admit that I feel a bit uncomfortable with some aspects of the contemporary model of CM. I am concerned about the emotional demands it puts on teachers and its lack of balance among priorities given to the central objectives of schooling. I am also afraid that it seems to ignore to a large extent the current harsh realities of schools worldwide. I suspect that this model would probably be particularly appropriate for elementary schools with relatively affluent and homogeneous populations of students, free of problems of poverty and racial tensions, violence, anti-social attitudes, underachievement, and disrespect for school.

In previous chapters I expressed reservations about approaches to schooling that are too ideological. Ideologies tend to lack tolerance for opposing views, and they are expressed in ideational homogeneity that allows no deviation (Babad et al., 1983). Much of the literature on CM that I had reviewed in this chapter demonstrates such homogeneity.

Contemporary schools (especially high schools) face tremendous, almost insoluble problems of lack of discipline, violence, aggression and student misbehavior. In their discussion of discipline problems and review of corrective programs, Freiberg and Lapointe (2006) drew a gloomy picture of antisocial behavior in schools. They described extremely high and sharply increasing rates of behavioral problems, violence and aggression, and mentioned the fact that the Center for Disease Control and Prevention had declared violence in school "a serious health hazard affecting students." Candidates are hesitant to enter the teaching profession fearing that they might fail to control their classrooms, and behavioral problems constitute one of the major causes of teacher burnout (Friedman, 2000). Under such conditions, to give up external control of behavior and to put such an intense stigma on behavioral approaches (the effectiveness of which cannot be denied), and to demand that teachers use only affective methods to create student connectedness and self-regulation seem unrealistic and really unfair to teachers. The objectives of developing students' self-monitoring and self-efficacy are indeed highly commendable. But like a Maslow-type pyramid, these goals represent the top level, and they can be tackled only after lower-level goals have been attained.

In the classic research on the three types of leadership (Lewin et al., 1939, Chapter 3, this volume), authoritarian leadership was found most effective in causing task performance, even though students preferred the democratic (or authoritative) leadership style and felt more content with it. The ideological stigma put on behavioral control and on authoritarian leadership may well prevent teachers from even considering the use of certain behavioral strategies when facing crisis situations in their classrooms. It seems that the CM ideology denies the legitimacy of achievement-oriented teachers.

I mentioned in Chapter 3 that the majority of teachers spend a very limited number of hours in each classroom, teaching only one discipline or sub-discipline. This is certainly true of high school, but more and more characteristic of elementary school as well. It is not realistic to demand that teachers would develop a complex system of emotional relationships with all students in all classrooms despite their limited access to the students and their instructional duties in their particular fields. In studies conducted in our Israeli project of teachers' research, we found substantial attitude differences between home-room teachers and professional teachers of particular subjects. The former indeed felt responsible for the social-emotional aspects and for students' development and socialization; but the latter (especially science teachers) saw their task limited to good instruction and promotion of student achievement in their particular fields.

When adults look back at the good old days of their early schooling, they often remember particularly memorable teachers. Many remember nostalgically very charismatic teachers (transformational leaders, see Chapter 3) who left a profound impact on their students' social self and identity. But many others remember fondly past taskmasters, very demanding, hard-driving and uncompromising teachers who led their students to unusual achievements despite their lack of people orientation.

In summary, then, I think that an appropriate approach of CM must be more pluralistic and tolerant to different styles of teaching rather than promoting only one exclusive image of effective management. Different types of teachers (as described in Chapter 3) should be able to discover and practice the most effective strategies that fit their personal style and teaching circumstances.

A Final Comment about the Expression of Emotion

Teachers are required to develop social-emotional relationships with their students. The literature (see Elias & Scwhab, 2006; and Everston & Weinstein's (2006b) discussion of common themes in the CM literature) emphasizes the importance of teacher–student relationships as the very core of effective CM and as the source for students' emotional, social and moral socialization. But teachers are thrown into the pond of the classroom and required to be emotional without appropriate preparation and without caution about potentially negative consequences of their emotionality.

What should teachers do with their negative emotions? Teachers are expected to be caring and supportive, to enjoy students and to hold positive expectations for all of them. But teachers also experience numerous and sometimes intense negative feelings in the classroom–frustration, anger, failure, threats, confrontations, and eventual burnout. Are they supposed to spontaneously express their negative feelings as well? One of the few writers who referred to teachers' negative emotions was Emmer (1994; Emmer & Gerwels, 2006). He studied teachers' positive and negative feelings in the classroom and pointed out that teachers must learn to cope with their negative feelings and to manage them. Teachers report that they often do that by masking and repressing their negative emotions. Thus, it seems that teachers are encouraged to express positive emotions but to hide their negative feelings. This kind of emotionality can hardly be considered authentic or spontaneous.

I am concerned about teachers' positive emotions as well. When emotionality becomes normative and teachers are required to express their feelings (at least their positive feeling) toward each individual student, it is quite difficult to channel the emotionality in desirable directions and to avoid other directions. Chapters 7 and 8 dealt extensively with TDB and the teacher's pet phenomenon. The emotional effects of TDB can be intense, and students are very critical of the preferential positive emotions teachers express toward their pets, and, to a lesser extent, toward their high-expectancy students. Preferential affect can potentially cause serious damage to CC and students' satisfaction. Given that a noticeable teacher's pet phenomenon is found in half or more of elementary school classrooms; given the strong findings on teachers' differential affective expression toward high-versus low-achieving students; and especially given the evidence on students' expertise in detecting the most subtle cues in teachers' NV behavior

(Chapter 14)—then teachers' free-floating emotions constitute a potential liability rather than an asset.

I think that the ideas about teachers' emotional expression and teacher–student relationships as a component of CM are valuable and important. However, to be helpful for teachers and for teacher education students, more information and guidance should be provided, in order to promote controlled and well-planned expression of teachers' emotions. Some of the salient CM writers had been involved in the past in research on expectancy-related TDB and on teachers' emotional attitudes, but they refrain from mentioning that research in their current CM writings. I was quite surprised to find almost no reference to the TDB issue and teacher's pet phenomenon in the CM literature.

10 Punishment and Effective Management of Discipline Problems

DISCIPLINE AND PUNISHMENT AS COMPLEMENTARY SOCIAL FORCES

For its survival, human society needs social order and sets of rules, norms and expectations for maintaining the lawful conduct of its citizens. This is true for society-at-large, but no less true for mini-societies such as the family, various organizations, and the classroom society. Discipline is the process of upholding the rules and the norms to ensure social order. Socialization is the educational process that develops individual self-control, character, and orderliness. Discipline can be forced upon the individual by authority figures and societal institutions, but the ideal and desirable state is for discipline to become internalized, part of the individual's inner world and value system. Therefore, the socialization of self-discipline is an important educational goal, a central objective of CM and value education.

But at the same time, lack of discipline and violation of social order are not unnatural—they are basic and deep needs that exist despite our conscience and value system. Some people are prone to be violators, and it might be assumed that the educative process had failed as far as they are concerned. However, every person sometimes acts undisciplined and in opposition to societal rules. There is a gap between values and behavior in every society and the violation of discipline is a common human phenomenon. Therefore, discipline must be enforced in that gap between the necessary standard and what people are willing to do of their own volition. The lower the inner standard, the more external enforcement of discipline would be required, and vice versa, the more effective the value education (and CM), the lesser the necessity for external enforcement of discipline.

Punishment is one of the central instruments for maintaining social order and discipline. A human society cannot exist without a penal code and a penal system, because (at least some) violations of discipline are inevitable. Even the strongest opponents of punishment cannot envision a state that has no mechanisms (such as the law, police, judges and prisons) to punish violators of social order. This is true as well for the educational system and for the classroom society. The educational context presents an interesting duality, because a major task of the educational system is to develop self-discipline and autonomy, so that the need for the application of punishment would be reduced. At the same time, school cannot exist without any exercise of punishment.

Our present times are characterized by lack of discipline and by severe and frequent violations of social order in all walks of life. This is true of most educational systems in Western society. On the day that the first draft of this chapter was written, all elementary school teachers in the metropolitan area of Tel Aviv conducted a two-hour strike to protest against frequent physical assaults of teachers by frustrated and angry parents. One of the major causes of teacher burnout (Friedman, 2006) is their difficulty in maintaining order and discipline in their classrooms and the great investment of effort that is required to deal with discipline problems. The great heterogeneity of contemporary classrooms—ideologically justified in our society—intensifies the challenges facing teachers in maintaining order in their classrooms.

LEXICAL DEFINITIONS OF PUNISHMENT ARE NOT EDUCATIVE

As mentioned, punishment is the mechanism employed by the legitimate authority to maintain social order and to reduce the frequency of violations of discipline. From a societal point of view, the ultimate test of the effectiveness of punishment is the evidence that the undesirable behavior had indeed been reduced and minimized. The punishment must be a powerful deterrent, and it might often be quite severe and harsh. But from an educational point of view, the main objective is initial prevention, and if that objective could be attained, there would be no need for punishment.

The next list presents a sample of lexical definitions of punishment picked up from the Internet. The gap between the administrative and the educational points of view becomes very clear from this list:

1. Suffering pain or loss that serves as a retribution.
2. A penalty inflicted on an offender.
3. Severe, rough or disastrous treatment.
4. An authorized imposition of deprivation of freedom or privacy or other goods because the person had been found guilty of some violation.
5. Infliction of some kind of pain or loss upon a person for a misdeed.
6. The practice of imposing something unpleasant on a subject as a response to some unwanted or immoral behavior or disobedience.
7. Penalty for doing something wrong.

These definitions have in common the unpleasant, painful, and aversive nature of punishment, and the educational element is missing in them. The causal link connects backwards from the painful punishment towards the violator's misdeed, but there is no apparent forward causal link to future behavior. From these definitions, it appears that punishment is a means used by society to protect itself, but no educational or learning element is defined in them. Given these definitions, no wonder that educators are not fond of punishment, and do not consider it a desirable educational practice.

The literature on CM demonstrates the ambivalence about the use of punishment in the classroom. The anti-punishment perspective is represented by the contemporary CM ideology (Chapter 9) and by the good parenting literature (next discussion). These educators maintain that punishment lacks in educational value and therefore oppose the exercise of punishment at home and in the classroom. They believe that careful planning and implementation of discipline can minimize the need for punishment, and these beliefs are pivotal in their educational ideology and in their image of the ideal teacher and ideal parent.

In contrast, the behavioral approach views the exercise of punishment as an integral element of CM, part of an overall attempt to lead teachers to maximal effectiveness in all aspects of their interactions with students. The behavioral approach is practical and data-based rather than ideological: The ideal teacher copes most effectively with all problems that arise in the classroom and leads students to the best school work with minimum obstacles, and that may well include the intelligent and effective exercise of punishment.

Because the debate between these two points of view is very important, I first discuss the two approaches in more detail. Subsequently, the main part of this chapter presents an integration of various literatures and delineates the relevant considerations and tactics for the effective application of punishment in the classroom when it becomes necessary to punish students.

CONTEMPORARY APPROACH TO PUNISHMENT IN THE CM AND GOOD PARENTING LITERATURES

Everston and Weinstein (2006b) summarized the common themes among the numerous authors in their recent handbook of CM research. Punishment was one of the common themes, with overriding consensus among the different writers about its disadvantages as an educational technique. Everston and Weinstein wrote that positive teacher–student relationships are at the very core of effective classroom management. The relational conceptualization of management overshadows a view of management as a set of rules, rewards and penalties. Authors repeatedly cite the importance of teachers' being warm, responsive, caring and supportive. Managerial strategies relying on external reward and punishment are not considered optimal for promoting academic and social-emotional growth and self-regulated behavior. Authors are critical of coercive, exclusionary methods of discipline. They argue that the approach to CM moves beyond a stimulus-response paradigm to an approach that emphasizes students' self-regulation, social-emotional learning, school connectedness, trust and caring. In students' perceptions: "Good teachers care. They know how to set limits and enforce expectations without being punitive and demanding."

In the same book, Woolfolk Hoy and Weinstein (2006) summarized students' perceptions of good teachers, and concluded that students react negatively to teachers' coercive strategies and find extrinsic control undesirable. In students' view, the worst teachers are characterized as shaming, humiliating, insulting and unfair.

This approach is also widely held today in the literature on good parenting (see, for example, Steinberg, 1996). The same concerns are voiced in trying to educate parents and future parents how to bring up and socialize their children. Both the good parenting and the CM literatures emphasize the distinction between punishment and discipline. Punishment (words that shame or ridicule the child; shouting; holding back rewards; penalizing the child or using physical punishment; etc.) involves physical or mental pain and is intended to make the child suffer. On the other hand, discipline is guidance to make the child think before acting and is intended to promote self-control. Discipline does not hinder the warm relationship and caring between the adults and the children as punishment may well do.

It is generally accepted that punishment is usually quick and easy to administer, and most effective in reducing disruptive behavior. But teachers and parents often use punishment to vent their own frustration when they are at means end. They assert their power and control, as if admitting that they do not know how to deal with the child otherwise. Instead of learning self-control and responsibility, punished children might learn that it is right to be cruel to people close to you; that those who care for you are those who make you suffer; and that harshness and violence are OK when other things don't work. Finally, severe and continuous punishment may hinder children's self-esteem and self-worth, possibly resulting in a decrease in efficacy motivation and an increase of misbehavior in different forms.

From an objective point of view it seems that the punishment issue puts the affective CM and good parenting advocates in an almost insoluble bind. Because punishment is undesirable and non-educational, it would be best to de-emphasize the issue and not take much of readers' attention in discussing punishment. However, if punishment is sometimes inevitable and must be used, it would be better to teach future teachers how to use punishment effectively, because inefficient exercise of punishment can seriously hinder CM.

THE BEHAVIORAL APPROACH TO PUNISHMENT IN EDUCATION

The behavioral approach in education is focused on students' actual behavior. It analyzes environmental factors (such as the reactions of teachers and peers) that increase and/or decrease rates of particular behaviors. The central assumption in the behavioral approach is that behavior is always influenced by its consequences, and therefore students' behaviors can be modified when there is a clear consequence as the result of the behavior. On principle, behavior does not continue to be enacted if it is not reinforced in some manner. Without reinforcement, a behavior is extinguished and its rate decreases. However, reinforcement is not always rational, and what might seem to be aversive to students, such as angry teacher's attention or scolding, might be reinforcing to some students and to increase the rate of their disruptive behavior. Numerous studies demonstrated that in many cases of classroom misbehavior, teachers' strategy of stopping to pay attention to the disruption can result in the reduction or even disappearance of the disruptive behavior—but only following an initial annoying increase in the rate of misbehavior first (see O'Leary & O'Leary, 1972).

The term that caused most controversy and trouble for the behaviorists was control (as in behavior control, classroom control etc.), because it was interpreted by opponents to reflect external, authoritarian and arbitrary control of students' behavior. The behaviorists had something quite different in mind: They thought of an operational and measurable definition of the behavior and of its consequences; and used the term control to refer in a practical manner to the causal chain of relationships between initial behavior, consequences, and subsequent behavior. Contemporary advanced behaviorism includes Albert Bandura's social learning (Bandura, 1986, 1997), Albert Ellis' cognitive-behavioral rational-emotive therapy (Ellis & Dryden, 2007), and many approaches that put a premium on developing students' self-monitoring and transferring to them the control over their own behavior (still, unfortunately, using the word control).

For the present analysis, the relevant concepts involve processes that influence students' behavior. Influence is divided dichotomously into effects of increasing or decreasing rates of behavior. Punishment involves the decrease of disruptive behavior—often while concurrently reinforcing and increasing other, more positive behaviors instead. Two additional elements in the matrix are the type of teacher operation (giving something or removing something) and the type of stimulus used by the teacher (desirable versus aversive). The combinations of these elements create what Landrum and Kauffman (2006) label as five basic behavioral operations (all behavior analysts discuss these basic operations in one manner or another):

1. *Positive Reinforcement*—Student's positive behavior leads teacher to give student a desirable stimulus (reward). Consequently, rate of student behavior increases. (Examples: rewarding student's

participation or positive performance by teacher's attention, praise or other rewards).

2. *Negative Reinforcement*—Student's positive behavior leads teacher to remove an aversive stimulus. Consequently, rate of student's behavior increases. (Examples: "when you finish the task, you can go to recess;" nagging is also an example of a negative reinforcer that increases rate of desired behavior—doing the right thing and behaving appropriately stops the nagging).

3. *Aversive punishment*—Student's negative behavior leads teacher to employ an aversive stimulus. Consequently, rate of student behavior decreases. (Examples include shaming or penalizing students, assigning extra work, or using physical punishment).

4. *Award loss punishment*—Student's negative behavior leads teacher to remove a desirable stimulus (loss of reward). Consequently, rate of student behavior decreases. (Examples: shortened recess, losing computer time, fines, confiscation of personal property).

5. *Extinction*—Stopping to reinforce a previously reinforced behavior. Consequently the rate of student behavior decreases. (Probably the best-known example is when a teacher ignores disruptive behavior, i.e., removes attention from the misbehaving student).

The most desirable and best-known behavioral phenomenon is the event of the positive reinforcement. Much of the socialization of children and most of the management of any human organization is, and should be, enacted through the process of reinforcing positive behaviors with positive consequences. The use of positive reinforcement is widely accepted as the best educational technique. All authors on CM (holding whatever ideology or perspective) would agree that educating students and managing classrooms via positive reinforcements is highly desirable (only that some of them would avoid using the term reinforcement). However, according to Landrum and Kauffman (2006), the accumulated evidence shows that teachers do not give enough positive reinforcement to their students, showing instead high rates of disapproval in the classroom.

In earlier chapters, I described the classroom situation as a scene of constant struggle between students and teachers. In behavioral terms, it is the struggle over the control of contingencies and rewards. Much as the teacher is the environment whose acts influence students' behavior, the teacher's environment consists of the students, and their behavior acts to reinforce or to punish the teacher. The teacher tries to modify students' behavior, but the students try to modify teacher's behavior (and they may often be quite successful). A famous behavioristic cartoon shows a rat in a Skinner box boasting to its mates: "Gosh, have I conditioned the experimenter. Every time I push the lever, he gives me food!" Of course, the teacher is in an advantageous position in this struggle, holding legitimate authority and controlling most of the resources for influencing students' behavior.

In that struggle, the actual reinforcing value of any particular stimulus for its receiver is not necessarily what was intended by the originator of that behavior. Most notably, teachers believe that their scolding and reprimands are aversive stimuli (and therefore should reduce rates of disruptive behavior), but for neglected students (see Chapter 5), the mere attention of the teacher (even if negative in nature) might act as a positive reinforcer and increase their rate of disruptive behavior. Another behavioristic joke describes the dialogue between a masochist and a sadist. "Hit me!" says the masochist, "Definitely not!" responds the smug sadist.

Generations of psychology and education students have experienced a difficulty in distinguishing between negative reinforcement and punishment, because aversive stimuli are involved in both. The key to a clear understanding of the distinction between negative reinforcement and punishment involves the idea that the definition of reinforcement and punishment is based on the final outcome (the effect) and not on the nature of the stimulus (positive or aversive): (a) If the rate student's behavior is increased, then a reinforcement had been involved (either through positive reinforcement in the form of a reward, or through negative reinforcement in the form of the removal of an aversive stimulus); (b) If the rate of student's behavior is decreased, then a punishment had been involved (either through the application of an aversive stimulus or through removal of a positive stimulus). In the case of negative reinforcement, the outcomes are rather pleasant, although an aversive stimulus had been involved in the process. In the case of extinction, the effect is reduction in rate of behavior, but that decrease is not a function of punishment but due to the fact that reinforcement had been stopped. (Extinction of one behavior is usually employed concurrently with the reinforcement of an alternative behavior).

Having clarified these basic terms, we can now discuss the status of punishment in the behavioral approach. Landrum and Kauffman (2006) lamented that "it is unfortunate that the general term punishment has come to connote a single type of punishment: the application of aversives" (p. 52). And indeed the contemporary CM literature relates almost unanimously to the use of punishment as the planned and intentional application of negative and aversive stimuli. Behavioral analysts agree that cruel and unnecessarily aversive punishments should indeed be avoided. O'Leary and O'Leary (1972)—in their early behavioristic book aptly entitled *Classroom Management,* stated that until recently many psychologists protected the myth that punishment is a most ineffective way of controlling behavior. Today, the effectiveness of punishment is not questioned, but the ethics and educational value of punishment remains controversial.

A great accumulation of empirical evidence shows that punishment is the fastest and most effective method for reducing disruptive behavior. It is much faster and more efficient than extinction and negative reinforcement, which require time and repetition to reach their effectiveness, whereas the effect of punishment is immediate. It is helpful in CM because—when effectively used—it removes the disruptive behavior almost instantaneously. This is important because many instances of disruptive behavior and disorder in the classroom create a crisis, and teachers need strategies for managing crises and for resuming the teaching/learning process with minimal interruption.

The behaviorists argue that it is an illusion to believe that teachers do not punish students and that CM can be effective without the use of punishment. Every loud call for order in the classroom, every scolding or reprimand, every cynical remark is, in essence, a punishment—the application of an aversive stimulus to reduce disruptive behavior. It is not possible at all to manage any human system without employing aversive stimuli in some manner, and punishment is a necessary component in management. Even prevention (as advocated in the CM literature) is done through a threat of potential consequences of misbehavior or violation of rules and norms, which means that future punishment is threatened, and students must learn how to behave to avoid punishment. Therefore, according to the behavioral approach, advocating that punishment should not be used at all in education is a ridiculous notion and an impossible demand. Rather, educators should think and plan how to use punishment in the most educational and productive way and how the educational disadvantages of punishment can be reduced or avoided.

TACTICS FOR EFFECTIVE PUNISHMENT

Having presented above both the anti-punishment view and the behavioral view, I feel like the rabbi in the classic Jewish joke. Two opponents came to the rabbi for a judgment in their dispute. One of them spoke first and presented his case. The rabbi responded by saying: "You are right." Next, the other presented his side, and the rabbi responded again: "You are right." The rabbi's wife, hearing this exchange from the door, turned to her husband in wonder: "How can both be right if one says exactly the opposite of the other?" The rabbi thought for a minute, nodded, and then said to her: "You know, you are also right!"

In my view, the behaviorists are right in their approach and in their practical ways of dealing effectively with the entire range of students' behaviors. The proponents of the child-centered approach to parenting and to CM are no less right in their advocacy of relationships, caring, and supportive ways of promoting self-growth. The question is whether an integrated approach to CM can utilize the advantages of both positions and avoid pitfalls in using punishment in the classroom.

Punishment should not be the cornerstone of CM, and education must not be based on external control and coercion. On the other hand, it is an illusion to think that teachers could manage all crises in the classroom through positive regard, understanding and preventive explanation without using any punishment at all. All teachers and parents sometimes encounter crisis situations that necessitate punishment and leave no other alternative. Even well-disciplined and well-behaved children sometimes tighten the rope intentionally and misbehave in order to test the limits of the adult educators. Therefore, to brainwash teachers that they should never use punishment is a mistake that would potentially hinder their effective CM. Teachers should be trained to avoid punishment as much as possible, and to resort to punishing students only when it is absolutely necessary. When they use punishment, teachers should do it in a wise, insightful and educative way, being aware of its disadvantages and trying to make the best out of the situation. For doing that, teachers should be well-versed in the language and findings of behavior analysis.

A detailed list of principles and considerations for effective punishment is presented in the remainder of this chapter, a synthesis from numerous writings and various educational orientations. Despite the salient ideological differences between various orientations, I was surprised to discover how much agreement one finds in the actual practice of how punishment should be planned and delivered.

    I. *Which behaviors should be punished?* Not every classroom disruption and misbehavior should be punished. Punishment should be the last resort after more positive methods had been tried and had not been successful. Teachers should carefully analyze the source of disruption and its possible causes, who are the offenders, and what is the effect of the disruption on the classroom process. Researchers agree, for example, that there is not much sense in punishing offenses that are not likely to be repeated. On the other hand, punishment is appropriate for intentional and premeditated offenses and for repeated offenses. Punishment is also recommended when the misbehavior is associated with significant impairment of the offender's social relationships in the classroom. In general, teachers can resort to punishment if the disruption hinders and damages the learning process of the entire classroom, and when other methods have not been effective to curb the disturbance.

   II. *Who should punish?* The teacher, and not someone else, should administer the punishment. The old fashioned notion of "the headmaster's stick" or "daddy's belt when he returns from work in the evening" is not acceptable. The person responsible for the management of the classroom, the teacher, is responsible to personally administer punishments. Another requirement is that punishment should be administered only by adults who are warm toward the student when his/her behavior is acceptable, adults who offer ample possibilities for positive reinforcement to the student for appropriate behavior. The previous history of the relationship between the punishing teacher and the punished student should include positive interactions, not only punishments and negative interactions.

III. *Pre-punishment considerations.* There is wide agreement that preliminary steps must be taken before punishment is actually administered, involving initial knowledge, warning and threat. Rules and procedures must be stated explicitly and be known as part of preventive CM, so that students would be aware of the expected consequences of behavioral infractions. Some writers even think that written guidelines should explicate specific punishment procedures for particular violations. Students should have a clear expectation of the contingency that particular misbehaviors would indeed lead to punishment. When punishment is likely to be delivered, the offenders should first be warned. It should be made clear that the teacher would rather prefer to avoid punishment, and the student therefore becomes responsible for bringing about the punishment. A threatened punishment (warning) is sometimes more effective than actual punishment in reducing disruptive behavior. However, in some cases, the fear of an unknown punishment would act as an effective deterrent, and specific knowledge of the consequences might reduce its effectiveness.

IV. *Characteristics of the punishment.* Punishment should be flexible and tailored to the specific situation at hand. On principle, reward loss punishment (losing a privilege) is preferred to the administration of aversive stimulus as punishment. Whenever possible, the punishment should be related to the misbehavior, enabling the student to make restitution or to practice a more adaptable related behavior. Imaginative punishments can correct the misbehavior by forcing the student to demonstrate the adaptable behavior that corrects the disruptive behavior. With regard to specific punishments, no overall consensus can be found about appropriate and inappropriate penalties, except for an overwhelming opposition to physical punishment. Some writers think that suspension is not a good punishment, and many writers believe that school assignments should not be used as punishments. There is consensus about the principle that punishment should be educative, but not about the details of what might or might not be considered educative.

V. *When to punish?* Here, there is wide consensus that effective punishment should be immediate and swift, and little time should elapse between the misbehavior and the punishment. Delayed punishment is generally held to be less effective.

VI. *How to deliver punishment?* There is wide agreement among authors about the manner in which punishment should be delivered—emphasizing teacher's cool, rational and deliberate manner. Most importantly, punishment should not be given in anger and should not appear as an involuntary emotional response or a spontaneous reaction to provocation. Even if the teacher does feel angry or provoked, s/he should suppress the negative feelings and deliver the punishment in a cool, detached and matter-of-fact aura, demonstrating rationality rather than emotion. The teacher should refrain from insulting, humiliating or demoralizing the punished student, and should take efforts not to appear capricious or revengeful. Preferably, students should not be punished in the presence of their peers. Teachers should attempt to demonstrate consistency in the manner in which they dole out punishment and should avoid deviation which might appear to differentiate between one punishing situation and another or to differentiate among students.

VII. *Intensity of punishment.* Punishment should not be excessive in quantity or in intensity. Repeated punishments might lose their effect through a process of satiation. Teachers should aim to use punishment rarely, and employ reasonable penalties, proportional to the punished offense and proportional to other punishments they had delivered in the classroom. Punishment should be short, mild as possible, yet unpleasant enough for the receiver to reduce the disruptive behavior and to motivate change. Mild punishments are sometimes very effective—they attain the needed behavioral change without leaving the recipients humiliated, angry or revengeful. It would be a mistake to think that the effectiveness of punishment grows as a function of its intensity. Very intense and harsh punishments are probably less effective than mild, reasonable punishments!

VIII. *Activity to accompany punishment.* Punishment is not supposed to be an isolated act and the teacher must plan other activities to accompany and to complement it, so that the reduction in disruptive behavior would be replaced by a more adaptable and positive alternative. At the very least, the teacher can accompany the punishing act with the expression of positive expectation about what the offender could do in the future. In the best situation, the punishment is embedded in the context of an ongoing instructional and/or management program that emphasizes positive consequences for appropriate behavior. Thus, the circumstances surrounding the unpleasant event of punishment must project hope and positive expectations about changed conduct.

IX. *Students' thoughts and cognitive processing.* The effectiveness and educational value of punishment can be enhanced if it is delivered in a way that evokes particular thoughts and cognitive interpretations on the part of the punished student. Every event is cognitively processed through comparison to other events and to other people. This comparison determines the attributed meaning of the event, the feelings experienced by the punished student, and the influence of the punishment on future behavior. Similar comparisons are made by all other classroom students when punishment is delivered. The comparison is twofold: (a) The punishment is compared to previous punishments received by the student and their particular circumstances; and (b) the punishment is compared to other punishments delivered by the teacher and their particular circumstances. The punishment would be more effective in attaining its goals if these comparisons yield a sense of proportion.

Let's discuss first the student's perception of the punishing teacher and the status of the teacher in his/her eyes. If the teacher is successful in transmitting the message that s/he really does not want to punish the student but acts because no other option is available, the student might feel more responsible for his/her offense, would understand why s/he is punished, and would see the punishment as justified. The more the teacher is perceived as non-punishing and as uncomfortable about using punishment, the more effective the punishment would be, and then even a very mild punishment would be meaningful. It is also important that the student's perception of the teacher and their unique relationship would lead to an understanding that it is not the student who is being punished, but rather, the deed is punished. In such case, the student would be more likely to feel ashamed and embarrassed having caused him/herself that trouble. In short, the status and image of the teacher in the student's eyes, the teacher's personality and past consistency, and the history of the relationship between the teacher and the student (as well as teacher's relationships with the other students), all influence students' perceptions and attributions about a given event of violation and punishment.

With regard to the student's thoughts about the punishment itself, it is important that the punished student would judge the punishment as justified, and its intensity would not be judged as excessive or spiteful. Sometimes offenders collaborate with their teachers in determining the appropriate penalty for their infractions. Teachers often marvel to see students' moral judgment and maturity in determining the appropriate consequences for their disruptive behavior (and often the students are harsher than their teachers). Children understand that punishment must be painful, unpleasant and aversive, but their sense of the appropriate dosage and intensity is critical.

Additional Considerations

Beyond the set of considerations just outlined, various authors offered additional thoughts concerning the enactment of punishment. One example concerns the dilemma about the fixed consequences for any particular infraction of rules. On the one hand, writers emphasize the importance of having detailed rules and procedures known ahead to all students, and students' knowledge should include explicit expectations about the specific consequences of every violation. On the other hand, punishment should not be automatic, and not all children should be punished in the same way.

Consideration of the circumstances of a given situation and the knowledge of the particular students involved in it should influence teacher's action. Another point concerns situations of mass disruptions, when many students are involved in particular violations. Collective punishment is not considered a good practice, because it might sometimes boomerang and make the situation worse (in addition to the ethical concerns about collective punishment). Teachers' wisdom and ingenuity might therefore be needed to handle mass disruptions. In any event, it is not recommended to punish for the sake of making an example. The last point concerns the situation when a delivered punishment had not been effective in reducing the disruptive behavior. Teachers might then tend to do more of the same or to repeat the punishment in greater intensity (Watzlawick, Weakland, & Fisch, 1974). Actually, punishment should be discontinued if it becomes apparent that it is not quickly effective. Unlike other types of reinforcement, the effectiveness of which builds up slowly with performance, the effectiveness of punishment should be apparent immediately. Continuing to deliver ineffective punishment increases students' tolerance to aversive stimuli, and therefore the damage might outweigh the desired consequences. Therefore, ineffective punishment should be stopped at once, and other alternatives must be sought.

SUMMARY

Having gone through the various arguments for and against the use of punishment and having delineated the principles and tactics for effective punishment, I think that the following conclusion is appropriate: Generally, teachers should try to avoid punishing students. Effective CM should be based on prevention rather than intervention, and strive to develop discipline through students' self-monitoring, internal control and responsibility. However, punishment is unavoidable in many classroom situations, and rigid adherence to a no punishment ideology might hinder effective CM. The extensive discussion above of the characteristics of effective punishment indicates that punishment can have an educative value and may contribute not only to necessary crisis intervention but also to promote the attainment of the objectives of student-centered CM.

11 Behavioral Analysis of Common Pitfalls in Classroom Management

ADVANTAGES OF A BEHAVIORAL VOCABULARY FOR ANALYSIS OF CLASSROOM MANAGEMENT

This book is written from a practical perspective and does not advocate one single educational ideology. I try to provide knowledge that would enable teachers to make their own choices about the style of CM best for them. There is no one correct way and no tyranny of the should (how one should act, what one should believe, etc.). Many ways and different alternatives of managing classrooms are available to different types of teachers. Future teachers should on the one hand consider their personality makeup and their resources and, on the other hand, consider the objective characteristics of their classroom, its composition, its past achievements and pitfalls. The student-centered ideology of contemporary CM might appeal to many teachers and they can be effective in implementing it. Other teachers might wish to emphasize academic aspects of teaching and learning and would not wish to give center stage to students' emotional well-being. Some teachers might prefer a competitive environment whereas others would prefer a cooperative classroom. Some teachers feel more comfortable in a firmly managed and disciplined classroom whereas others enjoy a more fluid and constantly changing classroom society.

But there is one goal that is important to all teachers regardless of their chosen approach, and that is to perform their task in the most effective way and to avoid mistakes. Every chosen way has its own unique pitfalls and obstacles, but some typical mistakes are common and frequently made by all types of teachers regardless of their classrooms' characteristics and chosen CM ideology. One example of such a mistake—discussed later in this chapter—is doing too much, where teachers' behaviors are exaggerated in a way that might boomerang and reduce their effectiveness. In this chapter, I discuss ten frequent and typical pitfalls, in the hope of increasing readers' awareness so that mistakes might be avoided or reduced.

I reached the conclusion that the most appropriate language and terminology for analyzing pitfalls in CM is that of behavioral analysis. The behavioral language can be very helpful to teachers for analyzing their conduct and their patterns of interaction with students without necessarily acting as behaviorists, and even without employing explicit behavioral methods and techniques in their classrooms. Throughout the previous chapters I expressed concern over the possibility that future teachers would start their teaching career having been led to believe that the behavioral approach is bad and potentially harmful to students' development. I am not a behaviorist, and my personal research and applied practice in working with teachers are strongly tied to the human relations approach and to social-emotional aspects of teacher–student interaction. And yet I have learned to appreciate the value of the behavioral language and behavioral analysis as an instrument to help teachers in reflection and self-analysis to improve their CM.

All characteristics of CM, of instruction, and of teacher–student interaction are expressed in specific behaviors and in exchange of behaviors between teachers and students. Caring, support, emotional relationships, promotion of students' self-monitoring, no less than rewards, reinforcements and punishments, are all expressed in the final analysis in behavior through specific stimuli and responses. The success and the failure of any process of CM is a direct function of its behavioral enactment by the teacher—not what teachers do, but rather how they do it. It must be made clear, however, that the behavioral view as presented here is quite wide and encompasses many aspects, extending beyond the mechanistic application of external reinforcements and punishments. The broad behavioral view in this chapter is founded on the following considerations:

1. The five basic principles of behavioral analysis (explicitness, planning, consistency, measurement and follow-up) are generally valid and would be accepted without reservation by holders of any CM ideology.
2. The analysis of exchange theories in social psychology is based on notions of psychologists and sociologists such as Thibaut and Kelley (1959), Homans (1961), and Eric Berne, (1964) who were not known at all as behaviorists. And yet, the analysis of social interactions and the prediction of future interactions is conducted in behavioral terms such as gain, loss, profit and price.
3. The inclusion of cognitive-social theorists such as Bandura (1986, 1997), Weiner (1992), Dweck (1999; Elliott & Dweck, 2005) and others widens the behavioral view to include students' self-efficacy, internal motivation and autonomy.

NOTIONS OF EXCHANGE AND CONTROL IN HUMAN INTERACTION

The term control has caused much trouble for behaviorists. For decades they have been criticized for promoting external control harmful to students' social and emotional development. A deeper meaning of control can be provided to the readers through the discussion of theories of social exchange. In the 1960s, a group of theories named Exchange Theories gained prominence in psychology and sociology—especially the theories of the well-known sociologist George Homans (1961), social psychologists John Thibaut and Harold Kelley (1959), and clinical psychologist Eric Berne (1964). The basic conception common to all exchange theories was that human interpersonal interaction is a process of mutual exchange of rewards and other possible positive and negative outcomes. As a universal characteristic of human nature, each side tries to gain maximal benefits out of the interaction. Homans and Thibuat and Kelley described interaction processes in terms of profit, gain, loss and price; analyzed comparison levels and other processes; and conceptualized about power relations and types of control in attempts to predict the outcomes of various interactions. Their analyses included equal-status interactions and unequal-status interactions (such as the interactions between bosses and subordinates, teachers and students). Berne discussed the interaction process in terms of exchanges of strokes and described typical games people play (that is, conduct aimed at maximizing personal gains at the expense of others) in various human situations.

The basic meaning of exchange involves the notion that the interaction process is never one-sided. Both sides participate actively in the interaction even if their status and power are not equal. The partner of lower status (a child in the family, a student in the classroom, a subordinate in the work place) is an active participant in the interaction and can often gain power through the enactment of particular behaviors. The behavior of one side (response) constitutes the stimulus (often the reinforcing stimulus) for the other side, and vice versa. Each side wants to maximize its positive outcomes, in the sense that its behavior would influence the other to act in a particular way. If the reinforcement given to the other side is effective, desired reinforcements are received.

As long as there is harmony between the two sides, their actions are complementary, each side gains its desired profits and both are satisfied. Equality of status between the sides is not required for harmony, and unequal-status interactions can definitely be harmonious. That happens when the lower-status side recognizes the higher-status of the other side and acts within that framework. However, both equal-status and hierarchical interactions are often characterized by lack of harmony, when the gains for one side can be attained only at the expense of the other side. The interaction then becomes more competitive, even combative, notions of winning and losing appear, and the concept of control becomes significant. In disharmonious situations, the power in the interaction is expressed in causing the situation to have particular outcomes.

The conceptualization of exchange can be demonstrated through the behavioral analysis of a commonplace parent–child interaction that constitutes a classic pitfall in parenting. This example involves a set of interactions between a young boy and his mother. The boy wants a cookie but the mother refuses to give him a cookie. The child begins to nag the mother by shouting: "Cookie, cookie" repeatedly. The nagging is unpleasant for the mother, and eventually she gives the boy a cookie. The boy eats the cookie quietly. In behavioral analysis, we should remember that the boy's behavior is the mother's stimulus, and the mother's behavior is the boy's stimulus. From the mother's perspective, the behavior of giving the cookie (finally, after repeated behaviors of not giving previously) caused the boy to be quiet, and the quietness is the mother's reinforcement for her act. From the boy's perspective, his behavior of shouting caused (at last, having been non-effective for a while) the mother to give him the cookie, which is his reinforcement. So what did the boy learn? He learned that it is worthwhile to nag more and more because eventually it brings about a positive outcome. Therefore, the probability that he will shout and nag next time is increased. The mother taught the boy to nag and reinforced him for nagging. Why would she do that? Isn't she opposed to nagging? Well, she is, but she bought temporary relief in this particular occasion. This is a classical mistake in parenting that happens very frequently, even to the most well-intentioned parents. Had the mother conducted a behavioral analysis at the appropriate time, she would have certainly selected a different course of action. Many other options do exist, each depending on the mother's ideology of good parenting—from reinforcing an alternative behavior, developing child's self-control over his behavior . . . to punishment. The analysis of this exchange indicates that a struggle for control had taken place, and the (lower-status) child won and controlled the behavior of his mother.

In Chapter 1, the classroom society was described as the arena of constant struggle between teachers and students and among students. Therefore, the discussion of exchange and control is relevant to CM. Naturally, the teacher is the authority figure in the classroom, dictating its ongoing process and managing it. Students accept the legitimate status of the teacher and enact the role of student in their behavior. Even if they try to challenge the teacher and influence classroom processes to increase their power and benefits, they rarely rebel openly against teacher's authority. Students' control is quite different than teacher's control, and they use strategies and tactics typical to low-status participants in unequal-status exchanges.

When we say that the teacher controls classroom processes, it does not mean at all that the teacher is a controlling person or that the teacher uses external control. Teachers can be authoritarian or democratic leaders (Lewin et al., 1939), or authoritative leaders in Baumrind's (1971) re-definition. Their leadership can be benign, participative, or even shared leadership. In all above possibilities the control is in the teacher's hands, and s/he decides how to exercise her authority. Teachers activate their classrooms; they determine tasks and performance criteria; they evaluate the students; and they control the resources and most of the expected benefits to all members of the classroom society. In a paradoxical manner it can be said that the benefits to the teacher are gained through the development, adjustment and success of the students. Part of the teacher's success is the creation of harmony, where students identify with the academic, social and emotional objectives of the teacher and become autonomous and self-regulating. But because students are required to invest great efforts (price) to attain these objectives, and because quite often their immediate rewards (like the mother in the cookie story) are attained through avoidance of effort, classroom reality is characterized very often by struggle between teacher and students. All of these aspects are included in the concept of teacher control, and in the best scenario, teacher's control facilitates students' self-control.

One final point should be emphasized for a deeper understanding of the issue of control in social interactions. In contemporary thinking on social learning and in current cognitive-behavioral analysis, the old notion of reinforcement as the expression of external control has been replaced by a notion that the stimulus behavior constitutes information that is internally processed by the receiver.

From teacher's behavior, division of attention, praise, criticism and NV behavior, students derive information which influences their self-image and helps them to conduct their own behavior. Therefore, the social reinforcement is not similar to appetitive reinforcing stimulus such as food given to a rat in a maze or a pigeon in a Skinner box to control its behavior. In my doctoral thesis decades ago, I showed that the reinforcing value of adult's praise for its recipients (children) is not simply determined by the quantity of reinforcement (like food). Rather, it is mediated by the children's judgments about the character and traits of that adult, information derived from her reinforcing behavior (Babad, 1972).

FIVE BASIC PRINCIPLES OF BEHAVIORAL ANALYSIS

As mentioned before, the following principles are global, not specific to the behavioral approach only. These principles are relevant for any empirical approach, when analysis and subsequent decision-making are data based and conducted in a systematic manner. In a practical approach, CM must be rational and evidence-based.

1. *Explicitness.* Teacher–student interactions cannot be discussed in vague terms. Every act and every behavior must be defined and analyzed in explicit and exact terms. For example, what exactly is the meaning of: "I was angry at the class"? Did I feel angry or did I express anger in my behavior? How exactly did I express my anger and what were the specific behaviors I used? Did I express anger toward the entire classroom or toward specific students? What was the length and the intensity of my expression of anger? What preceded and what followed my expression of anger? Was my expression of anger salient

and unique or was it part of my regular behavior? The problem with non-explicit description is that the actual occurrence of a specific behavior might be interpreted quite differently by the teacher and by the students. In addition, different students might have different interpretations of the same behavior. Therefore, terms must be explicitly and operationally defined in observable and measurable behaviors, and then their meaning can be consensual. In the common professional language and dialogue, teachers often use vague and inexplicit concepts that are not anchored in specific behaviors.

2. *Planning*. Effective intervention or reaction to a classroom situation must be well planned and executed according to the plan. In the words of my late colleagues and friends, Kenneth Benne and Max Birnbaum, pioneers in the human relations movement, "change does not have to be haphazard" (Benne & Birnbaum, 1960). Planning involves analysis of the situation and an attempt to understand the forces operating in it; identification of factors maintaining or strengthening particular patterns of behavior; and selection (among alternatives) of an appropriate course of action to be employed in a systematic manner. The more exacting and more specific the initial planning, the better are the chances of successful intervention. The problem is that many immediate teacher interventions in the classroom are unplanned and reactive—intuitive and often impulsive reactions to a given situation at a given moment. In the child–mother cookie story, the mother's act of giving the cookie to her son demonstrated a spontaneous unplanned reaction that reaped an immediate benefit but was harmful in the longer range. Few executives, teachers or parents are such gifted managers that their unplanned spontaneous reactions can be always effective. The importance of teacher planning is doubly important when repetitive patterns of students' behavior are involved.

3. *Consistency*. Consistency is a central key to effectiveness, and inconsistency is probably the central source of teachers' ineffective management. Sometimes one deviation from consistency is sufficient to cause exactly the opposite of the planned, desired outcomes. In the cookie story, the mother gave in to her son only once, after consistently resisting the nagging previously. By doing this, she gave partial reinforcement to the child's nagging behavior. The research literature on learning processes tells us that partial reinforcement is especially resistant to extinction, and behavior that had been partially reinforced would persist for a long time without additional reinforcement. In the classroom, teachers often plan to reduce particular disruptive behaviors by ignoring them, so that their attention would not reinforce the misbehavior. Even a single fall from their consistency can cause adverse effects, intensifying rather than reducing the problem. Maintaining consistency is a rather difficult task because specific circumstances often arise that seem to justify breaking the

consistency. This again reflects the dilemma between short-term benefits and long-term damage. Students are great experts in understanding their teachers, and they are particularly sensitive to discover any manifestation of inconsistency, such as rare slips of the tongue, when teachers leak some expression they really intended to conceal. Approaches to CM that encourage the spontaneous and authentic expression of teachers' emotions increase the danger of inconsistency and unplanned action. To act according to plan and maintain consistency the teacher must be detached in some way from the situation rather than being immersed in it. In that way teachers can maintain a critical eye in their own self-monitoring.

4. *Measurement.* To know whether a given intervention or a certain mode of teacher behavior is effective, systematic measurement is necessary. Measurement provides empirical feedback and can reduce the influence of various factors that might potentially distort perception and judgment. Such distortions might include: Halo effects, when our initial like or dislike for a person biases all subsequent judgments about the person; seeing a rare event as representative or vice versa, seeing a representative event as rare; exaggeration or reduction of differences due to processes of leveling and sharpening; and more types of distortion. When measurement is conducted objectively and utilizes explicit and operationalized behavioral terms, it can provide the teacher with valuable information for planning and for subsequent intervention. I don't think that any teacher should spend all or most of her/his time in the classroom in behavioral measurement, but a basic approach that values measurement creates a mental set where global and vague impressions cannot be counted as evidence, and systematic measurement is conducted when the need arises. A huge literature in social psychology exposes many types of distortions in information processing and demonstrates that our spontaneous social judgments are highly susceptible to a variety of cognitive and emotional biases. We cannot trust our own impressions and judgments, especially as they relate to our own behavior. Readers are reminded of findings on TDB reported in Chapter 7 (Babad, 1990a), where teachers reported giving more learning support to low-expectancy students and putting less pressure on them compared to high-expectancy students (confirmed by students' reports and by other, more objective measurements); and also reported giving more emotional support to low-achievers than high-achievers (disconfirmed by other measurements and found to be false). Because we are all susceptible to bias, skepticism is a serious teacher asset because it pushes one to seek more empirical, accurate information.

5. *Follow-up.* This principle is quite similar to the measurement principle—only that it refers to a longer time perspective. Follow-up is like a periodical check-up, where given interventions are evaluated along

the time dimension; the influence of various interventions is assessed in an integrated manner; side effects and unintended influences of particular interventions are examined; and teachers try to reach a general picture of the classroom situation as a basis for subsequent planning. Follow-up enables teachers to assess the situation more objectively, because it is free of particular events and particular contingencies at any given time, and it is conducted in a wider and more detached perspective. Many schools hold particular meetings and workshops to allow teachers to conduct follow-up activities, often in teams with other teachers.

BEHAVIORAL ANALYSIS OF COMMON TEACHER MISTAKES

We all learn from our mistakes and many training programs are constructed so that trainees can examine their own conduct, analyze their mistakes, and develop counter-measures for improvement. But the truth is that we probably stand a better chance to learn from the mistakes of others, because self-analysis always evokes some defensiveness. No guilt or shame is involved in observing and analyzing the misdeeds of others.

The remaining part of this chapter presents common pitfalls in CM, typical mistakes likely to be made by teachers in their classrooms. These pitfalls are analyzed in the language of behavioral analysis. By knowing these common mistakes and understanding their etiology, teachers can inoculate themselves and take planning steps to avoid such mistakes.

I. Satiation Effect—Doing too Much.

All approaches to CM require teachers to provide students with a lot of positive reinforcement—regardless of whether one uses a behavioral language (reinforcements, extinction, etc.) or a social-emotional language (with terms such as care, support, praise, positive emotions, etc.). If there is one contribution of the behavioral approach that is consensually accepted, it concerns the value of positive reinforcement. But many teachers (especially in preschool and elementary grades) adopt this approach a bit too enthusiastically, exaggerating and flooding the children with positive reinforcement.

The value of a reinforcer (and therefore its potential to influence behavior) is determined by the motivational state of the receiver. In animal learning, the value of food as a reinforcer increases when the animal is hungry. Therefore, it can be said that the reinforcement value of food is a reverse function of its previous availability, and higher reinforcement value is associated with greater previous deprivation (that is, stronger hunger). A satiated (non-hungry) animal would not make any effort to push a lever to gain food it does not need. With human beings, learning is usually not based on appetitive stimuli such as food, and learning is caused by secondary reinforcements—social reactions of the other which cause pleasant consequences. Adult praise, smile, stroke, attention, and of course high grades and positive evaluations are the most common social reinforcers for students. But the deprivation-satiation principle remains as valid in human behavior as it is in animal behavior. The lesser the previous availability of a social stimulus (e.g., praise) to the child, the higher its value to influence the child's behavior. In a sense, the child might be considered as hungry for praise. This is the deprivation effect, defined as the increase in the reinforcing value of a stimulus caused by its reduced availability. Satiation effect is the opposite (or complementary) process—the decrease in reinforcement value due to excessive availability. The satiation effect of social reinforcers had been demonstrated many times (e.g., Gewirtz, 1967, 1969; Babad, 1972). The more children were praised, the less they valued those praises, and the effectiveness of these stimuli to reinforce particular behaviors decreased considerably.

Having been socialized that giving a lot of positive reinforcement and positive regard is so important, teachers err by over-use and excess of praise and positive reinforcement, and this exaggeration reduces the value of their reinforcement in students' eyes. If a teacher wishes to maintain the high value of her praise, s/he must be frugal and deliver it in relatively small portions. Exaggeration causes a boomerang effect and makes the stimuli ineffective. And once the value of a stimulus had dropped, it is rather difficult to raise it again.

Contemporary behavioral analysis views social reinforcement in informational terms beyond the satisfaction of (an appetitive or acquired) need. Reinforcement value is influenced by two different components: One is the intensity of students' social need (as described, a function of relative previous availability); and the other is the image of the teacher in students' eyes (a function of previous teacher dispensation of praise and social reinforcements). That image is determined by students' perceptions of the cumulative behavior of the teacher over time. A satiating teacher is one who praises and reinforces students a lot all the time, and a depriving teacher praises or dispenses social reinforcement quite rarely. When the teacher praises a student at a given moment, the value of that praise is determined by the teacher's image. In the case of a satiating teacher, the value of praise would be low, whereas in the case of a depriving teacher, the value of the praise would be high. Therefore, the problem of exaggeration and doing too much is a chronic, rather than a situational phenomenon.

This phenomenon is demonstrated in an interesting way in the following scenario investigated by Dinah Avni-Babad (2002). The scenario described an old woman who was ill, and her two daughters: One daughter, Hanna, usually visited her mother very frequently, whereas the other daughter, Geula, visited the mother only rarely. One day only one daughter visited the mother. Respondents were asked to assess whether the mother would be happier if Hanna or if Geula visited the mother. On another day neither daughter visited the mother. Who (the respondents were asked) would the mother be angrier at for not visiting, Hanna or Geula? Following the logic of the deprivation-satiation effect, respondents were almost unanimous in predicting that the mother would be happier with the visit of Geula, the rare visitor, and more angry with the lack of a visit from Hanna, the frequent visitor. Perhaps it is not fair that Geula, the less devoted daughter, would reap all the benefits at the expense of her more devoted sister. But the lesson for teachers in their classrooms in planning how to use their praise and social reinforcement is quite clear.

Because the intensity of the receiver's need is also a component in the determination of reinforcement value, the characteristics of the students receiving the social reinforcement from the teacher should also be considered. Teachers tend to think that the weaker and the underprivileged students are more needy of reinforcement and encouragement. Therefore, they often praise and encourage the weaker students a lot. The danger is that the excessive use of social reinforcement with those particular students might cause a satiation effect that would reduce teachers' effectiveness in managing these students.

An additional possibility concerns the information derived by the students regarding a teacher's style in praising weak, low-expectancy and underprivileged students, which might cause a negative expectancy effect (see Chapters 6 and 7). If students come to associate gushy overflow of teacher's praise and reinforcement with low or problematic student's status, such behavior on the part of the teacher might boomerang and cause damage to its recipient.

II. Deprivation Effect—Doing too Little

As mentioned, deprivation and satiation might be considered the opposite poles of the same phenomenon. Reinforcing stimuli gain in value for their receivers if they are rare and given infrequently. Today, students have sessions with several different teachers every day, even in the lower elementary grades. After almost every break between lessons they experience a shift from one teacher to another. Their motivational state and their willingness to extend effort in order to gain teacher's praise would vary as a function of their perception of each teacher.

Let's consider a standard unit of hypothetical praise such as the word good from the teacher. In the shift from a satiating teacher to a depriving teacher after the break, the value of good would increase (regardless of the student's state of personal need for good); and in the shift from a depriving teacher to a satiating teacher, the value of the same unit of good would drop. Therefore, if the teacher wishes to maintain a high reinforcing value of her/his good, s/he must be frugal in dispensing her goods.

As in the case of satiation just described, exaggeration in the other direction can also be harmful. If teachers avoid giving social reinforcement and warm regard to their students, they lose the most important CM instrument for motivating students and for establishing a pleasant atmosphere in the classroom. Students of depriving teachers are frustrated or alienated, and classroom atmosphere can be unpleasant, similar to the effect of laissez faire leadership (Lewin et al., 1939). Thus, to maximize the benefits and minimize the price, teachers must find the appropriate balance in dispensing their social reinforcement toward the entire classroom and towards each student individually. Deprivation presents a real dilemma for teachers— whereas doing too much causes a satiation effect and the straight-forward recommendation to teachers is to avoid flooding their students with praise, depravation is a double-edged sword: On the one hand, delivering praise sparingly increases reinforcement value and teacher's effectiveness; On the other hand, teachers should ideally be as warm and positive as possible in praising and reinforcing their students.

III. Reinforcement of Incorrect Answers

Wishing to praise students and to create a positive classroom climate, a typical and frequent mistake that teachers make is to provide positive reinforcement for behaviors that should not be reinforced. When they conduct a question-and-answer dialogue with their students, teachers have two objectives: (1) To encourage as many students as possible to participate; and (2) To reward correct answers that promote the classroom discussion and advance the learning process. The academically stronger students are expected to provide correct answers, and therefore they are reinforced for their correct answers and not reinforced for incorrect answers. For the academically weaker students, the probability of answering correctly is lower, but the teacher wishes to encourage their participation, and therefore would praise them even if their answers were incorrect. Thus, in the same situation, some students are reinforced for correctness and other students are reinforced for their mere participation.

This is a classical pitfall. It is easy to understand why teachers commit this mistake, and we can feel empathy with teachers' wish to encourage the weaker students even if they cannot perform in a high academic standard. But this pattern has several psychological costs: First, when weaker students are reinforced for their mere participation, that behavior is reinforced, and they might continue to participate actively without being concerned about the correctness of their answers. Second, teacher's behavior in that situation demonstrates inconsistency, perhaps even a double standard that distinguishes between two groups of students. Because students are so sensitive to every nuance in teacher behavior, and because they care particularly about teacher fairness and equity (see Chapter 7), this TDB transmits positive expectancies toward some students and negative expectancies toward other students. Perhaps the potential gain in increased participation might be overshadowed by the price of lowered self-image of low-expectancy students and decreased classroom climate.

A similar process often takes place in teacher dispensation of grades and their evaluation of students' work. Teachers often show flexibility (or inconsistency, or a double standard) in their assessment criteria, awarding some students with higher grades than other students for similar performances. Again, the deviation from fairness and consistency is well intentioned. It stems from teachers' motivation to reinforce students whose performance does not provide their teachers with sufficient opportunities for rewards. But that deviation can carry a psychological price, hindering not only classroom climate, but causing damage to the very students that the teacher seeks to encourage. The protective reinforcement signals to the recipients their low academic status and low expectations in the teacher's eyes.

IV. Delayed Reaction

The effectiveness of praise and criticism, of reinforcements and punishments depends on their immediacy. To influence students' behavior, its consequences—positive or negative—must be contingent in time to the occurrence of the behavior. This principle is not always followed in the classroom, and consequences are often delayed, sometimes quite delayed.

Some delays in teachers' reactions are unavoidable. In some school situations—such as giving grades for assignments or evaluating students' performance—the delay is structured as a necessary factor in the classroom scenario. Initial knowledge of the expected delay helps to minimize its price. Even if students understand the necessity of the delay, an assignment returned on the next day has more reinforcement value than an assignment returned after two or three weeks. Delays reduce student motivation and change the immediate significance of their behavior and performance.

Immediacy is important in positive teacher reactions supposed to encourage students and to maintain their high motivation, but it is doubly important in negative teacher reactions in response to misbehavior or infraction of rules. In such cases, a delayed reaction might actually backfire and encourage students' misbehavior. Sometimes the reasons for a delayed reaction are legitimate and reasonable (for example, when the teacher tries to avoid humiliating a student in front of her/his peers, or when the teacher needs to consult with other school staff), but the lack of an appropriate immediate reaction reduces CM effectiveness.

V. Non-Contingent Reaction

For reinforcement to be effective, the contingency between student behavior and its consequences must be clear. But often the contingency is not clear, and students do not understand what caused the teacher's behavior. Contingencies must be as clear as possible and they must be made explicit to the students. This is important because the flood of events in the classroom is quite confusing for many students and might even be overwhelming for some students. The students look up to their teachers for clarity and explicitness. Lack of clear contingencies in teachers' reactions might be caused by unclear criteria, by rules and procedures that had not been explicitly defined, or by occurrences that are more visible to the teacher then to the students. Perhaps it might even be true that some teachers prefer to be vague and mysterious.

Chapter 7 dealt extensively with TDB and emphasized the frequent violation of fairness and equity in teachers' behavior toward different students. The chapter also demonstrated the negative effects of TDB on students and classrooms. I believe that the demand for clear and explicit contingencies is a strong antidote of TDB, and would deter teachers from demonstrating differential and preferential behavior. The other side of the coin is that teachers who are more differential toward different students might avoid demonstrating clear contingencies, because they employ different standards toward different students.

The importance of clear contingencies of reinforcement is demonstrated in the following experimental example. In my early research on the social satiation effect (Babad, 1972), an experimental situation was created in which young children waited for ten minutes in an experimenter's office to start a game. While they were waiting, the experimenter (who was presumably busy with paperwork as justification for the waiting period) raised her head several times and said to the child: Good. The number of goods stated to the waiting child constituted the experimental treatment of satiation (twenty goods in ten minutes) or deprivation (only two goods during the ten-minute period). The value of good as a reinforcer of a specific behavior was subsequently tested in a task where the children received good from the experimenter as reinforcement for a certain type of choice among alternatives (i.e., selecting a plant rather than an animal among two pictures). The satiation effect was demonstrated by the low value of good as a reinforcer in the test after having heard good for many times while waiting. In other words, the children in the satiation condition did not bother in the subsequent test to choose the option that would reward them with the reinforcing stimulus good from the experimenter.

Several years later (Babad & Weisz, 1977), the issue of contingent versus non-contingent satiation was investigated directly by adding a new experimental condition to the previous design. The 1972 study constituted the non-contingent condition, because the twenty (or two) goods delivered in the waiting period came out of the blue and were not associated with anything the child was doing at the time. The new contingent condition also consisted of twenty (or two) goods delivered in the ten-minute waiting period, but each good was explicitly made contingent upon some behavior of the child: Good that you sit quietly; Good that you are patient; Good that occupy yourself; Good that you wait, etc. The results showed that the satiation effect disappeared in the contingent condition. Making the goods contingent upon some behavior of the child erased the satiation effect, and children who received goods which were made contingent upon their behavior did make an effort in the subsequent test to gain more good reinforcements from the experimenter, despite the twenty goods they had received previously.

VI. Teacher Praise and Teacher Attention

Praise and attention are the two major positive reinforcers used by teachers in CM. Praise is volitional, usually enacted by teachers in a voluntary and planned manner to reinforce students and to influence their behavior. Attention can be a volitional reinforcer, but in many cases teachers' attention is dispensed haphazardly and without sufficient planning. Numerous teachers are not aware that their attention, in itself, can influence student behavior, and therefore do not plan as carefully how to dispense it among students.

The generic example of behavior modification in the classroom that is probably mentioned most frequently in psychology textbooks involves teachers' attention. It concerns disruptive students who often throw temper tantrums and seriously disturb their classrooms. Reprimands, warnings, punishments and all other means do not seem to stop the disruptive behavior. From a behavioral perspective it was incomprehensible why these behaviors persist, because no behavior can exist without reinforcement. Early behavioral analysts (see O'Leary & O'Leary, 1972) concluded that in a paradoxical manner, the disruptive behavior is maintained and reinforced by teachers' attention, even though this attention is negative and punitive. The analysts thought that those problem students probably crave for any type of teacher attention, even if it is negative and angry. Therefore, the experts advised teachers to ignore the disruptions and totally withhold their attention from those students (even during temper tantrums). In such cases, at first the disruptive behavior is intensified, and teachers are put to a difficult challenge to persist in ignoring the intensified disruption, but subsequently the disruptive behavior subsides and disappears.

In the language of behavioral analysis, removal of a positive reinforcer causes extinction, and the frequency of the previously reinforced behavior decreases. If teachers' attention reinforced disruptive behavior, then the removal of attention (that is, ignoring the disruptive student) causes extinction. This remedy has been tested thousands of times and keeps proving very effective. The lesson for teachers is very clear, and they learn that their attention, even if negative and intended to decrease particular student behaviors, might paradoxically function as a reinforcer of undesirable behaviors. Becker and colleagues published in 1967 an article appropriately entitled: "The Contingent Use of Teacher Attention and Praise in Reducing Classroom Behavior Problems."

Teachers' attention is often vulnerable to students' manipulation in the ongoing struggle for control in the classroom. Students sometimes wish to focus the attention of a teacher in a particular direction or to divert the teacher's attention away, and therefore the teacher's conscious awareness is crucial. With awareness, teachers can dispense their attention and divide it in the classroom as they find appropriate.

It is not easy to divide attention equally in the classroom: Some students are attention getters and others are not; some areas in the classroom (such as the activity zone in the middle of the classroom, close to the teacher, which was discussed in Chapter 8) attract more teacher attention; and sometimes dispensation of attention is unconscious (readers are reminded how teachers continue longer eye contact with high-expectancy students after a wrong answer compared to their shorter eye contact with low-expectancy students).

Turning back to teachers' praise, despite teachers' conscious awareness and planning, the situation is wrought with potential problems. Good and Brophy (1990) pointed out that teachers' praise is often ineffective and fails to achieve its objectives of increasing student motivation and improving student performance and classroom atmosphere: At times, praise is false and exaggerated (and there are no better experts than students to pick it up); sometimes it does not fit the character of the receiving student; and often it is not specific enough and not sufficiently contingent upon specific behaviors. Teachers' praise is scrutinized by the students in the social comparison process, and therefore it is possible that praise given to one student actually shames and hurts other students.

It is extremely difficult to maintain fairness and equity in the distribution of teachers' praise. The situation presents a serious dilemma: Should teachers' praise be given and distributed according to what students deserve by their actions and conduct, or should teachers seek less deserving opportunities in order to equalize their praise among students? Empirical equality in distribution of praise means that a differential standard must be employed. Keeping a systematic standard would result in unequal distribution.

The final issue concerns students who receive very little attention (or praise) from their teachers. Teachers' awareness about the distribution of their praise is usually focused on the extreme poles of their student body—the academically excellent, well-behaved and popular students at the top of the distribution, and the low-achievers, problem students and disruptive students at the bottom. But the sociometric literature (Coie et al., 1982, see Chapter 4) clearly indicates that each classroom has some neglected students, mediocre students in the middle of the distribution who are invisible and forgotten, and receive no attention (nor praise) from either teachers or students.

VII. Dependence on Students' Reinforcement

The view of teacher-student interaction in terms of social exchange implies that as much as the teacher tries to influence students' behavior, the students also attempt to influence teacher's behavior. The teacher receives (or does not receive) from the students positive reinforcements, negative reinforcements and punishments. It is true that students' power is limited because of the differences in status between the teacher and student roles which make the teacher more dominant and influential than the students.

The major reinforcements that students give to their teachers are the positive products of their learning, their developmental improvement and their social adjustment. Teachers are rewarded by the success of their planned instructional and managerial work through students' progress. Thus, in the frequent and desirable state of harmony, we can talk about a positive cycle of reinforcements for both students and teachers. But because teachers pose many demands and must structure and control students' activities, tension and conflict are unavoidable even in the most harmonious classrooms and students urge to attain some level of control to influence their teachers.

Teachers' dependence on their students for their own well-being is very strong, and the "games students play" (rhyming with Berne's famous 1964 book *Games People Play*) can be very subtle but also quite influential. The main source and cause of teacher burnout is the stress involved in their daily interactions with their students and the continuous tension of CM (Friedman, 1993, 1995, 2006). Students indeed can make their teachers feel miserable. In the central issues on the agenda (curriculum, learning objectives, rules and procedures, etc.) teachers' dependence on students' reinforcement is less problematic. Students' influence is more marked in small incidents and in daily events such as negotiations about tasks, exams and homework, protests about grades, dealing with discipline problems in the classroom, etc. In those situations students can influence teachers' behavior because of teachers' dependence on their reinforcement. The weaker partner in social exchange perhaps has a narrower range of possible tactics, but some can be quite potent. Students have the power to make the teacher feel bad, to be frustrated and nervous, and sometimes even to be ridden with guilt feelings. That dependence often breeds mistakes in CM that are intended, inadvertently and without conscious awareness, to make the teacher feel better.

In research on the teacher's pet phenomenon (Tal & Babad, 1989) we found consensus in students' reports that a major task of the teacher's pet is to be sent by the class to soften up the teacher in conflict situations. Thus, in order to avoid mistakes in this area, teachers must view the classroom situation from the students' point of view, recognize that students also play an active role in teacher–student exchanges, and try to overcome their dependence on students' reinforcement.

VIII. Partial Reinforcement

The topic of partial reinforcement was discussed several times previously. I described how teachers' and parents' attention can serve as a partial reinforcement and inadvertently increase disruptive behavior. In other words, relatively infrequent, unplanned teacher behaviors can boomerang and hinder CM by intensifying undesirable behaviors. This unintended outcome is often discussed in the literature (see, for example, Good & Brophy, 1990; Landrum & Kauffman, 2006). When a disruptive student gains teacher's attention as a consequence of disruptive behavior, that behavior might be reinforced and intensified. And because teachers' attention is not given all the time but only on some occasions, it attains the status of partial reinforcement, and the misbehavior can become more persistent and resistant to extinction.

But the discussion of partial reinforcement should not be limited to disruptive behaviors only, and we should examine the influence of partial reinforcement on students' positive and desirable behaviors. Potential mistakes of many teachers stem from the lack of understanding the differences between the effects of full reinforcement and partial reinforcement. Full reinforcement (that is, every time a goal behavior is performed by a student, it is reinforced by the teacher) is highly effective in acquisition of new behaviors. Behaviors are learned quickly and performed at a high rate under full reinforcement. But when full reinforcement is stopped or reduced, extinction is also very fast, and students stop performing the previously learned behavior almost as fast as they had acquired it. Under conditions of partial reinforcement, both acquisition and extinction are slower. When only some of a student's goal behaviors are reinforced, the goal behavior is learned at a slower pace. But when partial reinforcement is stopped or reduced, the extinction is also very slow, and the goal behavior persists much longer even when reinforcements are not given any more.

A wide range of student behaviors are relevant to this discussion of full versus partial reinforcement, and they pertain to appropriate student conduct in a harmonious, working classroom. Examples include turn taking, not interrupting other students, staying calm after completion of a task, appropriate manner of addressing classroom peers and the teacher, help-seeking and help-giving, and a wide array of additional behaviors. When the acquisition and the maintenance of such positive student behaviors are concerned, full reinforcement is advantageous for quick acquisition, and partial reinforcement is advantageous for persistence over time. In the long run, the advantage of partial reinforcement is more significant, because in effective CM many positive behaviors should be performed at a high rate with no need to maintain them through repeated reinforcements. Of course, the best strategy is to turn the control over these behaviors to the students themselves, so that they would reinforce themselves for their positive conduct. That is the meaning of self-monitoring and self-control in the CM literature.

In the reality of the classroom it is almost impossible, and certainly not desirable to use full reinforcement. Teachers cannot be expected to continue reinforcing every desirable behavior all the time. Even if possible, such continued reinforcement would quickly lead to a satiation effect which would reduce the reinforcing value of the teacher's behavior.

The integrated lesson that emerges out of the above sections is that, a common mistake among many teachers is to believe that more is better, that if they persist in providing a lot of positive reinforcements, the classroom would be more effectively managed and the atmosphere would be more harmonious. This belief is probably held more strongly among kindergarten and pre-school teachers and perhaps by elementary school teachers as well. But actually, reinforcers that are given quite rarely are more efficient and more highly appreciated by students. The high value of less frequent reinforcement is due to a combination of a deprivation effect and a partial reinforcement effect. Desirable behaviors can persist and be more autonomous with low dosages of reinforcement. Thus, a behavioral analysis from several directions leads to the conclusion that excess in teachers' positive behaviors towards students is not good and does not contribute to CM effectiveness.

IX. Dealing with Problem Students and Special-Needs Students in the Classroom

The common policy today in most educational systems is to integrate the special needs children in the regular classroom and to cancel the past segregation between special education and general education. This includes educable mentally retarded children, emotionally disturbed children, students with attention deficits, dyslexia, and other students of special needs that had been segregated in the past in special education classrooms. This policy is ideologically justified, but it makes the life of the regular classroom teacher more difficult. It is very hard to work effectively with a heterogeneous classroom, and both instruction and CM become more complicated by the presence of special needs students in the classroom. Not all children can be taught and managed in the same uniform way, and the teacher's overall style toward the entire classroom is not applicable to some of the special students. These students require special and different treatment, often diametrically opposed to the principles guiding the overall CM. Standards that lead to desirable states of students' self-control, self-monitoring and autonomy cannot be applied to many students with multiple problems and deficits. Teachers then face the dilemma of having to abandon fairness and equity, because they must employ differential treatment, and often even a double standard in their classroom conduct.

In contrast to the intense opposition to behavioral methods in the CM literature, there is much agreement that behavioral methods can be most effective and sometimes necessary with individual students who have special emotional, mental and behavioral problems. Methods considered inappropriate for overall CM or even harmful to students' development, are recognized as potentially effective in extreme individual cases. Without using external control teachers simply cannot deal with individual students demonstrating severe behavioral and emotional problems. Quite often, undisciplined and/or disturbed students can ruin the balance and harmony of the entire classroom. It is a mistake to believe that the same methods and strategies of student-centered CM that might be effective with the classroom-at-large would be equally effective with the problem students on the fringe.

In order to deal behaviorally with special students who present severe problems, it is not sufficient that teacher education students would learn about behavioral principles, but they must practice how to actually conduct behavioral interventions in the classroom. Once they master the skills for behavioral intervention in addition to other managerial skills, they can make reasonable decisions about their overall style of CM and about how to deal with problem students. Another task facing the teacher is to dull the sting of double standard and to make students understand the necessity for differential treatment of some students. Finally, the teacher has to do the impossible—to make sure that the great investment of time and effort in managing special students will not come on the expense of the full and fair treatment of the entire classroom.

X. Punishment

Chapter 10 was devoted to punishment and to the behavioral analysis of effective and ineffective punishment. Mistakes in the use of punishment can be particularly harmful to effective CM and to CC. It is widely agreed that teachers should try to avoid the use of punishment as much as possible. When deciding to punish students after all, teachers should follow the guidelines in Chapter 10 with extreme care. But one grave mistake is common among teachers who oppose punishment: They wish very strongly to avoid any form of punishment in their CM, and they resort to it only at wits' end, when nothing else seems to be effective in dealing with a given problem. Because of their predicament, those teachers often revert to punishment in a state of rage and frustration, angry with the disruptive students. But as was stated clearly in Chapter 10, for punishment to be effective, it must be delivered in a cool and detached manner. One should remember that strictly speaking, even shouting at students constitutes a punishment, that is, the employment of an aversive stimulus in order to reduce the rate of a particular student behavior. Hot-headed punishment is a grave mistake by all accounts, and punishing students in a rage should certainly be avoided. Unfortunately, teachers often punish students in a rage and cannot detach themselves from the anger caused by students' disruptive behavior.

Part V

Nonverbal Behavior in the Classroom

12 Basic Concepts and Issues in Nonverbal Research

WHAT IS NONVERBAL BEHAVIOR AND WHY IS IT IMPORTANT?

Nonverbal behavior (NV) is an integral part of human communication. It consists of all expressive aspects that have no verbal content, no words, and no spoken or written language. The visual and auditory aspects of behavior are all nonverbal: Facial expressions, gestures, body language, postures, movement, voice, tone and vocal clues (without verbal content), attire, and physical appearance. Also included in the NV domain are certain behavioral patterns in interpersonal interaction (e.g., personal space, touching, etc.) and characteristics of the setting and the environment.

We live in the era of the visual and are continuously exposed to NV aspects in television and movies. Children learn from a young age to understand NV language, to decipher implicit codes from what they see and hear and to make meaning of social situations from subtle NV nuances. We learn to understand social situations without having to receive verbal explanation. NV behavior is a rich source of information, whereas verbal behavior can be misleading and often deceptive.

A good example demonstrating the importance of the NV aspect is the popular internet chat in its form of the 1990s and the early parts of this century. Before the introduction of full picture chat, the chat was based on written verbal exchanges, and people chatted by writing verbal messages to each other. But something was missing in this form of interaction, and a special NV language—in the form of a library of NV icons and pictorial symbols to express emotional states such as happy, sad or smiling—was invented. A growing collection of icons was added to the software to enable the chatters to express NV emotional clues to accompany their verbal interaction.

DePaulo (1992) delineated the aspects of NV behavior which make it so important in social interaction: Its irrepressible nature; its links to emotion; its accessibility to observers; its speed; and the fact that it communicates unique meanings. The most important point is that NV behavior expresses and reflects emotional states (Ekman & Friesen, 1969a; 1971). In a way, NV behavior is the language of emotions, and feelings are expressed mainly in facial expressions (Ekman & Friesen, 1978). Emotions can, of course, be expressed in words and verbal content as well, but verbal expressions are more controlled and planned, and as we will see, they can sometimes be intentionally deceptive, compared to the more immediate and irrepressible nature of NV expression. People believe (with good reason) that NV behavior is more truthful and less susceptible to deception. Teachers and parents often tell children to "look me in the eyes," believing that attending to NV clues can help uncover and prevent concealment or deception. Finally, evidence shows that people (especially students) have an uncanny ability to decipher NV clues and to derive important social information about other people (especially their teachers) even from the briefest and most subtle NV nuances.

DePaulo and Friedman (1998) summarized the central research topics in contemporary NV psychology (see also Riggio & Feldman, 2005). The topics included:

- Person perception and personality judgments based on NV sensitivity;
- NV aspects in self-presentation;
- The study of deception and detection of lying;
- Social influence and attempts to manipulate impressions;
- NV aspects involved in interpersonal interaction;
- NV aspects involved in interpersonal attraction;
- The communication of expectations (by judges, doctors, and, of course, teachers);
- Studies on media bias and teachers' bias expressed in NV behavior have also been published in recent years (Babad, 2005a; Babad et al., 1989a).

This part of the book focuses on NV aspects and NV behavior of students and teachers, and analyzes the NV phenomena most relevant to teacher–student interaction in the classroom.

THE REPERTOIRE OF NV BEHAVIORS: FIVE TYPES OF NV BEHAVIOR

In a now-classic article, Ekman and Friesen (1969a) introduced and analyzed the five major types of NV behavior, laying the conceptual foundation for subsequent research on NV behavior. The five types are: Emblems; Illustrators; Affect displays; Regulators; and Adaptors. The types are described next, emphasizing their relevance to teachers and students in the classroom.

1. *Emblems* are complete NV acts that have a direct, clear and shared meaning. An emblem is a movement or a gesture which has a clear verbal definition consisting of one or two words or a phrase. They

are communicated intentionally in order to transmit a clear message. Examples of emblems include making a fist, pointing a finger and various obscene or sexual gestures, putting a finger at the temple to indicate lunacy (and, in another form, to indicate intelligence), hand movements indicating confusion or not knowing, head nod meaning yes and head side to side turning meaning no, etc. The smile might also be considered in some way as a generalized emblem expressing well-being and social facilitation. However, a substantial literature deals with different types of smiling expressions, intended and unintended, genuine and false. Sign language used by deaf people consists of sets of consensual emblems. Teachers often use emblems in their interactions with students, and also invent emblems to communicate particular messages to their students (for instance, a particular movement requiring silence in the classroom or inviting students to participate). Emblems are communicative and parsimonious, because they are complete, summative, consensual statements. Emblems are very often used in the visual language of the theatre and the movies, and viewers have no problems in understanding what is going on without actually seeing it in explicit pictures. Some emblems are universal across cultures, but most emblems are culture-bound and change from one culture to another. That is one of the reasons why new immigrants are usually confused at first in their new culture, because the emblems of the absorbing culture are not yet accessible to them.

2. *Illustrators* are face, hands, body and voice NV movements accompanying speech, serving to illustrate what is being said verbally. They are meant to emphasize and clarify intended messages or bits of instruction. Illustrators can sometime consist of emblems (though not always complete messages) and are often facial affect displays (see next). They are always intended to improve communication through illustration and amplification. Effective teachers are expressive and use NV illustrators continuously, and this is an important aspect of their effectiveness. In training for public speaking and in microteaching labs for teachers, trainees are taught and practiced in the use of illustrators.

3. *Affect displays* are the facial expressions of emotions, the movements of the facial muscles expressing the primary emotions. According to Ekman and Friesen (1969a), every primary emotion (e.g., happiness, surprise, fear, sadness, anger, disgust and interest) has unique, distinctive movements of the facial muscles that can be identified and measured, and these displays are universal to the human race. Ekman developed coding systems to quantify the measurement of facial expressions (e.g., Ekman & Friesen, 1978), and has led a very wide field of the study of emotions for several decades. Affect displays are extremely informative and important in every human interaction, but they are not deliberate and do not have a communicative intent as emblems and illustrators. Affect displays can be consonant or dissonant with intentional verbal messages, and the study of deception is

based on affect displays and on gaps between channels. In CM, teachers are supposed to be nonverbally expressive, and their genuine affect displays act as mediators in fostering student motivation and learning and in establishing positive classroom climate. Unfortunately, affect displays also play a crucial role in the transmission of teachers' negative expectancies, potentially hindering low-expectancy students via NV TDB (see Chapter 14).

4. *Regulators* are NV acts intended to regulate the back and forth interaction and to control the behavior of the other(s). Examples of regulators include head nods, eye contact, slight movements forward or backward, eyebrow raising, hand movements, etc. Regulators do not have a universal content and they are not necessarily deliberate or intentional. Affective displays, illustrators or adaptors (next) can function as regulators. Of course teachers must use NV regulators all the time, and these regulators are critical in CM and in teacher–student interaction.

5. *Adaptors* are anti-communicative NV acts, transmitting to the receiver that the person is busy with him/herself and with his/her own needs, and is not really available and attentive to the other. Examples of NV adaptors include self-referent behaviors such as grooming, nail-biting, head-scratching, fidgeting with self (self-touching) or with object (pencils, glasses, watch, etc.). Adaptors signal that the person is directed inside, toward the self and away from the other. In NV research, adaptors usually lead to negative predictions, contributing to negative impressions and leading to negative reactions. Teachers' sensitivity to students' expression of adaptors is highly important to maintain the learning atmosphere and to prevent student inattention (see Chapter 13). Conversely, adaptors expressed by teachers are detrimental to CC and to effective CM.

Display Rules

The expression of the human emotions is universal and measurable across cultures. However, display rules (Ekman, 1984) modulate and control the expression of emotion. Display rules are norms for the management of affective displays, to ensure that emotional expression would be appropriate. They prescribe who can show which emotion to whom and under what circumstances. Certainly not all the emotions that we experience at given moments are appropriate for direct expression, and we must learn display rules to control our expressive behavior. For example, sane workers would avoid expressing contempt toward their superiors, and students would more readily express their liking than their hate toward their teachers. Therefore, the NV expression of emotion is partly determined by automatic universal processes and partly by social regulation and self-control rules. Philippot, Feldman, and McGee (1992) reviewed various studies demonstrating the development of the ability to use display rules (for example, controlling one's facial expression when receiving a disappointing gift). In a way, the use of display rules and the exercise of self-control makes it possible to dissemble or to deceive others in social interaction.

Another line of research examines display rules in a cross-cultural perspective. Early research by Ekman and Friesen (in fact, Friesen's doctoral dissertation in 1972 under Ekman's supervision) analyzed culture specific display rules, demonstrating cultural norms about the expression of given emotions in given situations. Lee et al. (1992) discussed and illustrated cultural influences on NV behavior. This is highly important knowledge for teachers of culturally heterogeneous classrooms, because different students might be motivated by different display rules.

DECEPTION AND DETECTION

A sizable proportion of NV research is focused on issues of deception and detection, and this issue accompanies NV research ever since its early beginnings (see, for example, Vrij, 2000). In fact, Ekman and Friesen published two parallel seminal articles in 1969, one (1969a) on the repertoire of NV behaviors (presented above), and a second (1969b) on NV leakage and clues to deception.

Deception in NV Behavior

It is not adaptive for any individual—adult or child—to expose or express all emotions. We learn from a young age in the process of normal adjustment to control the expression of affect, to mask our emotions sometimes, and to express our feelings in useful and effective ways. The conception of display rules (above) represents self-regulation which is basically adaptive. Negative feelings are concealed more frequently, but sometimes positive feelings should not be displayed as well (as in the case of teachers' love of their pets in the classroom, Chapter 8). Concealment of affect can easily turn into dissembling, which is defined in the dictionaries as concealing feelings under some pretense, and this leads to putting a false appearance, that is, to emotional deception. This phenomenon exists, of course, in the verbal domain as well, but it is more pronounced in NV behavior because of its affective nature and its direct connection with emotions.

Because emotional deception is a common occurrence, the question arises whether we can detect the deception and identify the emotional false messages. A dynamic paradox is involved in the delicate balance between deception and detection. Concealment of some emotions and the use of display rules are adaptive and represent adjustment and mental health, but deception also hinders communication. Thus, much as it is important that children's self-regulation would include self-monitoring of their emotional expressions and deception, it is also important that teachers would learn to detect students' deception and to identify their concealed emotions.

Detection of NV Deception

As previously mentioned, investigation of deception and detection was prominent in NV research from its early beginnings, and various researchers were involved in it in addition to Paul Ekman, including Bella DePaulo, Mark Frank, Robert Feldman, Aldert Vrij, Robert Rosenthal and others. In a recent review of detection methodologies, Frank (2005) pointed out new practical implications of detecting deception in counter-terrorism and intelligence gathering, in addition to the implications of detection in many life domains, including customs checkpoints along national borders, marriage, the workplace, and of course the classroom. Very extensive research, and applied work of similar nature, were published by Vrij (2000) over the years. There is a commonly held belief that NV clues can be helpful in identifying deception and in tracing hidden feelings and meanings. The truth is that this belief is indeed borne out by empirical findings, but detection processes are not as simple and straightforward as some people would wish to believe. To quote Frank (2005, p. 342), "Scientists studying deception over the past century have noted one thing—that, unlike the fictional Pinocchio, whose nose grew in response to telling a lie, there is no specific verbal or nonverbal deception clue that appears in people in all situations to indicate deception" (see also DePaulo, 1994, DePaulo et al. 2003). However, these same reviews also concluded that some clues can identify deception quite reliably, because liars appear to be less forthcoming, their accounts are less compelling, they appear to be more tense, and their accounts are a bit too polished. Summarizing the conclusions and evidence from various sources (DePaulo et al., 2003, Ekman, 1985; Frank, 2005; Philippot et al., 1992; Vrij, 2000; and Zuckerman, DePaulo & Rosenthal, 1986), it can be said that concealed affect can potentially be traced in natural observations because often:

1. Liars are too planned, non-spontaneous and deliberate;
2. Liars exaggerate the expression of the false emotion;
3. Liars are tense and perhaps feel guilty, and their tension and guilt might be picked up; and because
4. Deception leaks through less controllable NV channels. The leakage phenomenon and the research methodology used to investigate leakage are delineated next in more detail.

Research on NV Leakage

The conception of leakage is based on the separation of NV channels. The theoretical assumption is that people cannot control all their verbal and nonverbal channels to the same extent, and controllability varies among channels. Therefore, when people lie and transmit a false message, they will be more convincing in the channels that they can control well, but their concealed emotion might leak and be detected through the channels that they cannot control. A separation of channels and the comparison between the perceived emotions transmitted in each channel would indicate a discrepancy when people lie.

Let's assume that one wants to conceal anger or boredom, transmitting outwardly instead a false sense of friendliness or of alert interest. In the leakage hierarchy, the channel that can be best controlled when lying is the verbal channel. Therefore, words expressing friendliness or interest might be quite convincing, and the lie would not be detected. I always tell my students that if they wish to lie successfully, they should convey their message in writing, through a note, a letter or an Email message. The next channel in the leakage hierarchy is the face. We cannot fully control our eyes and our facial expressions, and therefore the face leaks more than the verbal channel. The term poker face represents the relatively strong control when lying and transmitting a false emotion, whereas "look me in the eye" represents the potential leakage of the lie in the face. Body language and gestures are less controllable than the face and more likely to leak, and the tone of voice (without attending to words and verbal content) is very leaky. If we listen to the voice but ignore the words, or if we look at the body, we stand a good chance of identifying the true, concealed emotion and detect lying.

Thus, in the preceding example about deception in trying to transmit false interest, spoken words would be most successful in portraying interest, the face would be judged as showing less interest, and the body and the NV tone of voice would most likely expose the boredom. The leakage phenomenon is well established in research (Ekman & Friesen, 1969b; Rosenthal & DePaulo, 1979; see also DePaulo & Rosenthal, 1979), including a study on the leakage of teachers' concealed anger in the classroom (Babad et al., 1989b, see Chapter 6).

Research on NV leakage is conducted in lab-aided judgment studies. People's verbal and NV behavior when lying and when not lying must be first filmed or videotaped. Then, a given segment of behavior must be divided into separate clips, each depicting that same segment in one isolated channel. One clip would show the words spoken in that segment (written, with no video and no audio), another clip would show the face (with no sound), still another clip would show the body (no sound), and a fourth clip would carry the tone of voice (without being able to understand the verbal content). Each clip would be presented to a different group of judges, who would be asked to judge the actor's emotion through the one channel they were exposed to. In leakage of concealed anger, the verbal content (words) would be judged as being most friendly, the face would be judged as being less friendly, the body would be judged as expressing more anger, and the tone of voice would be perceived as the angriest.

In daily interactions with others we cannot conduct controlled judgment studies, but we can, and do, apply the principle of channel separation to detect concealed affect. If we try to separate the channels and attend to each alone, we can detect the inconsistency among the different messages we perceive, and inconsistency signals deception. Our social effectiveness depends on our ability to read social situations correctly and to identify false messages. Persons who lack the skill and ability of decoding NV messages correctly can easily fall prey to those who wish to take advantage of them.

THREE BASIC NV SKILLS: EMOTIONAL EXPRESSIVITY (ENCODING), EMOTIONAL SENSITIVITY (DECODING), AND EMOTIONAL CONTROL (DISPLAY RULES)

In recent decades, numerous NV researchers have focused on NV skills and the relationships between NV skills on the one hand and social competence, success in the social world and psychological well-being on the other hand. Their view of these phenomena as skills or abilities rather than personality traits is based on the assumption that such abilities can be developed and trained, so that people can increase their social competence. The three NV skills described next are distinct from each other in expressing different emotional abilities. However, the skills are correlated with each other, and people of high social competence utilize all three skills effectively. Ronald Riggio (1992) emphasized the importance of these NV skills in social interaction: in initial encounters with others; in impression management and in adaptive deception; in relationships formation and in relationship maintenance. Philippot et al. (1992) analyzed the role and importance of NV skills in the educational context.

1. *Emotional expressivity—Encoding ability.* This is the sending skill, the ability to transmit and communicate emotional messages to other people. Encoding ability involves the expression of emotions in NV ways beyond the verbal expression. Emotions are nonverbally transmitted through facial expressions and gestures, through tone of voice and paralinguistic cues, and through body movements and posture. In initial encounters with others, expressive persons have several advantages over non-expressive persons: Their behavior is more attractive and attention-getting, and they are more noticeable and more inviting to others to interact with them. And indeed highly expressive people (and expressive teachers, of course) are more popular and better appreciated than non-expressive people. In terms of social exchange, expressive people give more emotional stuff (including self-disclosure) to their partners in social relationships, and therefore tend to receive more in return. In this way they maintain and deepen their social relationships. In contrast, people with less developed encoding skills appear to be shy and remote, they refrain from expressing their feelings and they do not readily enter emotionally into interactions with others.

2. *Emotional sensitivity—Decoding ability.* The decoding skill complements the encoding skill. It is the ability to perceive, to interpret and to decode the NV displays of others. Since the publication of "Skill in nonverbal communication" (Rosenthal, 1979) and the PONS test for measuring decoding ability (Rosenthal et al., 1979), hundreds of studies on NV sensitivity have been published, and various instruments for measuring decoding ability were constructed. Archer (1980), who was partner in the development of several tests for decoding ability, argued that NV sensitivity is the key for social intelligence. Various studies in Feldman's (1992) book indicate that decoding ability is acquired naturally in normal development, but at the same time it can be improved through training and guidance. Effective decoders can read the NV behavior of others and to detect subtle NV nuances in order to improve the interaction. One example is to maintain effective turn-taking in classroom interaction by using NV cues, being in tune with the other(s) and enhancing a sense of mutual understanding. Decoding skill enables the person to avoid the pitfalls of deception in the interactions with others. Highly skilled decoders have keen detection ability, and therefore they can decide how to react to the deceptive messages of others (discussion in the next chapter describes students' ability in decoding teachers' NV behavior and deception). Philippot et al. (1992) reported that decoding ability was related to sociometric status (Chapter 4) and to various measures of social competence (Chapter 2).

3. *Emotional control—Display rules.* The third basic NV skill is emotional control, and it is the funnel through which NV skills lead to social competence. The advantages of encoding and decoding skills are complemented by emotional control. Based on a deep understanding of display rules, this skill helps individuals to regulate their NV behavior and to make it situation-appropriate. This ability of self-regulation (self-monitoring in Snyder's, 1987, terms) enables the person to avoid spilling over in NV expressiveness, to control her/his emotional displays, and to use deception when necessary. The contemporary conception of CM emphasizes the attainment of students' self-regulation as the primary goal of CM (Chapter 9). Similarly, the attainment of emotional control in the NV domain is critical for social adjustment and for attaining psychological well-being. Without skill in emotional self-control, expressivity can run wild and hinder the individual in impression management. Emotional control skill also enables the individual to deceive others when necessary, and some measure of deception can be adaptive in the social environment. This would be particularly true for individuals in a lower social position in the social hierarchy (such as students vis-à-vis their teachers). Emotional control is one of the more potent instruments in the hands of the low-status person. In maintenance of ongoing social relationships,

Riggio (1992) argued that "perhaps the most important NV skill is the ability to regulate the communication of affect" (p. 18).

Gender Differences in NV skills

This book does not deal with gender differences. However, an exception is made in the case of NV skills, because the most frequently asked question about NV behavior is whether the belief that females are more sensitive and more intuitive than males has any empirical grounding. Most of the leading researchers on NV behavior have written about this issue, and there is wide agreement that indeed the stereotype is well-grounded and, on average, women are better encoders and better decoders than men (see, for example, Hall, 1978, 1984, 1998; Riggio, 1992). Women are more emotionally expressive than men, especially in their facial expressions, and display greater frequencies of smiling and facial animation. Women are also superior to men in their decoding ability, they score higher than men on standardized tests of decoding ability; they are more attentive to NV stimuli; and they can detect deception better than men. On the other hand, men appear to have an advantage in the third NV skill—emotional control. They have greater ability than women to control their emotional displays and to inhibit spontaneous expression of emotion. This ability might be quite helpful in certain social interactions, where lack of emotional self-control might hinder the individual.

NV Behavior in the Classroom Context

The classroom is an arena of continuous social interaction. Teachers are supposed to advance students' development in all domains—academic, social and emotional. Presumably, students and teachers share school's educational goals and should act in unison to attain them, but the realities and psychological complexities of the classroom refute this idyllic image (as discussed in Chapter 1). The classroom is often an arena of continued struggle, and students and teachers have cross-purposes on many daily issues.

Strong emotions are experienced and expressed in the classroom—by each student, between pairs of students, among the students in the classroom, by the student group as a whole, by the teacher, and in teacher–student interaction. Because the NV is the language of emotion, most of this emotional flow is expressed through NV channels, with or without the conscious awareness of the students or the teacher. Greater NV sensitivity and decoding ability would provide teachers with a deeper understanding of the emotional undercurrents in the classroom, and greater encoding ability would enable them to be more effective in CM.

The central objectives of schooling are cognitive development and scholastic achievement. As far as academic learning is concerned, it is the verbal domain that is most important in education. Curriculum, didactics, pedagogy, thinking abilities, knowledge, information processing, reading and writing are enacted mainly through the use of language and verbal processes. In that sense, the role of the NV in education is secondary. But the NV is a critical factor in the delivery of instruction and in CM, mediating teachers' success in attaining the primary goals of education. Bad teachers most often fail in their NV delivery and NV skills, whereas excellence in teaching is always characterized by teachers' positive expressive style. The next chapters discuss students' NV behavior and NV skills, and teachers' NV behavior in the classroom. The focus and emphasis on NV behavior is relevant to all previous chapters in this book, illuminating and emphasizing the emotional aspects in the life of the classroom society.

13 Students' Nonverbal Behavior

NV SKILLS AS COMPONENTS OF STUDENTS' SOCIAL COMPETENCE

Students' success in school is a dual function of their cognitive abilities and learning skills (resulting in academic achievements) on the one hand, and of their social intelligence and social competence (resulting in well-being and psychological adjustment) on the other hand. Students must adjust socially and find their place in the classroom society, maintain mutual relationships with other students, and cope well with the teachers and their demands. Because of the importance of the emotional domain in students' lives in the classroom society, NV skills become critical for good adjustment and for attaining self-efficacy. All three types of NV skills are important for students' well being in the classroom: Decoding ability which enables students to have deeper and clearer understanding of emotional processes and undercurrents in the classroom; encoding ability that improves self-expression and makes the student better understood by peers and teachers; and emotional control which keeps students' NV expression within appropriate and acceptable limits and saves them from trouble with their teachers and peers.

Thus, self-monitoring and self-control are important end states of CM in both the verbal and the NV domain. The extensive literature on CM is not sufficiently detailed in specifying for teachers exactly how they should guide students into self-control, and the NV domain is particularly neglected in the CM literature. Perhaps CM in the verbal domain might be more explicit and easier to describe because of the mediation of spoken language, whereas NV CM is more subtle and hidden. But it is really important that teachers gain working knowledge in the psychology of NV communication so that they understand the central phenomena of teachers' and students' NV behavior.

Philippot et al. (1992) and Riggio (1992) reviewed numerous studies that indicate that NV skills (especially encoding and decoding skills) are related to students' social competence, to their (sociometric) status in the classroom society, and to their psychological well-being. Summarizing their chapter on NV skills in educational contexts, Philippot et al. (1992) wrote:

Educational settings can be considered as social contexts in which cultural and social knowledge is provided and exchanged. We have seen that nonverbal behavior plays an important part in this socially contextualized exchange of information. . . . We have also shown how the communication of motivation and emotion, according to socially prescribed rules, is a necessary component of the educational process. Hence, the "know-how" to express and understand nonverbal cues in social contexts constitutes an essential set of skills for all the participants involved. (pp. 208–209).

STUDENTS WITH PERCEIVED DEFICIENCIES IN NV SKILLS

Students with deficiencies in NV skills are usually problem students in the classroom. Their problems are not limited to the NV domain, and they have difficulties in all domains, verbal and nonverbal, academic and social. But without competence in the three NV skills (decoding ability, encoding ability and emotional control), these students find it hard to adjust and get integrated in the classroom society. They do not manage well with other children and their interactions with their teachers are problematic, subsequently influencing their academic performance.

Robert Feldman and his associates conducted numerous studies on NV skills of problem students in the classroom. Philippot et al. (1992) used the euphemism atypical populations to refer to all special students in the classroom. Atypical populations include students from low socioeconomic background and broken families, abused and neglected students, violent and aggressive children, students with various learning disabilities and children with emotional disturbances and various mental problems. In most school systems, the contemporary policy is to integrate all problem children in the regular classrooms whenever possible. That policy increases the heterogeneity in the classroom and forces teachers to cope with atypical populations within the classroom both in the academic/instructional domain and the social/emotional domain.

It cannot really be determined whether deficits in NV skills are a cause or a consequence—whether the lack of developed NV skills hinders the students and turns them into problem students, or whether their particular social or emotional problems cause faulty development of their NV skills. Possibly there is no clear cause preceding the consequences but rather a vicious cycle, where the deficits in NV skills and the emotional problems feed and intensify each other. In any case, Feldman and his associates provided evidence from many sources demonstrating the deficits in NV skills of various types of atypical populations.

It is difficult to remedy academic and social problems of students who do not possess well-developed NV skills. Quite often, special education and communication specialists decide that interventions to develop the NV skills of problem children must take first priority. The meaning of deficit is that some students simply cannot read social situations and do not understand NV nuances, and they lack the ability to express themselves appropriately in social situations. A deficit differs from a motivational problem in the same sense as the difference between "cannot do" and "would not do." Each requires a different response and a different treatment by teachers and school staff.

A very special and salient instance of deficits in NV skills is the case of autism and its mild version in the form of the Asperger Syndrome. Autism is a neuro-developmental disorder characterized by impairment of the ability to form normal social relationships, by inability to interact with others, and by rigid and stereotypic behavior patterns. Autism develops at a very young age, and autistic children cannot be students in a normal classroom because they are detached and cannot participate in conventional social interchange. Asperger Syndrome (Baskin, Sperber, & Price, 2006) is quite similar to autism but is much less severe—Asperger children study in regular classrooms and are not detached from the social environment, although they are usually considered quite strange. Asperger children have difficulties integrating socially, although their intelligence appears normal or even superior. They cannot read social cues (decoding), they lack the ability to communicate their own emotional states (encoding), and they find it hard to know what is acceptable and what is not (display rules). They often have an all-absorbing interest in a single topic, they appear clumsy and uncoordinated, and they often say things that other children avoid saying. Because of such expressions, their peers might consider them too honest, but these manifestations stem from lack of understanding what is appropriate, and inability to understand the thoughts and feelings of others. When they learn social skills, their learning is logical and intellectual rather than intuitive.

Feldman and his associates investigated NV skills of autistic and non-autistic students using different research designs, and found autistic children to demonstrate both decoding and encoding deficits. The same would probably be true for Asperger Syndrome children. Asperger children are usually isolated in the classroom society despite their high intelligence. Their peers, and often their teachers as well, cannot understand why the Asperger children fail to understand social situations and so often implicate themselves in strange and inappropriate situations.

A totally different source of phenomena that might have the appearance of deficits in NV skills involves cross-cultural differences in affective behavior in different cultures. The NV behavior of students of certain ethnic minority groups in the classroom might appear different and incomprehensible to majority culture members, and it often violates conventional norms and expectations. This stems mainly from cross-cultural differences in display rules. A behavior or a gesture that is appropriate and desirable in the majority culture might be considered offensive and insulting in another culture. A minority culture student who enacts certain behaviors according to her/his socialization might face a problem in the heterogeneous classroom and might be considered atypical, with perceived deficiencies in decoding and encoding. In Western culture, for example, looking the other person straight in the eye is desirable and encouraged, but in several cultures such behavior is considered very offensive and must be avoided. The same is true for other NV behavior expressing emotional states, and the Western expressiveness is considered vulgar and exaggerated in many ethnic groups.

In the early 1980s, my colleagues and I (Babad et al., 1983) investigated cross-cultural differences in smiling behavior between children in the USA and Israel. American children are socialized to smile a lot to acquaintances and to strangers, and the normative behavior would be to return the smile of the stranger. In Israel (and perhaps in other European countries as well), returning the smile of a friendly stranger would not be encouraged, and over-smiling is considered phony and undesirable. In an experimental situation where we actually measured the frequency of returning the smile of a friendly, non-threatening stranger, substantial differences in smiling were found between American and Israeli children. That would mean that children who would demonstrate their socialized NV behavior in the other culture (Israeli children in the USA, American children in Israel), would be considered "atypical" and deficient in their NV skills.

STUDENTS AS ENCODERS IN THE CLASSROOM

As mentioned, skill in NV encoding is a necessary condition for student success in the classroom society. Students are constantly interacting with each other and express themselves verbally and nonverbally. The ability to communicate—of which encoding ability is a central component—enhances their social relations and their status in the student society.

Students' NV encoding also plays a major role in student-teacher interaction. When students express themselves nonverbally, the teacher is the decoder of their messages. Students transmit to the teacher messages concerning their state and their feelings. Some of these messages are specific and situational, others are global messages beyond specific contingencies. In these global NV messages, each student tells the teacher about his/her well-being, level of motivation, wish to participate, or about problems and distress in any of these areas. Teachers who are sensitive decoders know a lot about each student from their NV expressions. Sensitive teachers can also pick up quickly any change in a student's well-being from the student's NV encoding.

Situational students' encoding (and complementary teacher's decoding) is critical for running each classroom session and for actual instruction. Through students' NV cues the teacher knows whether they understand, whether they are concentrated, and who requires more instructional attention at a given moment. Most of this information flows in great speed without being verbalized, enabling the teacher to keep the flow of the learning/instructional process. When the teacher and the students are involved in a dialogue, students' NV cues (and teachers' cues as well, of course) help to keep turn-taking as smooth as possible. Several writers have focused on the role of NV skills in interactional turn-taking, a process that combines encoding and decoding skills and enables people to take turns smoothly and effectively in any kind of interaction. Again, these NV cues are almost never verbalized, and if they need to be verbalized, that in itself signals a communication problem.

The other side of the classroom scene involves various disturbances, conflicts, avoidance of classroom work, etc. Here, again, the combination of students' encoding and teachers' decoding allows quick and early diagnosis which enables teachers to prevent problems before they escalate. Students' moods, especially the potentially disruptive ones, are usually signaled and transmitted, and early detection can save a lot of trouble.

As in many areas of human interaction, gaps between verbal messages and NV behavior are very informative. Teachers can detect such gaps through their decoding of students' encoded behavior. For instance, students hate to admit that they do not understand something, and would prefer to (verbally) say: "I understand." The teacher can use NV cues to know if a student had understood or not. This is actually a situation of leakage detection by teacher's intuitive decoding. Such situations are very frequent for adults and students alike. For example, when people bump their heads accidentally on a window or a door, the most common response is to pretend that nothing happened and no pain is felt. Similarly, when students (or adults) are reprimanded, a typical response is a show of "I'm OK, nothing happened to me." As was mentioned several times before, the ability to deceive nonverbally is important and quite adaptive for the maintenance of human interaction. On the other hand, teachers' ability to detect students' deception is very important for their effectiveness as classroom managers.

STUDENTS' AS DECODERS OF TEACHERS' NV BEHAVIOR

The decoding skill is part of social intelligence, and students' ability to understand underlying emotional processes and to decode fine and subtle NV cues is critical for social and academic adjustment. It is part of students' social survival kit, so to speak. Most of the emotional processes are implicit, subtle and hidden, and verbal messages are often deceptive and misleading. Good decoders have a social advantage because they can read and understand the subtle messages of their peers and their teachers. In a way, they have more social knowledge at their disposal. And if their decoding ability is accompanied by effective encoding ability, they can be successful in the classroom society.

In effective CM, teachers try to reach a state in which they would not have to repeatedly spell out everything in explicit verbal terms, and minimal NV cues would be sufficient to inform the students what is expected at a given moment. A facial expression, a short sound or a body movement of the teacher would be enough to invite students to involve in turntaking, to quiet down, to ask questions, to help each other, or to behave in one of many expected options. Because so many messages of effective teachers are not explicit, they must be picked up through students' NV sensitivity. Thus, both students and teachers utilize their NV decoding abilities to understand each other and to smooth the flow of communication in the classroom.

Beyond the usage of NV cues as shortcuts for effective CM, teachers have much to conceal from their students, especially in the affective domain. It is true that the contemporary model of CM requires teachers to express their emotions and to form emotional relationships with their students, but the model does not allow full spontaneity and expression of *all* teacher feelings. Most negative emotions and expressions of teachers' stress and anger must be suppressed, and teachers should express only their positive and productive feelings. The frustrations and stress in the teaching profession are tremendous, and teachers must learn to conceal their negative feelings. Therefore, teachers involve in NV deception no less than other people, perhaps even more. Babad et al. (1989b; see also Babad, 1992) demonstrated empirically NV leakage of anger on the part of biased teachers. Therefore, students' ability to decipher teachers' NV behavior becomes particularly important.

Students become experts in decoding their teachers' behavior. They are very sophisticated in absorbing implicit messages and in uncovering concealed emotions and leakage. Paradoxically, the fact that many teachers believe that they can easily conceal from their students whatever they wish to conceal just adds to the students' expertise and sophistication in decoding their teachers' behavior. Students learn to know what their teachers think of them and how smart they are (Weinstein, 2002; Weisnstien et al., 1987). In light of the teacher expectancy research and the extensive investigation of TDB (Chapter 7), perhaps it might be stated that students learn to decode what their teachers *really* think of them—often in contrary to teachers' verbal statements.

In a series of studies, Feldman and his associates (Allen & Atkinson, 1981; see Feldman, 1992) compared the ability of young students and adults (most of whom were teachers) in decoding students' NV expressions when listening to a very easy or a very difficult lesson. They found that the young students demonstrated decoding ability superior to the adults.

In my own research, the most impressive piece of evidence on students' uncanny decoding ability of teachers' NV behavior was found in high school (Babad 2005b). In that research, eleventh-grade students viewed ten-second video clips of teachers' NV behavior while lecturing to their entire classrooms. The teachers were unknown to them, and the students' exposure to these teachers was limited to ten seconds of public lecturing to unknown (and unseen) students. After viewing the clips, the students were asked to guess the degree to which each teacher would demonstrate differential behavior (TDB) toward high- versus low-achievers in other situations. Their guesses/judgments were compared to actual measures of those teachers' TDB from analyses of their NV classroom behavior and from the judgments of their actual classroom students. The amazing finding was that those eleventh-graders could indeed guess TDB beyond chance, although they did not see those teachers interact with any student at all and only saw them teaching their entire classrooms. These predictive correlations were significant and quite substantial. Adult judges who completed the same judgment task failed to make any prediction of TDB. Thus, students are really experts in deciphering and decoding teachers' NV behavior.

14 Teachers' Nonverbal Behavior

TEACHERS' NV DECODING AND ENCODING
IN CLASSROOM INTERACTION

Teacher–student interaction is an exchange process in which the parties play complementary roles vis-à-vis each other. Teachers' behaviors and responses are the students' stimuli, and students' behaviors (responses) are their teachers' stimuli. The same complementary process is relevant for NV exchanges between teachers and students, with decoding and encoding of students and teachers complementing each other. In the classroom, teachers are the decoders of students' encoded NV expressions, and the teachers are encoders who express themselves in NV behavior that is decoded by their students.

Because the emotional processes in the classroom are extremely important, the NV domain and NV behavior play a major role in the life and the management of the classroom. Teachers' decoding skill make it possible for them to read their classrooms instantaneously. They can decipher fine nuances of students' NV behavior and understand their influence on the flow of the classroom process. By decoding students' NV expressions they know when students understand the study material and when they do not. In this way, teachers receive immediate NV feedback on the effectiveness of their instructional and social activities. Therefore, they know how to modulate their behavior toward the entire class and toward particular students. Their decoding skill is also very helpful in managing the turn-taking process that is so important in academic interchanges. Finally, teachers' decoding skill enables them to identify potential problems "in the bud," so to speak, and to take preventive action that can reduce the severity of a full-blown problem.

Through their encoding skills, teachers control their classrooms, direct various processes and facilitate the desired atmosphere and the appropriateness of students' behavior. Teachers' expressions provide students with important information: They know when the teachers are patient or not, when they are angry, when they are satisfied, and when they are determined. Teachers' expressions give the cues for the appropriate atmosphere at any given moment—solemn, amused, task-oriented, challenging, punitive, and so on and so forth. Teachers actually use their NV expression as a shortcut in CM, where things become known and understood instantaneously with no need for long verbal explanations. Through their NV encoding, teachers also keep guard that the appropriate display rules are maintained by the students.

Effective teachers use the entire repertoire of NV behavior types (Ekman & Friesen, 1969a) in their classrooms (see chapter 12):

1. *Emblems.* Because emblems are complete NV messages with a clear, consensual meaning, and because they are very concise, effective teachers find emblems very useful as parsimonious shortcuts in classroom interaction. Because the classroom is a closed society, teachers can invent new emblems that would be valid only for that classroom and for that particular teacher. Particular NV gestures can become emblems through systematic application. The students can learn that a distinct type of teacher's silence, raised eyebrow or wink, or a particular finger or arm movement would always carry a given message in that teacher's classroom. Thus, these NV behaviors become classroom specific emblems and serve their communicative objective in that classroom.

2. *Illustrators.* Illustrators are the bread and butter of effective instruction. The NV joins the verbal to clarify verbally taught material through NV illustration. Our understanding of words, terms, phenomena and sometimes of whole sentences can be greatly enhanced through NV illustration. Sometimes the illustration alone can cause understanding. Effective teachers use NV illustration very frequently in their instruction. I believe that illustrators are particularly important for instructional processes, whereas emblems and regulators, and to some extent affect displays, are more relevant for the CM components of teachers' work.

3. *Affect displays.* Affect display is the central medium and the major instrument of emotionality and expressivity. The demand for expressivity is especially important as part of the teacher's role, because of teachers' responsibility for the emotional development and adjustment of their students. And indeed by all accounts good teachers are expressive teachers. Teachers should not necessarily express all their emotions, they should not necessarily show high intensity of expressivity, and they should be selective situation-wise—but they should be generally expressive. Non-expressive teachers whose affect displays are minimal are not considered good teachers. Expressive teachers serve as models for their students and encourage them actively to be expressive, and this is an important part of the facilitation of students' growth.

4. *Regulators.* As mentioned several times, NV regulators are important mechanisms in CM. Effective teachers use regulators as parsimonious

shortcuts for maintaining the order and controlling the instructional and social flow in the classroom.

5. *Adaptors.* Adaptors are anti-communicative and hinder the effectiveness of teacher–student interaction. When students perceive their teachers as expressing the self-referent behavior typical of adaptors, they may lose their concentration and their task-orientation, because the teacher does not seem to be concentrated and task-oriented. It would be inhuman to demand that teachers refrain totally from expressing any adaptors in the classroom throughout their daily long presence in the classroom. However, it is reasonable to demand that teachers would become aware of their typical adaptors and would attempt to minimize their appearance and reduce their intensity.

DISPLAY RULES AND TEACHERS' DECEPTION

The basic meaning of display rules is that NV expression of teachers and students alike should stay within appropriate boundaries and would not spill over beyond them. We all remember isolated dramatic instances from our school days when a student or a teacher (or both) violated the display rules and their emotional behavior deviated from the acceptable norms. After such a break, it is difficult to remedy the situation and return to the legitimate boundaries. The struggle between students and teachers about norm-setting in the classroom society (Chapter 1) also involves a struggle over display rules and the determination of boundaries for legitimate and illegitimate emotional expression.

The role of teacher requires strict limits and self-control over emotional expression. Teachers should avoid extravagant self-presentation and their expressive style should demonstrate their boundaries. Teachers' violations of display rules have more severe consequences than students' violations.

I believe that the contemporary conception of CM (Chapter 9) might be somewhat misleading for inexperienced teachers. It over-emphasizes the demand for teachers' emotional expressivity and spontaneity in the classroom but fails to provide a complementary emphasis on display rules to direct teachers how to rationally control their emotional expression. It is implied in that literature that teachers should be mature and responsible in their emotional expression, but no serious guidance for teachers is provided, and the issue remains unattended. Statements like: "Be firm—but never punish" or "Express your emotions, but avoid being negative" leave teacher-training students quite confused. I am reminded of a fortune cookie I once received in a Chinese restaurant that read: "Be spontaneous—even if you do not mean it".

Teachers should try to avoid expressing some of the emotions they experience in the classroom, and there is substantial playacting in teacher's classroom work. Intense feelings in reaction to personal events external to the classroom should of course be suppressed, but many classroom-related feelings should also remain unexpressed. Anger at students, frustration about failings in instruction or in CM should be held under control and not expressed spontaneously.

Sometimes teachers must transmit positive feelings of sympathy that perhaps they do not really feel, and positive beliefs in the potential of particular students that perhaps they lack. On the other hand, teachers sometimes experience positive feelings that they should lock inside such as their love for their pets (Chapter 8), or when they are amused by some students, but a show of their amusement might be offensive to those students. The same holds for being bored in the classroom.

Teachers must sometimes control the expression of both positive feelings and of negative feelings. The same holds true in the expression of differential feelings toward different students (Chapter 7) which can pose a real threat to classroom climate. As is demonstrated later in this chapter, TDB in teachers' NV behavior can have very negative consequences in their classrooms.

Thus, we have a dual perspective in viewing teachers' NV emotional expression. The overall consensus asserts that teachers must be emotionally expressive in their classrooms. That pertains both to their interactions with their students and to their enthusiasm about their subject matter, and about their role as teachers. This demand is a central component of the social and academic classroom atmosphere that contributes to harmony and students' satisfaction and achievement. On the other hand, much of teachers' affect cannot be freely expressed in the classroom, spontaneity must be controlled, and sometimes teachers must be deceptive, that is, to express feelings they do not really experience.

TEACHERS AS LIE DETECTORS

Truth is a supreme value in our culture. All value orientations—regardless of other differences among them—emphasize the importance of truth-telling as a most desirable cultural goal. The educational system should socialize children to value truth, and teachers should serve as role models in the appreciation and expression of truth. And yet, from a social psychological point of view it is clear that people should sometimes deviate from truth-telling. On many occasions social harmony is possible only if people avoid telling the truth or even deceive others.

Lying is sometimes functional and adaptive, and we need the ability to lie in order to be socially competent. White lies, such as dinner guests asserting that the food is very tasty or that a given dress is really beautiful on somebody, are normative and socially necessary. When someone wakes you up by ringing your phone, a normative response would be to lie and say: "No, I was awake." When we hit the door clumsily in front of other people, a typical reaction would be to avoid showing pain and to pretend that nothing happened.

Theories of social development emphasize that an important social skill that must be acquired in childhood is the ability to lie. Children learn both how to lie and how to detect when other people are lying. Once this social skill is developed, the choice when to lie and when to tell the truth should be based on a combination of (acquired) moral judgment and considerations of social expediency. Mordechai Nisan, a developmental psychologist who theorized about moral development, stressed the moral balance that people learn to calculate for themselves in the conflict between different considerations of how one ought to behave in particular social situations. His concept of limited morality (Nisan, 1991) contends that people allow themselves some deviations from what they judge to be proper behavior (and in this case, truthfulness). He argued that such deviation does not stem from weakness of will or imply any departure from morality.

Therefore we sometimes lie to others and we do not necessarily expose every lie we detect in the behavior of others. Bella DePaulo, one of the early experts on gender differences in NV detection, said that women with a developed skill of detecting NV leakage sometimes decide to avoid demonstrating their detecting skill when people lie, because such sensitivity might cost them in social status among their acquaintances.

As managers of a complex and volatile society, teachers are not expected to always tell the truth, the whole truth, and nothing but the truth. On many occasions they have to be deceptive, and often they detect students' lying but decide to avoid exposing the liars. Such behavior does not contradict teachers' overall value of pursuing the truth. Teachers would lie only when necessary, and hope that they are skillful enough to avoid being detected by their students.

Students' lying is a very common phenomenon in the classroom. Because of their low status and lack of power vis-à-vis the teacher, and because of many other social reasons, many students lie often, trying to make various social gains or avoid social losses by not telling the truth. Their lying might be acceptable on some occasions but unacceptable on many other occasions. Effective teachers exercise some leeway in allowing or disallowing students to be deceptive. Typical examples where students might lie include: not admitting that one does not understand something; denying that one did not do an assignment; cheating on an exam or assignment; insisting that the other started a fight or dispute; receiving a reprimand with a poker face although one is steaming inside, and so on and so forth. When mediating between fighting students or between disputing versions of the truth, teachers should be skilled in separating liars from truth-tellers. They must not expose every deception they detect, but they must be able to detect the underlying truth and then make a rational decision how to deal with the information they had decoded.

Teachers' overall objective is to reduce students' lying and to teach students how to make social gains and avoid social losses without lying. In any event, because lying is a common occurrence in the classroom, teachers' skill in lie detection is a key element in their psychological toolbox as classroom managers. Their effectiveness is enhanced if their students believe that their teacher always sees everything and cannot be manipulated.

As lie detectors, teachers use all the clues to NV deception known in the literature (see Chapter 12):

1. They observe gaps in emotional expression between spoken words, facial expressions, body movements and the voice.
2. They perceive exaggeration in students' expressions.
3. They diagnose over-planning, deliberate and non-spontaneous behavior.
4. They trace hints of tension and guilt.
5. Their detection is aided by their previous history of interaction (of lying and truth-telling) with each student, so that atypical conduct becomes quite noticeable.
6. The verbal domain is also available to teachers in lie detection situations, and a dialogue with the student and a verbal inquiry can also be helpful. However, on the basis of the literature on deception and the fact that students are very sophisticated in dealing with teachers, I tend to believe that NV clues might be more helpful to teachers, because lying is less detectable from verbal behavior!

POSITIVE NV BEHAVIOR: TEACHERS' ENTHUSIASM AND IMMEDIACY

Some of the NV aspects discussed up to this point—deception, leakage, lying and violation of display rules—might be considered negative. The next discussion is focused on the most positive and desirable NV phenomenon—teachers' overall expressive style. Teachers' expressivity contributes to harmony, satisfaction and positive climate in the classroom. This discussion shifts from specific aspects of teacher-student interaction and CM to teachers' overall instructional style and the role of NV behavior in their general conduct. Overall style includes how teachers appear, sound and behave when they teach, how they relate not only to their students but also to the subject matter and to their instructional role. Substantial evidence demonstrates consistently that teachers' overall expressive instructional style can contribute to students' learning and motivation.

Next, I discuss two branches of literature dealing with teachers' overall expressive style. Readers must be aware, however, that these lines of research were largely focused on higher education, characterizing university instructors and their students. At the university level, instruction is more teacher-centered compared to the more student-centered instruction of the early grades. Therefore, teachers' instructional style may gain in its relative importance. One of the reasons why these lines of research were conducted mainly in higher education contexts is the availability of standard students' ratings of their teachers and their evaluation of instruction as outcome measures. Such student evaluations of teachers are usually not collected in the elementary and high school levels. However, some studies had been conducted in the lower grades, and the conclusions of the various studies are generally applicable to all levels of schooling.

Since the beginning of the 1980s, two separate and totally independent research literatures examined the impact of teachers' expressivity on students' learning, motivation, and evaluations of their teachers. Amazingly, researchers in the two branches have ignored each other almost totally, although they investigated the same phenomenon (under different titles, it must be admitted), used almost identical measurement instruments, and reported very similar findings. One group originated in a Psychology Department in Canada (Murray, 1983a, 1983b, at the University of Western Ontario) and investigated the phenomenon of *teacher enthusiasm*, and the other group was located in the Communication Department at West Virginia University in the U.S.A. (Andersen, 1978; McCroskey & Richmond, 1992), and they investigated the phenomenon of *teacher immediacy*.

In both cases, the investigators wanted to compare the instructional style of excellent compared to non-excellent teachers according to their students' testimonies. Both groups focused on teachers' expressive behavior, irrespective of specific instructional methods or subject matter. Therefore, both branches concentrated on instructors' NV behavior. Following behavioral observations and analyses of students' reports about teachers' behavioral style, lists of the most typical behaviors characterizing teacher enthusiasm and/or teacher immediacy were constructed. Subsequently, the associations between enthusiastic/immediate style and teacher effectiveness were investigated. The term enthusiasm is self-understood, but the term immediacy requires some explanation. Actually, the term was borrowed from the writings of Albert Mehrabian (1966, 1971, 1972), who concentrated on the degree of closeness between people in the communication process, as expressed in mutual positive affect and liking. The term immediacy is, in fact, somewhat misguided with regard to teacher immediacy, because what is actually measured is not teachers' closeness to students or their relationships with them, but rather teachers' expressivity with regard to their subject matter and their enthusiasm in teaching as a global style.

Babad (2007) called attention to the identity between the two instruments measuring teacher enthusiasm and teacher immediacy. Both instruments include the following teacher behaviors:

1. Gestures when talking to the class.
2. Uses monotone/dull voice (a reversed item).
3. Looks at the class and at the students.

4. Smiles at the class.
5. Has a tense body position (a reversed item).
6. Moves around the classroom.
7. Looks at board or notes (a reversed item).
8. Has a relaxed body position.
9. Smiles at individual students.
10. Uses a variety of vocal expressions.

Murray (1983a, 1983b) and subsequent investigators of teacher enthusiasm (e.g., Wood, 1998) measured the associations between teacher enthusiasm and teaching effectiveness as measured by the student evaluation questionnaires that are used in almost all colleges and universities. Investigators of teacher immediacy measured teacher effectiveness through students' self-reports about their learning: In one item students rate "how much you learned in this class?" and in a second item they rate "how much you could have learned if you had an ideal teacher in this class?" The first rating is subtracted from the second to yield a measure of students' learning, better learning indicated by a smaller gap between the ideal and the actual. Additional items in teacher immediacy research focus on students' satisfaction and behavioral intentions to learn more in this area or with this teacher.

Two recent meta-analyses summarized the results of the numerous studies on teacher NV immediacy and teacher enthusiasm and their relations to educational outcomes (eighty-one studies in Witt, Wheeless, & Allen's, 2004, meta-analysis; and thirty-seven studies in Harris & Rosenthal's, 2005, meta-analysis). Both meta-analyses demonstrated that teachers' expressive style was strongly related to many positive student outcomes: Liking for the course and the instructor; willingness to take more classes with the instructor and more classes on that subject; and especially students' reports that they have learned a lot in the classes of teachers high in enthusiasm and NV immediacy. What was not clear in those analyses was the degree to which these positive outcomes were translated into objective gains in actual, empirically-measured student achievement. Without going into a host of methodological reservations about these studies (Babad, 2005c, 2007, 2009), it can be concluded with confidence that teaching effectiveness, as perceived and judged by students in college and in high school, is a function of teachers' positive and warm expressive NV style in the classroom.

POSITIVE NV BEHAVIOR IN THIN SLICES RESEARCH

In teacher enthusiasm and teacher immediacy research, global NV behaviors (such as: "uses a variety of vocal inflections" or "moves around the classroom" from the previous list) are judged by students according to their perceptions of teacher's typical and frequent behavior. Thus, the measurement of teacher expressiveness is conducted through students' self-reports on global behaviors in retrospective questionnaires. This is high-inference measurement (see Chapter 5), where NV behavior is inferred from students' perceptions. However, NV researchers usually prefer to analyze specific NV behaviors and to isolate the smallest elements of facial expressions, gestures, body movements and voice intonations. Therefore, NV research tends to rely more often on low-inference measurement. In thin slices research (Ambady, Bernieri, & Richeson, 2000; Ambady & Rosenthal, 1992, 1993) very brief instances of NV behavior (typically only a few seconds long) are viewed by judges who had never been exposed to the videotaped persons. Subsequently, researchers examine whether the judges' ratings of the NV behavior in the brief segments can predict direct outcomes or remote outcomes for the videotaped target people—such as end-of-semester student evaluations of their teachers or candidate's success in a job application interview.

Thin slices research often evokes a "wow!" reaction in its audience, because it consistently demonstrates that there is enough information available in extremely brief instances of NV behavior to predict important outcomes. Here are several dramatic examples of thin slices predictions:

- Babad et al. (1991) and Babad and Taylor (1992) demonstrated that after viewing unknown, foreign teachers for ten seconds without understanding their speech content, fourth-grade students could accurately guess whether the teachers were interacting with unseen high- or low-achievers.
- Blanck, Rosenthal, and Cordell (1985) showed that ratings of brief excerpts of judges' NV behavior while delivering instructions to jurors in actual criminal trials were correlated with judges' expectations for the trial outcomes and with the criminal history of the defendants.
- Hart (1995) used these videotapes of trial judges from actual trials in mock jury research, and found that even when admonished to disregard the judge's behavior, participants returned verdicts concordant with the judges' bent.
- Babad (1999) demonstrated that thin-slices of content-free NV behavior of television interviewers (averaging seven seconds) provided ample information to accurately detect interviewers' favoritism and preferential treatment.
- Gada-Jain (1999) examined NV behavior in job interviews, focusing on initial greeting and settling into chairs, and reported that thin slices depicting the initial handshake and introduction predicted the outcome of the subsequent structured employment interview.
- Babad (2005b) demonstrated that after viewing ten-second clips depicting unknown teachers lecturing to their entire classrooms, eleventh-grade students could accurately guess those teachers' differential treatment of unseen low- and high-expectancy students in other classroom situations.

Two studies (Ambady & Rosenthal, 1993; Babad, Avni-Babad & Rosenthal, 2004) tried to predict university students' end-of-course evaluations of their instructors from thin slices of the instructors' NV behavior while lecturing to their classes. Extremely brief video clips (six to ten seconds long) of the teachers' behavior (without comprehension of verbal content), were rated by judges who had never been exposed before to the videotaped teachers. Their ratings were then correlated with teacher evaluations filled out by the actual students in these courses. In both studies, strangers' impressions based on a few seconds of teachers' NV behavior while lecturing significantly predicted the end-of-course evaluations of teachers' effectiveness. The 2004 study investigated prediction of SRT from several instructional situations, and it must be added that the positive prediction from NV behavior was found only for the lecturing clips.

Micro-analysis of the specific molecular elements contributing to this prediction (Babad et al., 2004, Babad, 2007) made it possible to formulate from these thin slices the nonverbal behavioral profile of the successful and effective lecturer. Highly-rated lecturers were very expressive in their faces, hands, voices and body orientation toward their audience. They made continuous shifts in the various channels of their NV behavior, thereby preventing boredom and increasing student interest. And yet, despite their high level of activity, they were quite relaxed and avoided showing negative behaviors. These results from low-inference measurement confirmed and supported the results obtained through high-inference measurement in teacher enthusiasm and teacher immediacy research. An expressive instructional style is probably a very important component of teaching effectiveness, independent of CM techniques in interactions with students.

In a parallel study on the predictive power of judgments of thin slices of teachers' NV behavior in high school, a different pattern of results was found (Babad et al. 2003). In the high school study, teachers were videotaped in several instructional situations, and the most positive prediction of students' evaluations of their teachers was not found for lecturing behavior, but rather for NV behavior videotaped while the teachers were involved in disciplinary action. The more teachers' NV behavior while disciplining students for ten seconds was judged positively by the stranger judges, the more those teachers received positive evaluations from their high school classroom students at the end of the year. It seems that in the relatively tense atmosphere of the high school, the warmth and NV expressiveness of the teachers is more important in disciplinary situations than in frontal lecturing. Thus, in high school, teachers' NV expressivity in activities involving CM had a positive effect on the students.

CONCLUSION ABOUT TEACHERS' POSITIVE NV BEHAVIOR

Studies using disparate, almost contrasting methodologies lead to the same conclusion that teachers' emotional expressivity in the classroom contributes to classroom climate and harmony, increases students' motivation, and creates optimal conditions for learning. The ideal teacher is indeed expressive, enthusiastic, very active, interested, pleasant, and never boring. In college teaching, the enthusiasm characterizes the instructor's lecturing behavior, whereas in high school, the value of teachers' positive NV behavior is demonstrated when they deal with complex CM problems.

It is important to emphasize that teachers' NV expressive style, as investigated in the various studies, is impersonal, not focused on emotional relations with students. Despite the implication of the borrowed term immediacy—which Mehrabian (1966) described as expressing interpersonal closeness—the phenomenon measured in the various studies characterizes the teacher's conduct rather than the teacher's relations with students. The teacher is enthusiastic and joyful about her work and about her task, and she loves the material she teaches. She enjoys transmitting her enthusiasm to students and to facilitate their learning and development. In a sense, the teacher has a positive emotional relationship with the entire class and with the subject matter, but personal emotional relationships with the students are not part of the investigated phenomenon.

NEGATIVE NV PHENOMENA: TEACHER EXPECTANCIES AND DIFFERENTIAL BEHAVIOR

Much as teachers' enthusiasm, their overall expressive style and their positive emotionality can contribute to teaching effectiveness and to positive classroom atmosphere, the expression of other parts of teacher emotionality might hinder students' satisfaction, cause anger, and damage the academic and social climate of the classroom. Here, again, NV behavior plays a central role because of its strong connection to emotions and its irrepressible nature (DePaulo, 1992). Some teacher feelings must not be shown, and certain aspects of expressivity are unnecessary and potentially damaging to students. This statement refers mostly to teachers' deviations from equity in their differential emotional treatment of high-expectancy and low-expectancy students. Research consistently demonstrates that even when teachers try to conceal their differential feelings, their emotions can leak out in their NV behavior and become known to their students.

I must reiterate my opposition to some ideas advocated in the current CM literature. The sweeping legitimatization given to teachers by some CM writers for free-wheeling emotional expressivity and the fact that teachers are urged and demanded to be spontaneously emotional in the classroom might cause damage to students. The following discussion of the potentially negative outcomes of teachers' NV expressive behavior is based on six studies on teachers' NV behavior that I have conducted with colleagues from the 1980s to 2005. Some of these studies were discussed in Chapter 7. In all studies, we used clips of video recordings of classroom teachers. The stimuli were thin slices of teachers' NV behavior, usually lasting no longer than ten seconds per clip. Comprehension of verbal content in those brief instances was removed either by keeping the volume down (that is, by eliminating the audio aspect), or by having clips of Hebrew speaking teachers rated by non-Israeli judges who simply could not understand the spoken words at all.

The short clips of teachers' NV behavior were rated by judges who were not familiar with the videotaped teachers, and therefore their judgments were based solely on the few seconds of NV behavior they had viewed. Even when the judges were school children, they were not students in the videotaped classrooms and were not familiar with the teachers. Most of the studies were categorized as judgment studies, based on a within-teacher design. This design means that judges rate independently different clips of each teacher, and the analysis consists of a comparison between teacher's mean ratings in one aspect compared to another aspect. In other words, the teachers are compared to themselves. This design is typically used in studies of expectancy-related TDB, comparing teachers' behavior toward high-expectancy students to their behavior toward low-expectancy students, and also in leakage research (where teachers' behavior in one NV channel is compared to their behavior in other NV channels).

Studies on TDB were discussed in detail in Chapter 7, and relevant results will be mentioned here in brief. TDB was concluded to be a largely negative phenomenon. It was recommended that teachers should largely avoid treating low-achievers differently than high-achievers. One exception to this conclusion is the excessive learning support teachers give to low-expectancy students, which is not criticized by elementary school students but is criticized by high school students. As to teachers' differential emotional expression towards different students—the overwhelming conceptual, empirical and ideological consensus is that teachers should treat all students equitably and refrain from demonstrating differential or preferential affect.

Leakage of Negative Affect by Biased Teachers (Babad et al. 1989b).

This study was designed to provide direct educational evidence of the leakage phenomenon. It tested the hypothesis that biased teachers (those more susceptible to stereotypically biasing information in scoring children's drawings, see Chapter 6) would have stronger overall feelings of anger, and therefore would be more likely to demonstrate leakage compared to unbiased teachers. Biased teachers were those who demonstrated Golem effects in a previous study (Babad et al. 1982a), that is, negative expectancy effects toward low-expectancy students. Leakage of suppressed negative feelings is discovered empirically when NV channels differing in controllability are compared to each other (Chapter 12). Judgments of the same behavior through different NV channels would then show growing negativity with the decreased controllability.

This study compared judges' ratings of the transcript of words spoken in the brief ten-second instance (most highly controllable channel) to ratings of the face (less controllable) to ratings of the body for the same behavioral instance (least controllable). A clear leakage effect was indeed found for the biased teachers, with greater hostility, tension, anger and rigidity judged for the less controllable channels. No such trend was found for the unbiased teachers, presumably because they were not angry at their classrooms and did not have to try to conceal anger.

The importance of this study was in the fact that it was the first empirical demonstration of the NV leakage phenomenon by teachers in actual classrooms. If concealed anger and negative affect can be picked up from ratings of judges who are unfamiliar with the teachers after viewing only ten seconds of the teachers' behavior, it is very likely that the negative affect of those teachers leaks quite freely in their classrooms and influences the academic and social climate of those classrooms.

Teacher Expectancy Effects in Talking About and Talking To Low- and High-Expectancy Students (Babad et al. 1989a)

In this study, the NV behaviors of biased and unbiased teachers were examined in situations where they talked about a high-expectancy and a low-expectancy student, and then in brief instructional situations where they interacted with these students and taught them a topic of their choice. In all video clips viewed by the judges, only the teachers were seen and heard, and the students were left out of the frame. Judges rated the brief clips with the different channels (face, body, voice, etc.) separated or combined in different conditions. We were aware of the fact that when teachers are requested to talk about students or to teach those particular students in front of the camera, they would perform by enacting their best behavior. That would minimize potential expectancy effects and work against the researchers, whereas in the natural setting of their classrooms teachers might be more differential than in those videotaped instances.

Adult Judges

In this version of the study, the judges were adult university students who viewed and rated the video clips. The findings showed that, when talking about low-expectancy compared to high-expectancy students, teachers were rated as showing more negative affect in the nonverbal channels, and as more dogmatic in the nonverbal and the transcript channels. That is, they talked differently about the two students, and their facially and bodily transmitted affect was more negative when they talked about low-expectancy students. When talking to the students and interacting with them, facially communicated expectancy differences were found in ratings of negative affect and active teaching behavior—with low-expectancy students receiving more teacher activity (assumed compensation, see Chapter 7) together with more negative affect (leakage) compared to high-expectancy students. In this study, expectancy effects were found for both biased teachers and unbiased teachers. Babad et al. (1989a) concluded that teacher expectancy effects and the resultant TDB were very pervasive, emerging in affective nuances of NV behavior even when teachers attempt to control their behavior and to help low-achievers.

Students as Judges (Babad et al. 1991; Babad & Taylor, 1992)

This research examined what young students actually perceived in teachers' NV behavior when the teachers were talking to and about their students. The judges were sampled from different grade levels, the youngest consisting of fourth-grade students (ten years old). The 1991 study was conducted in Israel, and the 1992 study was conducted in New Zealand. For Israeli judges, speech volume was turned off (silent video) so that they could not understand the verbal content. The NZ judges did not understand teachers' language (Hebrew), and the volume of speech did not have to be turned off. Therefore, the NZ fourth-graders were exposed to the fullest NV (visual and auditory) information without any comprehension of verbal content. Some changes were made to make the investigation more appropriate for young children: The numbers of teachers and channels were reduced, and the judgment task was changed to a detection task. Children are not accustomed to make judgments about teachers (such as, flexible, clear, or dogmatic). In the detection task, the young judges were asked to make guesses about the student that teacher talked to or talked about, even though they never saw that student and viewed only teacher's behavior. They were asked to guess (on 1–9 scales) whether the unseen student was academically weak or excellent, and also to guess the degree to which that student was disliked or liked by the teacher.

Student-detected expectancy effects were stronger than the previous results derived from the ratings of adult judges. The students, including the very young ones, did not hesitate in guessing that the unseen target child was a better student and was better liked by the teacher in clips based on teachers talking about and to a high-expectancy student, and as a weaker and less liked student in the clips involving the low-expectancy student. The children in both countries detected teacher expectancies from their facial expressions and body language. Thus, teachers give away their differential expectations through their NV behavior!

Predicting Student Evaluations from Teachers' NV Behavior in the Classroom (Babad et al. 2003)

This study in high school, together with another study conducted at the university level (Babad et al., 2004) was designed to examine whether students' evaluations of their teachers at the end of the term could be predicted from judges' ratings of 10 seconds of teachers' NV classroom behavior in several instructional situations. The high school situations included performing an administrative task, using the board, lecturing to the entire class, disciplining students, and interacting with individual students. The interactions were later divided into interactions with distinguishable high-achievers and low-achievers. All of the ten-second clips of teachers' NV behavior were rated by adult foreign judges who were not familiar with the videotaped teachers. At the end of the year, all classroom students filled out questionnaires evaluating their teachers (SRT), and also filled out a questionnaire measuring their perceptions of their teacher's differential behavior toward two hypothetical students (high and low, see Chapter 7).

Thus, two measures of TDB were available in this research, one based on judges' ratings of ten seconds of actual teachers' NV behavior toward low- and high-achievers, and the other based on the perceptions of the classroom students of their teacher's differential behavior. The empirically-measured differentiality from the NV clips was strongly validated by the students' perceptions, showing that TDB can be readily diagnosed from thin slices of teachers' NV behavior.

The teachers' NV differentiality was found to be very strongly related to their students' end-of-year evaluations. Students were very angry with differential teachers, giving them lower evaluations on almost every dimension. In Chapter 7 I reported that students in the upper elementary grades criticized teachers for differential emotional support but were more lenient about teacher differentiality in learning support. In this study, upper high school students were angry at any manifestation of teachers' deviation from equitable treatment, in emotional support and learning support alike. Thus, teachers' NV behaviors expressing differential treatment of low- and high-achievers in the classroom are conclusively negative.

A surprising finding in this research (contradictory of the college results in the 2004 study) was that judges' ratings of NV behavior in the instructional situation of lecturing to the entire classroom were negatively related to students' end-of-year evaluations. It was not clear why teachers who made a better impression on the adult foreign judges in their lecturing would be evaluated more negatively by their own students. Subsequent analyses revealed a relationship between public lecturing and TDB, so that teachers who were rated more positively as lecturers by the foreign judges were actually found to be more differential in their treatment of individual high/low students.

Students as Judges

To further investigate the surprising relationship between more positive ratings for lecturing to the entire class and higher intensity of differential treatment of individual students, a study was designed with high school students in another town (who were unfamiliar with the videotaped teachers) serving as judges (Babad, 2005b). These students viewed the ten-second clips of each teacher's NV behavior when lecturing to their entire classes, and were asked to guess how differential each teacher would be in her/his interactions with low- and high-achievers in their classrooms. The young judges were encouraged to make these guesses despite the fact that the clips they viewed did not depict any interaction with any individual student. Amazingly, those students/judges were quite accurate in guessing teacher differentiality from the lecturing clips. A parallel group of adult judges could not guess TDB from lecturing clips at all, and this keen sensitivity in knowing teachers and reading their most subtle NV nuances is solely a students' expertise.

Thus, teachers' expressive NV behavior in their interactions with low- and high-achievers transmits their differential emotions, and TDB can be picked up from judges' ratings of ten seconds of NV behavior. But beyond that, teachers' global expressive style (i.e., lecturing) also provides cues about negative NV aspects of inequity and preferential behavior that students (but not adults) can readily pick up.

CONCLUSION ABOUT TEACHERS' NEGATIVE NV BEHAVIORS

The studies above provide a consistent picture that indicates that teachers often transmit in their differential NV behavior emotional messages that have negative effects on their students and their classrooms. These negative effects are probably experienced more strongly by low-achievers and by the weak students, those who are the recipients of teachers' negative subtle NV behaviors (see also Weinstein, 2002). The research also demonstrates students' uncanny sensitivity and expertise in picking up the most subtle cues in teachers' NV behavior.

When I present in various forums research findings demonstrating differential and preferential NV behavior of teachers (Babad, 1998) and TV interviewers (Babad, 2005a) and describe to the audience the psychological damage that such behavior can cause, I often encounter a defensive reaction. Some people shrug the phenomenon off, arguing that emotional differentiality is only natural, that nothing can anyway be done about it, and that we should be lenient in accepting some failings of human nature. But much as we educate children to overcome innate human shortcomings and to learn to share with others and adopt cultural ways, we should not ignore out human failure because it is natural. There is sufficient evidence that NV skills can be improved through awareness and training, so that people (certainly teachers) can improve their self-control and avoid behaving in ways that can damage their receivers.

I believe that the root of the problem lies in the illusion of control and in the ability to deceive others. Many parents, teachers and managers convince themselves that they can control their behavior and transmit to others exactly what they wish, and that others would not be able to read through the deception. The more people believe in their control and in the inability of others, the greater the chances of bias and preferential behavior. Three decades ago I discovered (Babad, 1979) that the most biased people perceived themselves as the most objective, fair and unbiased. The research shows again and again that students have uncanny decoding ability and cannot be deceived by their teachers.

To summarize, the issue of teachers' NV expressivity and emotionality in the classroom presents a duality of contrasting implications. On the one hand, teachers' overall enthusiasm about their work, about their subject matter, about their classrooms and about their teaching tasks represents a most positive phenomenon that contributes to a variety of positive educational outcomes. On the other hand, maintaining emotional relationships with individual students can easily (often unwittingly) lead to differential and preferential behavior and cause psychological damage in the classroom. Studies on TDB (Chapter 7, and additional findings in the domain of NV behavior in the present chapter) and the research on the teacher's pet phenomenon (Chapter 8) demonstrate potential pitfalls of teachers' free wheeling emotionality in the classroom.

Unfortunately, the current literature on CM ignores the potentially harmful consequences of teachers' differential NV behavior. The advocates of affective CM (Chapter 9) seem to be trapped in an ideology that urges teachers to be emotional and to create emotional relationships with their students, and they dull the mention of phenomena that might signal problems evoked by teachers' uncontrolled emotionality. Everston and Weinstein's (2006a) edited book *Handbook of Classroom Management: Research, Practice, and Contemporary Issues* best illustrates my argument. This heavy volume (which includes fifty chapters by close to ninety authors) is an up-to-date and authoritative statement on contemporary CM. The book has no chapter on teachers' NV behavior at all, nor any chapter on teacher expectancies and TDB. Scrutiny of the subject index shows that these topics were almost not mentioned at all by the different writers. While advocating student-centered emotional CM, the book neglects to provide any caution regarding the danger in free-wheeling emotional expression of teachers in their classrooms.

Part VI

Educating and Changing Students

15 Educating Students

"TO EDUCATE" AND "TO CHANGE" STUDENTS: A SOCIAL PSYCHOLOGICAL PERSPECTIVE

The last part of the book deals with processes of social influence employed by the school and particularly by teachers in order to educate and to change students. Nobody would contest the educative role of the modern school, but not much has been written about the psychology of education—how students actually get educated in school.

The processes of educating and changing students are presented here from a social psychological point of view. The concept of "education" and the issues involved in educating students have, of course, been approached from numerous perspectives—philosophical, developmental, sociological, moral and religious. From a social psychological view, the central products of processes of educating and changing students would consist of students' attitudes, beliefs, values, world perspective, social behavior, group belongingness, socio-identities and good citizenship.

In the analysis of educative processes, it is useful to distinguish between formation (of attitudes, values, etc.) and change. School is perceived as responsible mainly for the formation (or education) stage, and change is often seen as more relevant for older people, when change in various aspects is needed after a social system had already been formed. But school is equally involved in formation and in change, and intensive efforts are invested in changing students from the very early grades. Children do not come to school tabula rasa, and social change is intertwined with formative education throughout all levels of schooling. The transition from the home environment to the social framework of the school (or rather, preschool) must involve change processes. The same is true for children's transitions from one age level to another, where old values, beliefs and social outlook must change together with children's developing cognitive and social abilities.

This chapter is devoted to a social psychological analysis of the educative process, and the next chapter (Chapter 16) is devoted to strategies of psychological change, with a special section on psychological resistance to change. The main difference between formative processes and change processes is the power and influence of resistance to change. Once attitudes, values and habits are formed and put to use, individuals and groups struggle to maintain the existing system and to resist change.

LEXICAL DEFINITION OF "TO EDUCATE"

The *Merriam-Webster Online Dictionary* provides the following options for the definition of "to educate":

1. To provide schooling.
2. To train by formal instruction and supervised practice, especially in a skill, trade or profession.
3. To develop mentally, morally or aesthetically, especially by instruction.
4. To provide with information (as in, "to educate myself about X . . .").
5. To persuade or condition to feel, believe, or act in a desired way.

And the dictionary adds: For synonyms see "teach."

These lexical definitions provide different meanings and implications of the process of educating, including the reference to teaching as a synonym of educating. Those definitions include the instructional aspects (with a heavy weight attached to teaching) but also the social psychological aspects, especially in the last definition.

The next parts of this chapter discuss the components and psychological mechanisms that are involved in the process of educating students. Readers are forewarned that the aspects are not as distinct and as separate from each other as they appear in the presentation. The educative process is an integrated process and all parts are intertwined with each other, but for the clarity of presentation, each aspect is delineated and discussed separately.

EDUCATING THROUGH INSTRUCTION AND TEACHING

Above all, school educates by teaching and instruction. This is done through both direct and indirect paths: The direct impact of instruction is in fostering intellectual development, and the indirect influence is enacted through specific subject matters and fields of knowledge.

Intellectual Development through Instruction

The brain—the human mind, is the major instrument of human civilization and progress. The central role of schooling is to develop students' thinking and mental capacities and to raise them to the maximal intellectual level possible for each individual student. Students must learn to think rationally, to absorb and process numerous and distinct types of information, to be effective in solving concrete and abstract problems, and mainly to know how to reason effectively in all life domains. To reach a high intellectual level, students must learn to master various methods and methodologies in different areas (mathematics, life sciences, historical analysis, geography, etc.), and they must also acquire endless knowledge and information to be utilized in their higher mental processes. Intellectual development means learning to reason and to be rational, and to deal with the challenges of reality in an empirical fashion based on data and systematic assessment of reality. Intellectual development also means to separate reason from affect and to reach a level of self-control so that underlying emotional processes would not bias or distort people's rationality.

In our culture, just attaining the highest possible educational level and to be intellectual are achievements of good citizenship and a demonstration of high values. The person is expected to always want to learn more, to seek new knowledge and to reach deeper understanding in many areas. The grandmother who decides to learn Italian is appreciated because she seeks new knowledge and skills, even if she does not plan to go on a trip to Italy or ever to use her acquired Italian. I tell my students that our society seems to appreciate individuals who reach higher educational levels, and also sees them as being better people. Of course this stereotypic generalization has many exceptions, and many highly-educated people could hardly be viewed as better people. However, attaining more schooling and making a visible effort to learn more are generally appreciated as demonstrating a higher human level. Persons who seek knowledge and appreciate knowledge would better reason their attitudes and plan their behavior, would be more open to absorb new knowledge and accommodate to it, would know how to analyze accurately what is going on, and would be considered as less given to negative influences, demagogy, bias, etc. Therefore, society rewards people who acquire more years of schooling both in financial terms and in social status.

High educational status is not necessarily related to a given discipline or a particular content area. In past centuries, enlightment had been tied to the classics, languages and philosophy, but no such views are held today. Still, a special honor is given to those who choose to be teachers and to dedicate themselves to teaching and to educating others. Unfortunately, due to economic pressures this appreciation is not necessarily expressed by higher pay.

Therefore, intellectual development through the accumulation of years of schooling in various educational frameworks is an educative process of the utmost importance. It is true, of course, that the accumulation of schooling also provides the opportunities for all the other educative processes (to be discussed next) to contribute to one's education.

Education through Academic Instruction in Content Disciplines

The different content disciplines and study areas serve diverse objectives in schooling. Some domains have a clearly defined focus of values education (e.g., religious studies), whereas other domains educate students in more indirect ways. It is important to understand that all disciplines and content domains serve concurrently several different functions. Indeed, most classroom sessions (in reading, math or grammar) are not taught with a conscious intent of educating the students. The objective of preparing students for their future life as citizens is not on teachers' minds all the time. The different disciplines are taught academically for the specific types of knowledge they provide and for the intellectual task of developing students' thinking. Their educative gains, including unintended gains, appear more clearly in the long run.

The different content domains are next classified into four large categories that represent different psychological functions. Instruction specialists and philosophers of education would not necessarily agree with this categorization:

1. Basic skills which are absolutely necessary for elementary functioning of every citizen in modern society. These basic skills include reading and writing, reading comprehension and arithmetic. Without having minimal skills in these areas, one cannot function at all in our society, and school's first task is to make every student acquire these basic skills. In earlier centuries the majority of the world population was illiterate, and no effort was taken to assure acquisition of these basic skills by all citizens.
2. School domains that provide elementary knowledge for functioning in society. Beyond the basic skills above, the elementary knowledge enables people to understand daily situations and to communicate with other people. Included in this category would be civic studies which provide knowledge for understanding society and its various institutions, geography, the study of the mother tongue, basic notions in music and arts, and even physical education.
3. School disciplines that provide for a deeper understanding of our universe. This category includes the various domains in science education (biology, chemistry, physics, and, of course, mathematics). These domains also serve for intellectual development through logical and scientific thinking, empiricist approach, etc.
4. School disciplines where the content itself is directly important for educative purposes, because it represents values and attitudes that are important for our society. These disciplines are usually not as universal as mathematics, and they give premium to the specific knowledge and contents important for a given society and a given country. This category includes domains such as history, biblical and religious studies, civic studies, and most areas of the humanities which provide

students with the cultural heritage. In these disciplines, the content is very important in shaping students socio-identities, world perspective and value system. The study of literature provides a dual cultural purpose of learning and acquiring universal values from world literature, and developing a national identity through the study of the local national literature. With regard to the study of history, I am doubtful whether politicians improve their professional conduct through learning insightful lessons from historical events. But for students, there is great value in knowing the history of their nation, of their culture, of their religion and of their ethnic group as bases for their various socio-identities.

Teachers often use specific examples from the study contents to illustrate various processes, to draw analogies, and to educate students through the learning contents. This is most obvious in the humanistic domains where lessons for students' present life can be derived from literary, historical or biblical events. But it might also be true of the sciences, with examples such as the importance of environmental conservation, concerns about medicine, etc.

Sometimes specific educational programs are constructed on the basis of specific contents to serve other educational objectives. Bibliotherapy, for example, involves programs that use literary contents for advancing students' mental health and psychological adjustment (Abdullah, 2002; Jack & Ronan, 2008), much as literary contents can serve to develop a national identity or a gender identity. I was impressed to see in Argentina how students' enthusiasm about the world soccer championship (the Mondial) was harnessed in a specially designed educational program to develop tolerance to different others and to learn about stereotypes and prejudice. In religious and biblical studies, the contents are used most directly for preaching to students about proper values, beliefs and behavior.

EDUCATION THROUGH INCULCATION AND PREACHING

Years ago, when I was trying to formulate my ideas about educating students for a course on the social psychology of the classroom, I asked our son, who was then a teenager, how he acquired his values and world view. He looked at me, seemed a bit surprised, and said: "But, of course, you told me!" (you in plural). I think that, as much as educators would not like to admit it, much of the formulation of students' values, beliefs, attitudes, world perspective and good citizenship is attained through repetitious preaching. We all follow the Biblical dictum: "And you shall tell your son" (Exodus, 13:8), by telling our children and our students again and again what they should think and what they should value, how they should view the world and how they should be and behave. Ideally, other means for educating and formulating values are preferable to preaching. The students themselves should take a more active and autonomous role in self-education through their experiences in interacting with the environment, and the educator's role should be more indirect. But I still think that it must be admitted that preaching is one of the most effective means of educating children.

Superka, Ahrens, and Hedstorm (1976) delineated in their *Values Education Sourcebook*, five approaches to values education, and they labeled the primer approach "inculcation." According to the *Merriam-Webster Online Dictionary*, to inculcate means "to teach and impress by frequent repetitions and admonitions." Much inculcation takes place in the daily life of the classroom. When rules and expectations are explicated and subsequently enforced as a necessary component of CM (Chapter 9), teachers explain to the students the values and the ideals represented by those demands. Effective teachers do not miss opportunities emerging from current events and classroom occurrences to inculcate values and to develop students' social perspective. Students should accept these ideas, accommodate themselves to them, and eventually come to own these ideas in a process of identification. In the words of Superka et al., (1976), inculcation occurs by students identifying with and accepting the norms and standards of institutions and society, incorporating the specific values into their own value system. In his classic work on attitude formation and change, Herbert Kelman (1958) discussed the depth of conviction of attitudes and values, moving along a continuum from compliance to identification to internalization.

The important point is that teachers take a very active role in the inculcation process through repeated statements that explicate the desirable attitudes, values and behavior. I believe that most teachers seize on the occurring possibilities to inculcate values and to preach to their students, and they are probably quite successful in this educative effort. Repetition of value clarification and preaching are important because the process of education is tedious and requires hard work and repetition. However, sometimes teachers might be successful in impressing a value on students in one dramatic instance. We all carry unique memories where a certain value-laden conviction flashed into out minds following one particular statement of a charismatic teacher.

The term inculcation is perhaps more acceptable than the term preaching. I think that only educators who strongly advocate a particular religious or social ideology, those who view themselves as "ideologists," are not ashamed of being perceived as preaching. In the view of strong ideologists, the values they advocate are so important that they must repeatedly be preached. Perhaps they believe that students' autonomous choice and self-selection of values fade in light of the need that they would hold particular religious or social values and not others.

The important point that I want to emphasize to teachers and to teacher education students is that, preaching and inculcation of values in teachers' interactions with students are OK and not anything to be ashamed of.

Telling students what they should think and what they should value is an effective way of educating them—students accept teachers' authority to do that, and perhaps they even see teachers' as responsible to direct them and to teach them right and wrong. Of course all educators are happier when preaching and inculcation are accompanied by additional educational methods that involve students in a more active and responsible capacity.

EDUCATING THROUGH BEHAVIOR MODIFICATION

Every system of human management is involved—explicitly or implicitly— in behavior modification. In school, the continuous modification of students' behavior by their teachers serves clear educative functions. Desirable student behaviors that express positive values are encouraged and rewarded by the teachers. The controversy over the appropriateness of the behavioristic approach to CM has been discussed in previous chapters (Chapters 9, 10, and 11). But the reality of behavior modification and its actual existence in teacher–student interactions in the classroom cannot be doubted at all. Regardless of teacher's educational ideology, students' behaviors are strengthened or weakened by their outcomes. Teachers react to students' behaviors with a variety of approving and encouraging responses on the one hand or disapproving and discouraging responses on the other hand. Teachers who are committed to a behavioral approach try to modify students' behavior in explicit, methodical, planned, and perhaps somewhat mechanistic ways. Teachers who oppose behaviorism also modify students' behavior, but they do it in a more intuitive, less planned and less mechanistic way. Such teachers do not measure empirically the behavioral outcomes, and perhaps they make more use of their emotional reactions compared to other types of reinforcers. Thus, behavior modification—formal or informal, explicit or implicit—always exists in every classroom and in every human interaction.

Much as teachers' reactions to students' behavior are important as the central component of CM, teachers' reactions to students' behavior are central in the process of education. CM is not only a managerial tool, but can be considered as an educational instrument as well. In fact, CM and education are intertwined and concurrently attained. Life within the classroom society requires students to enact value-laden behaviors such as responsibility, truth telling, mutual support, sharing, tolerance through turn-taking, and so on. Behaviors that express various values are rewarded by the teachers, and behaviors negating important values are shunned and disapproved, and teachers attempt to remove those behaviors from students' behavioral repertoire. Thus, teachers educate their students by modifying students' behavior while managing their classrooms. In effective classrooms, the students share the educative responsibility and try to influence each other to behave in ways reflecting positive values and good citizenship.

Enlightened teachers would not modify students' behavior without trying concurrently to employ other methods to make students understand
and appreciate the value of the desired conduct. Such synthesis of methods turns the behavior modification into a more reasoned and a more
cognitive process.

The focal point in the dilemma about the educative value of behavior
modification concerns the issue of internalization, that is, how the implicit
meaning involved in a particular behavior can be internalized and owned
by the student as a value that would determine future behavior. Most students' behaviors can be controlled and modified, but internalization is a
different issue altogether. In Kelman's (1958) terms, the issue is expressed
in the transition from compliance to internalization. An internalized value
would become in itself a source of self-reinforcement for the autonomous
individual and would determine future value-laden behavior. And indeed,
the opponents of the behavioral approach have always argued that the great-
est disadvantage of this approach is its external and mechanistic nature and
the absence of internalization in behavioristic practice. They claimed that
when behaviors are acquired and maintained by external reinforcement,
those behaviors would decrease and extinguish when the external reinforcement is removed. Externally controlled behaviors are performed only
when one is within the restriction of that given environment (like school,
or prison, if readers would excuse the analogy) but would disappear when
one leaves that environment.

This issue was addressed several times in the previous chapters about
CM (Chapters 9–11). Enlightened modern behaviorism has integrated cognitive approaches, and it emphasizes the development of self-control and
self-efficacy. Internalization thus becomes in itself a behavioristic goal that
can be pursued in planned and carefully executed behavioral steps.

Beyond the application of operational methods to increase internalization, several conceptual considerations can contribute to the internalization of acquired behaviors, and therefore behavior modification can
indeed become an important means of values education. Several theories
in social psychology—such as Bem's (1972) self-perception theory, but
more importantly, cognitive dissonance theory (Aronson, 1969; Festinger,
1957)—maintain that people justify in retrospect and come to believe in
what they are actually doing. Therefore, if teachers can bring students to
behave in a certain way, most frequently the students would convince themselves that they are doing the right thing. Second, we must understand that
rewards, reinforcements and teacher approval are not necessarily limited to
influencing external aspects of behavior. Rather, students can be rewarded
and praised for their internal states (both cognitive and emotional), com-
plimented for holding particular values and beliefs and for being a person of values. Third, people enjoy becoming autonomous and self-directed
by reinforcing themselves for good deeds. Internalization of values provides the person with internal standards that become means for enhancing

self-image and self-efficacy. Therefore, students would most often be motivated to internalize the values implicit in their actual behavior.

EDUCATION THROUGH CULTURAL/SOCIAL FRAMEWORKS AND NORMATIVE INFLUENCE

School educates students about good citizenship and provides values education by creating a society, a life framework in which students become active citizens. To succeed in school, students must adjust and learn to live in this society by its rules and standards. More than that, students' should reach a state where they can be happy in their lives in school and know how to reap the benefits of that citizenship. Besides their family life, school is students' central life framework for a sizable proportion of their young lives. Membership in school society is important to the students, and they are motivated to accommodate and succeed. Thus, school educates students simply by being a micro-cosmos of society-at-large and by managing students' lives in that society.

For the students, the classroom society becomes both their membership group and their reference group. They do not only belong physically in the classroom group (membership), but usually they value this belongingness and become proud of it (reference group). Despite the fact that they are a captive audience and are assigned to their particular classrooms, most students usually see their classmates as their reference group. They internalize the standards, norms, rules and expectations of the classroom society and come to own the values, attitudes, beliefs, and life perspective that are implied by those norms and standards. School is therefore a normative cultural/social framework that rewards its participants for their good citizenship, their values and their good behavior. Children's other important social framework—the family—usually encourages and rewards the children for their good citizenship in the school society, and adds normative pressure toward good and deep adjustment.

Some students do not fit well in the school society due to a wide range of problems. They become problem children and deviants in the school society. For those students, school actually fails to fulfill its role as a normative cultural framework and does not succeed in socializing them properly. But problem children are most often a small minority, and most students accommodate to school and its normative pressure and become good citizens of the school society. It is very rare that an entire school, or even an entire classroom totally fails in its socializatory mission.

Some types of schools are especially and explicitly designed as a mini-society (such as the well-known Democratic Schools). In such cases, all the processes discussed above are made more explicit, and special norms and procedures are designed and implemented in those schools to emphasize students' active roles in school governance. But the main point is that, by definition, schools function as normative cultural/social frameworks, socializing and educating their students for good citizenship.

The preceding information is the ideal image of education through the normative framework of school society, but some limitations must be considered. First, the failure in socializing problem students damages the rosy picture, and such phenomena are frequent occurrences in every school (no less than in society-at-large). Second, it must be remembered that in all of its major objectives (social and educative no less than academic and instructional objectives) school never brings all students to full realization of its goals, but rather produces a normal distribution of success, where a large majority of students attain only mediocre status and some students always remain in low status positions. Many children do not enjoy their school citizenship, and some children actually suffer in school. The roots of dissatisfaction in many students' future citizenship in adult society can be found in their formative experiences during the school years. Third, the picture of the socializing school drawn above is true particularly for the younger age range at the elementary grades. With adolescence and its trials and tribulations, after the long accumulation of schooling years until adolescence, many students become fed up with school and rebel against its limiting framework. Among adolescents it is more normative to hate school and to reject its efforts to educate, and students who state that they like or enjoy school would probably be rejected as some type of freaks.

EXPERIENTIAL LEARNING AND ACTION LEARNING AS MODES OF EDUCATION

In all theories and models of values education and change, central conceptual mechanisms involve experiential learning, action learning, and integration of cognitive and emotional processes (see for example Superka et al., 1976; Chin & Benne, 1976). Much effort and many resources are invested in every school worldwide to create encounters, experiences and various activities that would affect students emotionally. The assumption is that exciting and touching experiences can have formative educational impact, especially on impressionable young people. Such events evoke intense emotions and subsequent cognitions that form the foundation for the development of social-identities and the future value system of the individual.

Consider the following example: The State of Israel was established in the late 1940s only a few years after the defeat of Nazi Germany in World War II. Six million Jews were slaughtered in Europe during the holocaust. The survivors, and all Jews, vowed to commemorate the holocaust and never forget the genocide. The State of Israel, as the home of the Jewish people, established an official memorial day, the Day of the Holocaust, when all entertainment stops countrywide, and the media and schools focus on commemorating the holocaust. The Day of the Holocaust is a very sad and touching day for all Israelis, and it is certainly a formative educational experience for the development of Jewish and Israeli identity.

In the last decades, Israeli high schools began to organize every year large expeditions of eleventh-graders (aged sixteen to seventeen) who fly to Poland to commemorate The Day of the Holocaust. They visit the death camps and the remains of the Jewish ghettos and attend the Day of the Holocaust ceremonies in Auschwitz, the camp where more than two million Jews were murdered and burnt by the Nazis in the early 1940s. Considerable expense and effort is invested (by the families, by the schools, and by the State of Israel) to facilitate those trips. According to many testimonials of the youngsters, this is the single most important event in the formation of their adult identity. The importance of the visit is not in the informational domain but in the experiential domain. With the advanced media means and the electronic capacities we have today, all facts and all pictures could be shown to the students on the small screen more fully and more extensively than any personal trip could provide. And yet, the personal experience and the possibility to feel past events in their original locations have a tremendous impact on the students.

Conceptually, personal experiences can be very instructive. Experiential learning integrates cognition, emotion and behavior, and therefore its influence can be more profound. Unfortunately, the same can be said about negative or even traumatic personal experiences, which can scar people for life in their psychological impact. The experiential elements are important because of the powerful combination of cognition, emotion and action. Some experiential learning is provided in school through the academic studies themselves, but many unique experiential events are especially designed throughout the school year.

We need to distinguish here between experiential learning, where the student is the passive recipient or audience in a designed event, and action learning (see Superka et al., 1976) where the student is an active participant in a designed event, and learns through her/his own action in that situation.

Examples of experiential learning might include:

1. The experiential impact of books and literature, theatre, motion pictures and the study of religion and history.
2. The impact of special events—holidays, memorial days, ceremonies, etc.
3. The impact of testimonial visits (to Auschwitz, to an old people's home, to a poverty-stricken neighborhood, etc.).

Examples of action learning might include:

1. Writing action assignments and compositions (such as: "If I were a school principal . . ." or "My plan to combat poverty").
2. Participation in planned student governance (in school council, etc.).

3. Planned social encounters with different others in workshops, and exercises in taking on the perspective of the other.
4. Various activities in community service. Court judges often replace imprisonment to convicted felons by more educative community service.

EDUCATION THROUGH MODELS AND MODELING

Identification is one of the ways of acquiring values and morality. In Kelman's (1958) model of attitude formation and change, identification is presented as one of the three central mechanisms, preceded by compliance and followed by internalization. In social learning theory (Bandura, 1977, 1986) a central concept is vicarious learning, which involves imitation of a model to whose behavior the learner was exposed. The models referred to by Bandura are figures who illustrate how one should or could behave, and they are not considered as identification models. The process of identification is deeper and involves strong emotions invested in one selected model, whereas people can imitate several models with no emotional investment. In Freud's theory of personality development, identification is the process where the boy accepts and internalizes his father's inner world, moral system and values (superego) as part of the resolution of the Oedipal conflict. Therefore, in Freud's theory an entire internal world is adopted all at once through identification with the father.

Cultural Models

Identification (not necessarily in the Freudian connotation) is a central component in the educative process, and cultural models serve a central role in the formation of values and social identity. Particular figures and personalities become models because of special, admirable features in their personality or in their conduct. When they gain model (or idol) status, it is expected that the values they represent will be internalized by their followers. This is the process involving selected Biblical figures, historical figures, some political leaders, military heroes, and inadvertently actors, pop stars, etc. Moses, Jesus, Churchill, Paul Revere, Wilhelm Tell, Jean D'Arc and Yanosh Korchak are examples of cultural models whose cultural heritage is promoted by our civilization as models for all of us, teaching us how we should be, what we should think, and how we should act in selected situations.

In the social psychological and philosophical literature on leadership, charisma is often mentioned as the utmost level of leadership (see Chapter 3). Charisma is a rare trait found in a few leaders who have extreme charm and a magnetic quality of personality along with a powerful ability to communicate with people, to attract them, and to persuade them for a cause. Charismatic leaders have a very strong impact on their followers, who would follow those leaders through fire and brimstone; would be willing to sacrifice for them, would worship them as their cultural model and identification figures, and might even be willing to sacrifice their lives for their leader's cause. The more charismatic the leadership, the more it has a chance of intensely influencing the internal world of the followers. In fiction and folklore about admirable teachers, stories are often told about charismatic teachers who overcome tremendous difficulties, and through their virtues and charisma attain incredible educative success that other teachers fail to achieve. The image of the charismatic teacher exists in the historical ethos as a certain type of cultural ideal. Most of us remember nostalgically charismatic teachers we had had in the distant past, and cherish their educative impact on us.

Still, some consideration must be taken to clarify what exactly might be and what might not be learned, imitated and internalized from charismatic teachers and from models of identification. A Swiss child would not become Wilhelm Tell, a British child would not become Winston Churchill, and a student would not imitate the specific behaviors of the charismatic teacher. The educational intent is that students would adopt certain values and attributes of the identification figures in abstract, but would not necessarily imitate their mannerisms and specific behaviors. Imitation of dress, hairdo and mannerisms of pop idols is considered rather childish and stupid. Thus, the transmission of values and mental perspective is vague and somewhat problematic, and it is not sufficiently clear how cultural or personal identification actually works in behavioral terms.

Teachers as Models

Charisma is a rare social phenomenon, an infrequent integration of special traits and characteristics that emerges in particular situations. Nobody could demand that teachers should become charismatic models of identification. But in a milder form, teachers are expected to be leadership figures in their classrooms, and to serve as models for their students. In a way, this imperative represents the perception of school and teachers in loco parentis (teachers serving as substitute parents). Parents are held to be models of imitation and identification for their children, and children have a need to seek and emulate such figures. This process characterizes the younger age range, when children are not critical of adult figures. As they grow in age and mental development, children discover the clay feet of their idols, and then they refuse to accept so readily (or they might even reject) the moral authority of parents and cultural models. But in the younger age range children indeed imitate their parents and their teachers and accept them as models.

Parallel to the conceptual distinction between imitation and identification, we must distinguish between the image of the teacher as a model for imitation and personal example, and the image of the teacher as a model for identification. With regard to personal example, there is no doubt that much social learning is attained through cognitive and emotional emulation of human examples, and teachers indeed model for their students many behaviors and ways of responding to the environment. However, the demand that teachers would serve in their personality and behavior as identification models is exaggerated, and even more so if teachers are expected to become charismatic leaders. Such demands would put undue pressure on teachers (see discussion of this issue in Chapter 3). I am sure that some teachers are charismatic and they may have intense educative influence on their students, but for most teachers the demand is unattainable and anxiety producing, and therefore unjustified. It should be remembered that most students inherently accept the authority of the teacher as the representative of society, and therefore would accept cultural dictums from their teachers. Such acceptance is not determined by the personal attributes or status of any particular teacher, but rather by the social structure and the complementing features in the role definitions of teacher and student. When discussing the issue of the teacher's role in Chapter 3, I emphasized two minimal demands: One is that every teacher would have some special attribute that would characterize her/him as a unique model for her/his students; and the other is that no teacher would be a negative model for students. If these demands are met, teachers would indeed serve as educative behavioral models for their students. The important point is to remember that students come to school with readiness to be educated, and they inherently accept the position of the teacher as a model. Therefore, unless something goes wrong in teacher–students interaction, teachers would have considerable educative influence on their students.

16 Changing Students

SIMILARITIES AND DIFFERENCES BETWEEN EDUCATING AND CHANGING STUDENTS

The general strategies and tactics for changing values, attitudes, life perspective and behavior are essentially similar to those employed in educating students as described in the previous chapter. However, there are several differences between the formation process and the change process:

1. Not all strategies effective in formation are as effective in change. For example, it is probably easier to educate than to change through academic instruction and through inculcation and preaching.
2. It is more difficult to change existent attitudes and values than to form them on an empty slate, because the change requires the removal of existing beliefs and involves some distress.
3. Change almost inevitably involves psychological resistance that must be overcome, whereas formation of new values does not necessarily involve resistance.

Values and attitudes have three central components: cognitive; affective; and behavioral. The cognitive component includes beliefs, knowledge, expectations and information processing. The affective component consists of positive and negative emotions, feelings and sensations. The behavioral component focuses on action tendencies and habits. Every attitude has an underlying belief, positive or negative affect, and a tendency to act in a particular way. The same three components are operating in the formation process and in the change process. We can talk about changing cognitions, changing emotions and changing behavior. Most often, the change process integrates all three components. However, change in each component might involve a different strategy and a different conception, and each has its advantages and disadvantages, strengths and weaknesses for particular changes desired. Resistance to change can also be characterized by its cognitive, affective and behavioral components.

Schooling is a continuous process of change, where new knowledge and new methods of information processing replace former ones as part of students' intellectual development. In essence, this is a process of cognitive change, but it also involves affective, and certainly behavioral components. Even cognitive change requires teachers to overcome students' psychological resistance. Teachers must constantly encourage students, excite them, evoke their interest, and maintain their motivation to learn. It can be said that people do not want to change (together with, and despite the fact that they do want to change), in the same way as it can be said that students do not want to learn (again, together with, and despite the fact that they do want to learn).

RESISTANCE TO PSYCHOLOGICAL CHANGE

People resist change, and from their point of view, their resistance is often justified (especially when someone else wants them to change). The same generalization holds true for groups of people and for organizations. Resistance to change is a widespread human phenomenon. Every plan for changing people's values, attitudes or feelings must take into account how to deal with the expected psychological resistance. It is easy to understand resistance to change in conceptual terms borrowed from exchange theory (discussed in Chapter 11). Exchange theory views human interchange in terms of gains and losses, assuming that people wish to maximize their psychological profits and to minimize their losses. On the basis of expected gains and losses, it tries to predict whether people would pursue a given interaction or not. The same conception can be applied to intrapersonal processes (that is, the inner debate within each person), concerning our values, attitudes, and choices how to be in the world.

As a rule, we would like to feel comfortable with the way we are, with our value system and views. We usually believe that our behavior and conduct are fine and balanced. The demand for change usually comes from the outside (from teachers, parents, bosses, spouses, peer group) and it violates our balance. It often seems, subjectively, that moving towards the required change might increase our losses, whereas it is not clear at all that any profit might be involved. The transition period in itself certainly involves a loss in terms of uncertainty, confusion, anxiety, and lack of effective habits. One would then naturally tend to maintain the existing balance and try to resist change. Resistance is less intense when people are distressed with their current situation and wish on their own accord to improve it. In such cases, the existent price is high, and the change might reap better benefits.

Political campaigners know very well that in order to win people's votes—a change process where a change in political view is expressed by actual voting behavior—they must convince prospective voters that (a) the current situation is very bad (loss), and (b) that the new situation that would result from their vote would be much improved (gain). An incumbent candidate who tries to get re-elected must do the opposite: convince voters that the current situation is good (or less bad compared to other options) and that a changed vote would be costly in its expected results.

Teachers are change agents who spend most of their professional time at the frontline of educating and changing students. Teachers, parents and other change agents would act in the same way as the political campaigners in the preceding example, emphasizing the losses inherent in the current situation and the prospective profits of the changed situation. They must also communicate to students that the change process in itself, the transition from old to new views and conduct, can be smooth with little or no price to pay. The more successful and convincing they are, more psychological change would be likely to take place. Psychological resistance is a defense mechanism, and therefore, when resistance is overcome or reduced, much mental energy becomes available for the change process.

All human beings are motivated by two contrasting needs: The need for stability and the need for fluidity. The need for stability is aimed at maintaining and protecting the consistency of who we are and what we think, whereas the need for fluidity is our adventurous side, our curiosity and our need to seek and conquer the unknown. The need for stability is more dominant and powerful and would usually win over the need for fluidity. Therefore, parents and teachers must stimulate and coax the need for fluidity and evoke a more fluid perspective in the children. Indeed, the essence of education is the spirit of inquiry which is epitomized by a strengthened need for fluidity. But the need for stability cannot be ignored, and students' willingness and openness to psychological change cannot be taken for granted. This is true in the academic domain no less than in the social or emotional domains. The essence of effective CM is the facilitation of students' motivation to advance and explore new horizons and to feel competent and efficacious in pursuing their need for fluidity.

Cognitive Aspects of Resistance to Change

The cognitive foundation of resistance to change is the necessity "to know for certain," an expression of the need for stability. Doubt or lack of knowledge bother us and cause tension which we must somehow reduce. Therefore, we are often willing to accept ready-made answers (for example, by inculcation and preaching, see Chapter 15), so as to know what to think and to understand how we ought to be in a complex world. It would have been better to form our values and attitudes on our own, but the cognitive effort required in order to do that on our own is immense. Therefore, people are often willing to accept external influence without asking too many questions.

We are constantly bombarded with a great overload of information in every area and every domain. We simply have no time and no mental capacity to process all the available information in a sufficiently quick pace when we interact with other people. Computers have an almost limitless memory capacity and structured programs for speedy processing of information. But human beings are not computers, and their mental capacities in retaining and processing social information are rather limited. Therefore, people need shortcuts for speedy yet sufficiently effective information processing.

Social perception and impression formation can be taken as a good example. To know what to think of the other person and how to behave toward that person (a peer, a teacher, etc.) we would need to collect and process a lot of information. That is what employers do when they need to select new workers and want to make the best decisions. In daily interactions, people must react to other people instantaneously, and they need to have mechanisms that would help them to know as quickly and as validly as possible. In our analysis of resistance to change (Babad et al. 1983) we discussed the balance between accuracy and effort in social cognition. Every person needs to have a certain level of accuracy in information processing, otherwise s/he could not interact competently with the other person. But to reach increased accuracy more investment of effort is required, and people want to minimize the required effort. The solution lies in a compromise (or a shortcut) that would provide sufficient accuracy through the investment of the smallest effort possible. The compromise perhaps reflects a certain mental laziness, but this solution is an effective way given the overload of information on the one hand and our inability to fully process all information on the other hand.

Stereotypes provide an excellent example of shortcuts in impression formation and social interaction. A stereotype is a generalization about an attribute that characterizes a whole group of people (e.g., Italians are warm and temperamental; redheads are hot-headed; women are intuitive and nonverbally sensitive). If we are about to enter an interaction with an Italian, a redhead, or a woman, we have stereotypic information available to us that enables us to know how to behave toward that person without expending much effort. Of course the stereotype is always biased, because even if the generalization about a group characteristic is data-based and statistically correct, the stereotype ignores the variation within the group and characterizes all members of the stereotyped group as if they are identical in that attribute.

All people use stereotypes continuosly despite their built-in biases. Stereotypes are cognitive shortcuts that are quite effective, because they provide sufficient accuracy and at the same time require minimal effort. But people should be aware that they are using stereotypes and should make mental corrections to avoid being inflexible and over-dependent on stereotypic thought. A serious pitfall of stereotypes is that sometimes they are not valid generalizations about given groups and might be misleading for their users. This is particularly true of negative stereotypes about minority groups that really represent prejudices rather than valid generalizations. If one accepts uncritically stereotypes about girls being stupid, Jews being conniving, or Scotsmen being misers, one has inadvertently become prejudiced.

Many other cognitive shortcuts in information processing have been investigated by social psychologists over the years. All of them are biases, but they serve the function of knowing enough without expending too much effort. These include the halo effect (the tendency of general liking or disliking to influence other, more specific judgments about persons); attribution errors (where particular positive or negative behaviors are perceived as representing either stable traits or situational factors); biased judgments and expectations (as discussed in Chapter 6) and more. Since the 1980s, much attention (and a Nobel Prize award) has been given to heuristics that had been defined and investigated by Daniel Kahneman and Amos Tversky (Kahneman, Slovic, & Tversky, 1982; Tversky & Kahneman, 1974). Heuristics are rules of thumb that serve as cognitive shortcuts, simple efficient rules that are used for making decisions and judgments (such as the availability heuristic, where people assume that what is more available is more correct, or the representativeness heuristic, where commonality between objects of similar appearance is assumed). When people use heuristics (or other biases) they do not really process information on their own, and their conclusions might therefore be biased.

Thus, resistance to change in the cognitive domain stems out of a tendency to avoid effort and to rely on existing solutions and generalizations that had already been established, even if they are far from perfect in their accuracy. Cognitive resistance can hinder openness to change in attitudes, beliefs, values and life perspective. But these ideas are equally relevant to the academic domain, where students often avoid learning processes that might demand extensive efforts, preferring various shortcuts instead. Unless they see the benefits that might be gained by investment of effort, people often do not want to learn and do not want to work hard.

Emotional Aspects of Resistance to Change

The strongest base of resistance to change is found in the affective domain, in the negative emotions evoked by a demand for psychological change. Resistance to change is a central characteristic of the defense system. The function of defense mechanisms is to protect the person's well-being and to minimize threat and anxiety. Social adjustment is a complex and difficult process, and people cope incessantly with difficulties throughout their lives. We are threatened by dynamic forces from inside ourselves and from the outside world. Never-ending efforts are required to create and maintain a healthy and functioning self-system that enables well-being. Pressures and threats of the outside reality include: Complex tasks to be performed and goals to be attained; gaining status and other people's respect and positive regard; competing with other people and maintaining balance; succeeding in our love and work relations, etc. Stress from within stems from needs and wishes; unfulfilled fantasies; uncontrolled rage and various negative emotions; sexual desires; past failures, etc. The healthy ego must be able to deal with all of these pressures and allow the person to live well and to feel well.

Defense mechanisms help people to cope with these pressures. These mechanisms—like rationalization, projection, suppression, repression, denial, displacement, counter-formation, etc.—were delineated by Sigmund Freud's daughter Anna (Freud, 1946). The common conceptual characteristic of all defense mechanisms is that they distort internal or external reality in some way, to the extent that enables people to reduce anxiety and to maintain their well-being. Distortion of external reality (such as in rationalization or displacement) or of internal reality (such as in suppression or repression) dulls the stress of particular knowledge by creating a less threatening substitute knowledge.

It is commonly held that it is not good to be too defensive. Defense mechanisms that are used too rigidly and too intensely might hinder, rather than help that individual. In the terms of accuracy and effort previously discussed, stronger defense mechanisms would involve greater distortion, and therefore accuracy might drop and the person would not be able to function effectively in social settings. Dynamic psychotherapy has dual purposes with regard to defense mechanisms. On the one hand, its objective is to expose patients' defense mechanisms and to decrease their intensity. On the other hand, stripping persons totally from their defense mechanisms is dangerous and would expose them to intolerable anxiety. Actually, psychosis represents a total collapse of the defense system, and then the individual cannot function in the real world and must be hospitalized in a special protective environment. The ideal situation is to have defense mechanisms that would distort external and/or internal reality to a degree that would preserve well-being and self-image and yet enable one to adjust and function well in one's social environment. Thus, much as it was argued before that the balance between accuracy and effort is dominant in the cognitive domain for dealing with information overload, the same kind of balance is highly relevant in the emotional domain for maintenance of well-being. In both cases the human need for such balance contributes to increase resistance to psychological change.

The preceding discussion implies that resistance to change can in itself be considered a defense mechanism. People are invested in who they are and in what they think and hold important, and their goal is to preserve their self-image, attitudes and values as long as they feel that they can function effectively. The demand to change usually comes from outside, and it can cause pain and anxiety. People must then first recognize that their existing values, attitudes or conduct are inappropriate, that they must adopt new and different views and way of conduct. Calling attention to limitations immediately evokes a defensive stand, and the person would attempt to preserve the existing system.

Behavioral Aspects of Resistance to Change

Resistance to change in the cognitive and affective domains is eventually channeled into the behavioral domain, because change is expressed not only in inner thoughts and feelings but also in explicit behavior and in the choice what to do and how to act. The most relevant term for understanding resistance to change in the behavioral domain is habit. There is something very reassuring and mentally relaxing in the existence of a routine, in the almost automatic behavior based on well-learned habits. Routine behavior means that we know what we are doing and we can react to situations without having to expend any effort to decide how to act. The requirement to change one's behavior is unsettling, because one cannot be sure how to behave and one's habits are no longer appropriate. Therefore, people prefer to behave in well-learned and practiced ways and to avoid new, unknown ways.

FOUR GENERALIZED STRATEGIES FOR PSYCHOLOGICAL CHANGE

Four strategies for attaining psychological change are presented next, concluding Part VI on educating and changing students, and appropriately concluding this entire book. The discussion is adapted from Chin and Benne's (1984) model of generalized strategies for planned change in human organizations. Chin and Benne's chapter was a major contribution in the classic book *The Planning of Change* (Bennis, Benne, & Chin, 4th edition, 1984). Four editions of the book were published over a span of twenty-five years, and it had a substantial impact on applied psychologists, organizational consultants, educators, human relations specialists and behavioral scientists involved in psychological change. Chin and Benne discussed three strategies, but I took the liberty to divide one of their strategies into two separate ones, and therefore four strategies are presented here.

The strategies describe four distinct approaches that can be applied in a process of planned change. Each is based on different assumptions about human nature (such as "man is a rational being," or "people wish to belong in a group," or "emotions influence thinking") and employs different tactics of implementation. Each can be successful for particular change objectives. The planning of change involves the selection of the most appropriate strategy and subsequent tactics given the particular circumstances and the characteristics of the persons or groups involved. Despite their disparate assumptions and tactics, the strategies are not contradictory of each other. Quite often a combination of several strategies, each dealing with a different aspect of the change situation, might be most effective.

The four strategies represent distinct types of concepts and processes that had been extensively discussed throughout this book. These processes are fundamental in the process of education and central in the social psychology of the classroom. The phenomena represented by the four strategies might be labeled in short by the following objectives:

1. To understand;
2. To act;
3. To feel;
4. To accommodate.

THE RATIONAL-EMPIRICAL STRATEGY OF PSYCHOLOGICAL CHANGE

The rational-empirical strategy is the most positive change strategy because it maintains that people can change out of their own conviction and free will. The cognitive change process is based on the image of the rational man who chooses and decides what to believe and what to think in the most balanced and effective way. Change is rational, data-based, well-reasoned, and follows a systematic examination of alternatives. In this strategy, people change their values, attitudes or behavior because they become convinced that the change is in their best interest and would serve them well. The role of the change agent is to convince, and the receivers would think, reason, consider all sides, and eventually make a decision how to change their views and their behavior. Educators would prefer to change their students in this manner, and would probably wish to change themselves in that manner, too. The task of the educator as a change agent is to bring the facts and the data to students' knowledge, and if the students can be convinced they would do the work themselves. Teachers are also responsible to create the necessary conditions for a rational-empirical process to take place—develop students' thinking, their knowledge base, and their abilities to analyze data and to reach logical conclusions.

The institution that best represents this strategy and its underlying ideology in society-at-large is the school. The great investment of societal resources in the schooling process proves the strong commitment to the rational-empirical ideology. A common belief in our culture that was discussed in the previous chapter holds that people who are more highly educated are also better people in their value orientation and enlightenment. School is intended to develop intelligent and autonomous citizens who choose their own ways, who are open to new information, and who are willing to change if they become convinced that change is warranted. To get to this stage, students must improve their intellect and their thinking, they must learn and master methodologies for information processing, and they must obtain much knowledge in various content areas. Thus, it can be said that a major objective of school is to socialize rational-empirical citizens. This ideology and conception characterizes the dominant contemporary approach to CM, as described in Chapter 9.

Modern democracy clearly subscribes to the rational-empirical ideology. In a democratic decision-making process, the collective creates groups and committees that discuss various issues, teams are appointed to collect relevant information, all alternatives are examined and weighed vis-à-vis each other, and change is collectively planned. The participation in such processes contributes to all individual participants, and provides credibility to the change process that might emerge out of such rational-empirical deliberations. Teachers often design such joint activities in their classrooms, and involve the students in all stages of the change process.

There is no doubt that the rational-empirical strategy is ideal, and teachers would almost always prefer to give it first priority in their efforts to influence students. When problems arise in the classroom or in any other setting and change is needed, the best approach would be to convince students or other people to change. People take personal responsibility for the change process and make their own decision out of conviction, and therefore the change is likely to be stable in the long run.

By this time, the reader must be wondering about the limitations of this strategy. If it is so ideal, can it work all the time? Well, obviously not, and rational-empirical change efforts often fail. In fact, this strategy seems to ignore most of the issues raised in the previous discussion of resistance to change. Arguing that people are rational and can apply their rationality to change situations is actually based on an assumption that psychological change can be attained without encountering resistance. Indeed, I think that this strategy can be most effective in situations of no, or weak resistance, where the proposed change is not threatening. Rationality can be strongly influenced by emotions, and threat and anxiety almost automatically reduce people's rationality and hinder their objective thinking. For example, people can be far more rational with regard to other people (as consultants) than with regard to themselves.

As mentioned, change is usually required in areas where the current behavior or attitudes are faulty, and the change would constitute an improvement. But human vices are extremely resistant to change, and people do not like to become aware of their faults and weaknesses. Therefore, people become particularly defensive and irrational when their vices are exposed and change is demanded. To give but a few of many possible examples, if one's style of interacting with others is demeaning, or if one demonstrates prejudice against some minority group members, if one is inconsiderate of others, or if a student bullies other students—chances are that employing a rational-empirical strategy would not be very successful in attaining the desired change. On such occasions, people are likely to resist to feedback that might expose their faults. Similarly, the notice that "cigarette smoking is hazardous to your health" printed on every cigarette box (a rational-empirical change tactic) does not seem to reduce the habit of heavy smokers, those who are most frequently exposed to this information.

People are particularly defensive and irrational in protecting their ideology. Ideology is a set or cluster of beliefs that are very central to their holder as a socio-identity. Ideology is expressed in a set of interrelated values and attitudes, in behavior, and in patterns of social interaction. One can have a religious ideology, a political ideology, a professional ideology, etc. Once acquired and adopted (see Chapter 15) ideology is clung to and not given much to change anymore. Most people are not capable of maintaining a rational discussion about ideological subjects. Think of the futility of arguing politics with a person (even a good friend, a rational person, basically) whose strong political ideology is opposite to yours. That is, if you can even have a close friend whose ideology is opposed to your ideology! People have subtle ways of telling others when rationality is futile and logical arguments would not be even considered. For example, when people say: "For me, this is a matter of principle" or when they say: "I hear you"—what they are really saying is that they are not going to listen at all.

THE BEHAVIORAL ("POWER-COERCIVE") STRATEGY OF PSYCHOLOGICAL CHANGE

This strategy is in many respects the opposite of the rational-empirical strategy. In the rational-empirical strategy, the conceptual continuum leads from thought to behavior: People must be convinced first, and then they would change their conduct. The power-coercive strategy reverses the order, and the conceptual continuum leads from behavior to thoughts: Behavior must be changed first, and subsequently, attitudes, beliefs and values would change to fit with the changed behavior. Thus, the change process is behavioral, and the change effort is invested in modifying people's actual conduct.

The term power-coercive chosen by the late Chin and Benne so many years ago was exaggerated and somewhat unfortunate, because of the totalitarian associations is evokes in modern day readers. Today, Chin and Benne would have probably used a more appropriate term such as behavioral change.

Successful change is based on the exercise of authority and the explication of rules and sanctions as part of the maintenance of social order. The assumption is that people (certainly students) accept legitimate authority and are willing to be good citizens. Many theorists (such as Erich Fromm in his classic book *Escape From Freedom*, 1941) and developmental psychologists believe that people (and especially youngsters) need rules and need guidance what to do and how to be. All human beings need a clear and explicit social framework that would spell out the appropriate and inappropriate conduct—and inadvertently, also direct people what to think. When students hear the term power-coercive, many of them think that the social institution best representing this strategy is prison. But this is not necessarily true, and the more relevant societal institutions best representing this strategy are, in my opinion, organizations, management, and government. Every society determines behavioral rules and modes of conduct that citizens must accommodate to. In education, all theoreticians of CM agree about the critical importance of the requirement for clear rules and clear expectations of consequences in effective CM.

This strategy assumes that, in order to change values, attitudes and life perspective, people's behavior must be changed first by available methods and tactics. The theoretical assumption (discussed in Chapter 15 and in previous chapters) is that people would retrospectively fit their attitudes and values to what they are actually doing. The strategy is therefore based on a dual conception—a behavior modification approach for changing behavior, and a complementary cognitive approach to deal with the process of internalization that causes change in values and attitudes. One relevant theory that would explain the internalization following behavioral change is Cognitive Dissonance Theory (Aronson, 1969; Festinger, 1954, 1957). Dissonance theory is still popular today as it had been a half century ago. It posits that attitudes and behavior must be consonant with each other, and there would be internal pressure to reduce any dissonance when thoughts differ from ex post facto behavior. And because it is easier to change behavior than to change inner thoughts (especially in a hierarchical institution with an existing legitimate authority such as the school), this strategy can be useful to effect psychological change.

As Chin and Benne pointed out in the various editions of their article, this is the most commonplace and frequently used change strategy, and probably the most effective, too. Human beings are social animals who live within clearly defined social frameworks, and they must adjust to the dictums of society in both their behavior and their inner thoughts and attitudes. Even adults accept the authority of those in a superior role to determine their behavior patterns and even to force them to behave in particular ways.

The behavioral strategy is frequently used, it is easy to operate, and it is usually quite effective with great speed. Its major weakness lies in the link between changed behavior and internalization. There is no guarantee that changed behavior would necessarily lead to the desired internal change. Individuals might often resist the internal change and would struggle to maintain their independence and autonomy of thought. They might behave mechanically as required, but would separate outward behavior from inner thoughts, and refuse to change their values and attitudes. And then, when the external behavioral pressure would cease, they would revert back to their old behavior. In such cases, the change objectives would not be attained despite the observable change in behavior. This scenario is more likely to take place in totalitarian situations, when excessive authority and exaggerated pressure are exercised. Adolescents often feel that their parents are totalitarian and force them to act against their will, and many students often have a similar feeling in the classroom. In such cases, the behavioral strategy would fail to achieve internal psychological change.

The overuse of authority might boomerang and spoil the change process, and over-eagerness of the change agent may well lead to such excess. Therefore, the literature recommends against the exclusive use of the power-coercive strategy. Behavioral methods (with their obvious advantages) should best be integrated with other strategies of change that would help to facilitate the process of internalization. Most experts in psychological change believe that the behavioral strategy should not be the one to be selected first. Other strategies should be tried first, but if they are difficult to operate or fail to succeed, a plan for behavioral change should be implemented, subsequently supplemented by intervention based on one of the other strategies, in order to deepen the behavioral change and to lead to internalization of the changed attitude.

THE EXPERIENTIAL (RE-EDUCATIVE) STRATEGY OF PSYCHOLOGICAL CHANGE

This is the affective strategy, based on the assumption that psychological change can best be facilitated through the emotional experience. Chin and Benne defined one generalized strategy labeled normative-re-educative, which I divided into the present experiential-affective strategy and another normative strategy dealing with social accommodation (see next discussion).

Following a previous comment that Chin and Benne's choice of the term power-coercive for the behavioral strategy is out-dated today and perhaps unfortunate, I think that their choice of the term re-educative for the experiential strategy was also problematic in our current professional language. Chin and Benne borrowed the term re-educative from the theory of their mentor, Kurt Lewin. In his field theory, Lewin (1951) discussed re-education as the process of learning through emotional experience and changing through discovery and insight, often following attempts to take on the perspective and point of view of others. However, in the 1950s and 1960s the American public was concerned about the phenomenon of brainwashing conducted by the Koreans and the Chinese on American prisoners. The Koreans labeled their brainwashing as re-education. It could therefore be mistakenly suspected that Chin and Benne had brainwashing in mind when they discussed this change strategy.

The characteristics and importance of learning through personal experience were described in Chapter 15, and this approach is equally important in attitude formation (education) as in attitude change. Personal experiences can have a profound impact that may lead to psychological change. Witnessing personally a serious automobile accident or having a close person injured in an accident can be more influential on attitudes and behavior than the dry statistics on highway deaths. Similarly, actually meeting people who are different in ethnic background or social and economic class and feeling them experientially can have a profound impact. The journey of Israeli youngsters to the Nazi death camps in Poland to foster their Jewish identity (Chapter 15) and numerous other experiences can contribute to meaningful psychological change.

The experiential strategy is integrative rather than exclusive. The emotional experience alone is not intended to bring about psychological change. Rather, the integration of the affective experience with rational-empirical data-based thinking and with other strategies and tactics is expected to contribute to change. Where data and rational arguments are not sufficient to mobilize a change process, the addition of a strong emotional experience can tip the balance and result in change.

The human relations movement that bloomed for several decades in the second half of the 20th century was strongly based on this strategy. Kenneth Benne, together with Lleland Bradfort and Ronald Lippitt, were the founders and the leaders of that movement after the death of Kurt Lewin. Thousands of people (managers of all types, medical and military personnel, teachers, educators and students from all levels of education) participated in human relations workshops and laboratories, where learning and change were based on the personal experiences of the participants in group formation and in interaction with others. The strong emotional personal experiences in the here and now were accompanied by rational-empirical learning and conceptual analysis, and group members underwent change processes of values, attitudes and behavior through their participation. Numerous structured exercises were constructed to provide participants with pointed experiential learning focused on particular issues such as leadership, cooperation and competition, stereotypes and prejudice, and management strategies. Effects of such structured experiences were cognitive, affective and behavioral. One example of a structured exercise used heavily today to promote experiential learning is role playing—where participants take the role and point of view of others and try to enact reality through the perspective of different others.

Today, experiential workshops are commonly held in educational settings for teachers and administrators and for students at all grade levels, from the early elementary grades to higher education. It is commonly thought that experiential processes, especially if integrated with relevant cognitive learning (and with behavioral change as well) may contribute to education and to the facilitation of psychological change.

THE ACCOMMODATIVE (NORMATIVE) STRATEGY OF PSYCHOLOGICAL CHANGE

The last strategy of psychological change is the normative, or accommodative strategy. As mentioned, only three strategies were originally presented by Chin and Benne, the third labeled the normative-re-educative strategy. I separate the normative strategy and present it as a fourth option, because the normative-accommodative process is unique and distinct from the previous three strategies. The normative approach is focused on the attempt to change individuals through changes in their social environment.

In all three former strategies, the planned change interventions are applied directly to the individuals who are the prospective targets of psychological change. The change agents try to convince them, to change and modify their behavior, and/or to have them go through various emotional experiences. In the normative strategy, the focus is put on changing the social environment within which the individual or the group is operating. The purpose is to elicit accommodation to the changed environment, which would ultimately cause individual change in values and attitudes. The central psychological assumption is that people need to accommodate to their social environment and to fit as best they can into that environment. Because of the importance of norms, rules and expectations (Chapter 1), if we change the norms of the classroom environment, students would inadvertently accommodate and change their attitudes, values and behavior to be consonant with the norms in order to be effective citizens in the school society.

Nickols (2003) wrote his version of Chin and Benne's change strategies. He also added a fourth change strategy, which he labeled the environmental-adaptive strategy, assuming that people need to adapt to new environments. Nickols suggested that for radical organizational change, the old organization should be let to die on the vine, and the participants should be moved to a newly created organization with a different normative structure. He assumed that participants would accommodate quickly to the new environment. Nickols' terminology might be a bit extreme and perhaps more appropriate to the realities of organizational frameworks than to educational settings, but the emphasis on normative environments and people's need to accommodate to their social environment is as valid to the classroom as it is to organizational settings. In fact, teachers do create and change normative environments in their classrooms every year. It is therefore quite feasible that they would change certain aspects of the classroom environment in order to elicit particular psychological changes in their students.

The normative strategy is frequently applied in the classroom. The norms characterizing a particular classroom—especially if they are distinct and explicitly different and better than the norms of other classrooms—can be quite meaningful in shaping students' values and behavior. In our classroom students help each other and we act as one body. In our classroom students respect and listen to each other. In our classrooms students never lie! And so on. Students are often quite happy to identify with such norms and to be proud of them. Then they internalize and own the relevant values and attitudes. Therefore, teachers make frequent use of the normative strategy.

Another frequent use of the normative strategy is to apply normative pressure not on the collective of the classroom society but on individual students. Teachers know from their personal experience that one of the ways of dealing with disruptive students is to appoint them to an important, salient and responsible role in the classroom. Because—in the language of Goffman's (1956) dramaturgical perspective—"the role makes the person," it can be predicted that disruptive students who are appointed to be responsible for important social tasks in the classroom would accommodate to the new role and begin to demonstrate responsibility and commitment. Their disruptive behavior would then decrease or disappear.

The power of normative accommodation to social environments is very strong. Much of the strategically planned influence of political propaganda and commercial advertising is founded on people's normative needs to belong in particular reference groups and to fit in particular social environments. The need to be like certain people (famous people, smart people, high-status people, sexually attractive people, etc.) is a normative influence that can cause attitudinal and behavioral change—to vote for a certain candidate, to believe in someone and in his beliefs, or to buy a certain product. And if a certain newspaper is advertised as the exclusive newspaper of thinking people, many people would wish to belong in the imaginary group of thinking people by subscribing to that newspaper. In a larger perspective, it can be said that the process of acculturation and social adjustment is heavily founded on people's normative needs and subsequent accommodation.

Teachers and managers in all types of organizations use the normative strategy quite heavily. It establishes and modifies the nature and the uniqueness of social bodies, gives an identity to the citizens of a given society, and helps to effect psychological change through accommodation. But like all previous strategies, this strategy can sometimes backfire and fail to attain its objectives. Norms cannot be arbitrary, and exaggerated or excessive use of this strategy might hinder its effectiveness, because participants might shy away from identification and accommodation to such norms. The norms must be convincing for the participants, so that the accommodation would not be external and temporary. As in the power-coercive behavioral strategy, people do fit their behavior to powerful social norms even if they do not believe in them, but they would cease to follow them when the normative pressure will be removed (after graduation, for example). As in the case of the behavioral strategy, the process of psychological change would be completed only after internalization, when people take ownership of the normative attitudes and values and identify with them. Because psychological change often involves giving up previously held attitudes and values, a phony accommodation is undesirable. Therefore, the application of this strategy requires wisdom, moderation and good timing, and overzealousness of the change agents might boomerang.

CONCLUDING COMMENTS: THE TEACHER AS EDUCATOR AND CHANGE AGENT

The conclusion to Part VI on educating and changing students is, in fact, an appropriate conclusion for the entire book. It emphasizes the educative role of the teacher in the social environment of the classroom. Kenneth Benne (1943) was among the first to present a conception of authority in democratic society and to delineate the desired collaborative nature of the exercise of authority in our culture. Benne also coined the concept change agent in the first edition (1961) of the book: *The Planning of Change* (Bennis et al. 1984).

In several discussions of the teacher's role throughout this book, I argued against the demand that teachers should serve as identification models for their students. I thought that the demand for perfection which is implied by such requirement would be exaggerated and might cause stress, hindering rather than facilitating the work of future teachers. But there is one area in which teachers must serve as models for their students, and that is the spirit of changeability or spirit of inquiry. For the classroom to serve as a social environment where psychological change can take place, it must be characterized by a normative atmosphere of openness to change, and teachers must demonstrate such openness to their students. The contemporary conception of CM (Chapter 9) emphasizes the collaborative efforts of teachers and students and the openness to mutual inquiry and exploration. The meta-goals of the human relations movement, formulated almost a half century ago by Warren Bennis (1962) emphasized the same conception. The goals were:

- Spirit of inquiry;
- Authenticity of relationships;
- Expanded consciousness and recognition of choice; and
- A conception of collaborative relationships.

Of all role holders in our society, teachers are the most important and salient change agents. Their authority to educate and to change students is generally accepted and almost never challenged, and they are expected to exercise their authority and to influence students. The teachers are the first to be held accountable for breaks in social order in the form of violence, crime, lack of respect or lack of values (in school, but no less in society-at-large), and the demand to improve the education of the young is pointed directly at the teachers and the schools.

As discussed in Chapter 3, all the different bases of social power are available to teachers (reward power; coercive power; legitimate power; referent power; expert power; and information power), and they can employ them to teach, educate and change their students. The social powers of the teachers are legitimate not only from the external, societal point of view, but the students themselves also accept teachers' authority and teachers' use of social power. Except for relatively rare instances of rebelliousness (especially in adolescence) students are susceptible to teacher's influence and do not challenge it. This gives teachers perfect starting point to be effective in educating and changing their students. But the process is not automatic and its outcomes are not guaranteed at all, and very often the school and the teachers fail in their role as change agents. Effective change must be carefully planned, and as Benne and Birnbaum (1960) argued many years ago, change cannot be haphazard.

Teachers can educate students and facilitate the formation of their values, attitudes, beliefs, life perspective and behavior through all modes described in Chapter 15 (educating through instruction and learning; inculcation and preaching; behavior modification; normative pressure and cultural/social frameworks; experiential learning; and by serving as models), and they can change students' values, beliefs and attitudes through the four generalized strategies discussed in this chapter. Teachers' educative success can be enhanced through the numerous elements of CM discussed in various chapters in this book: norm and rule setting; appropriate and equitable teacher–student interaction; effective treatment of discipline problems and classroom disruptions; and competent application of NV behavior.

The key elements for teachers' educative success and effectiveness are knowledge and planning. Knowledge is a necessary, but not sufficient component for educative success, and it should be applied through careful and meticulous planning. Knowledge and planning are equally important to teachers' success in their other central task, namely instruction. However, the potentially negative consequences of lack of sufficient knowledge and of faulty or inadequate planning are far more intense and costly in the educative, compared to the instructional domain.

References

Abdullah, M. (2002). *What is bibliotherapy?* ERIC Clearninghouse on Reading, English, and Communication Digest #177, EDO-CS-02–08.

Adams, J. (1965). Inequality in social exchange. In L. Berkowitz (Ed.), *Advances in experimental social psychology* (Vol. 2, pp. 267–299). New York: Academic Press.

Adorno, T., Frenkel-Brunswick, E., Levinson, D., & Sanford, N. (1950). *The authoritarian personality.* New York: Harper.

Allen, V., & Atkinson, M. (1981). Identification of spontaneous and deliberate behavior. *Journal of Nonverbal Behavior, 5,* 224–237.

Ambady, N., Bernieri, F., & Richeson, J. (2000). Toward a histology of social behavior: Judgmental accuracy from thin slices of the behavioral stream. In M. Zanna (Ed.), *Advances in Experimental Social Psychology* (Vol. 32, pp. 201–271). Boston: Academic Press.

Ambady, N., & Rosenthal, R. (1992). Thin slices of behavior as predictors of interpersonal consequences: A meta-analysis. *Psychological Bulletin, 111,* 256–274.

Ambady, N., & Rosenthal, R. (1993). Half a minute: Predicting teacher evaluations from thin slices of behavior and physical attractiveness. *Journal of Personality and Social Psychology, 64,* 431–441.

Ames, C. (1992). Classrooms: Goals, structures, and student motivation. *Journal of Educational Psychology, 84,* 261–271.

Andersen, J. (1978). *The relationship between teacher immediacy and teaching effectiveness.* Unpublished doctoral dissertation. West Virginia University, Morgantown, W. V.

Archer, D. (1980). *Social intelligence.* New York: M. Evans & Co.

Aronson, E. (1969). The theory of cognitive dissonance: A current perspective. In L. Berkowitz (Ed.), *Advances in Experimental Social Psychology* (Vol. 4. pp. 1–34). New York: Academic Press.

Avni-Babad, D. (2002). *Routine, action-inaction, and regret.* Doctoral Dissertation, Hebrew University of Jerusalem, Israel.

Babad, E. (1972). Person specificity of the social deprivation-satiation effect. *Developmental Psychology, 6,* 210–213.

Babad, E. (1979). Personality correlates of susceptibility to biasing information. *Journal of Personality and Social Psychology, 37,* 195–202.

Babad, E. (1980). Expectancy bias as a function of ability and ethnic labels. *Psychological Reports, 46,* 625–626.

Babad, E. (1990a). Measuring and changing teachers' differential behavior as perceived by students and teachers. *Journal of Educational Psychology, 82,* 683–690.

Babad, E. (1990b). Calling on students: How a teacher's behavior can acquire different meanings in students' minds. *Journal of Classroom Interaction, 25,* 1–4.

Babad, E. (1992). Teacher expectancies and nonverbal behavior. In R. Feldman (Ed.), *Applications of nonverbal theories and research* (pp. 167–190). Hillsdale, NJ: Lawrence Erlbaum Associates.

Babad, E. (1993a). Teachers' differential behavior. *Educational Psychology Review,* 5, 347–376.

Babad, E. (1993b). Pygmalion—25 years after: Interpersonal expectations in the classroom. In P. Blanck (Ed.), *Interpersonal expectations: Theory, research, and application* (pp. 125–153). London: Cambridge University Press.

Babad, E. (1995). The "teacher's pet" phenomenon, teachers' differential behavior, and students' morale. *Journal of Educational Psychology,* 87, 361–374.

Babad, E. (1998). Preferential affect: The crux of the teacher expectancy issue. In J. Brophy (Ed.), *Advances in research on teaching: Expectations in the classroom* (Vol. 7, pp. 183–214). Greenwich, CT: JAI Press.

Babad, E. (1999). Preferential treatment in television interviewing: Evidence from nonverbal behavior. *Political Communication,* 16, 337–358.

Babad, E. (2001). On the conception and measurement of popularity: More facts and some straight conclusions. *Social Psychology of Education,* 5, 3–29.

Babad, E. (2005a). The psychological price of media bias. *Journal of Experimental Psychology: Applied,* 11, 245–255.

Babad, E. (2005b). Guessing teachers' differential treatment of high- and low-achievers from thin slices of their public lecturing behavior. *Journal of Nonverbal Behavior,* 29, 125–134.

Babad, E. (2005c). Nonverbal behavior in education. In J. Harrigan, R. Rosenthal & K. Scherer (Eds.), *The new handbook of methods in nonverbal behavior research* (pp. 283–311). Oxford: Oxford University Press.

Babad, E. (2007). Teachers' nonverbal behavior and its effects on students. In R. Perry & J. Smart (Eds.), *The scholarship of teaching and learning: An evidence-based perspective* (pp. 201–261). Holland: Springer Publications. Also In J. Smart (Ed.), *Higher education: Handbook of theory and research* (Vol. 22, pp. 219–279). Dordrecht, The Netherlands: Springer Publications.

Babad, E. (2009). Teaching and nonverbal behavior in the classroom. In L. Saha & A. Dworkin (Eds.), *International handbook of research on teachers and teaching* (pp. 797–807). Holland: Springer Science + Business Media LLC.

Babad, E., Avni-Babad, D., & Rosenthal, R. (2003). Teachers' brief nonverbal behaviors can predict certain aspects of students' evaluations. *Journal of Educational Psychology,* 95, 553–562.

Babad, E., Avni-Babad, D., & Rosenthal, R. (2004). Prediction of students' evaluations from brief instances of professors' nonverbal behavior in defined instructional situations. *Social Psychology of Education,* 7, 3–33.

Babad, E., Bernieri, F., & Rosenthal, R. (1989a). When less information is more informative: Diagnosing teacher expectancies from brief samples of behaviour. *British Journal of Educational Psychology,* 59, 281–295.

Babad, E., Bernieri, F., & Rosenthal, R. (1989b). Nonverbal communication and leakage in the behavior of biased and unbiased teachers. *Journal of Personality and Social Psychology,* 56, 89–94.

Babad, E., Bernieri, F., & Rosenthal, R. (1991). Students as judges of teachers' verbal and nonverbal behavior. *American Educational Research Journal,* 28, 211–234.

Babad, E., Birnbaum, M., & Benne, K. (1983). *The social self: Group influences on personal identity.* Beverly Hills, CA: Sage Publications.

Babad, E., & Ezer, H. (1993). Seating locations of sociometrically identified student types: Methodological and substantive issues. *British Journal of Educational Psychology,* 63, 75–87.

Babad, E., & Inbar, J. (1981). Performance and personality correlates of teachers' susceptibility to biasing information. *Journal of Personality and Social Psychology,* 40, 553–561.

Babad, E., Inbar, J., & Rosenthal, R. (1982a). Pygmalion, Galatea, and the Golem: Investigations of biased and unbiased teachers. *Journal of Educational Psychology,* 74, 459–474.

Babad, E., Inbar, J., & Rosenthal, R. (1982b). Teachers' judgments of students' potential as a function of teachers' susceptibility to biasing information. *Journal of Personality and Social Psychology, 42,* 541–547.

Babad, E., & Taylor, P. (1992). Transparency of teacher expectations across language, cultural boundaries. *Journal of Educational Research, 86,* 120–125.

Babad, E., & Weisz, P. (1977). Effectiveness of social reinforcement as a function of contingent and noncontingent satiation. *Journal of Experimental Child Psychology, 24,* 406–414.

Babad, Y., Alexander, I., & Babad, E. (1983). Returning the smile of the stranger: Developmental patterns and socialization factors. *Monographs of the Society for Research in Child Development, 48(5),* 1–93.

Bagley, W. (1907). *Classroom management.* New York: Macmillan.

Bales, R. (1965). *Small groups: Studies in social interaction.* New York: Alfred A. Knopf.

Bandura, A. (1977). *Social learning theory.* Englewood Cliffs, NJ: Prentice-Hall.

Bandura, A. (1982). Self-efficacy mechanism in human agency. *American Psychologist, 37,* 122–147.

Bandura, A. (1986). *Social foundations of thought and action: A social cognitive theory.* Englewood Cliffs, NJ: Prentice-Hall.

Bandura, A. (1997). *Self-efficacy: The exercise of control.* Englewood Cliffs, NJ: Prentice Hall.

Baskin, J., Sperber, M., & Price, B. (2006). Asperger syndrome revisited. *Review of Neurological Disorders, 3,* 1–7.

Bass, B. (1998). *Transformational leadership: Industrial, military, and educational impact.* Mahwah, NJ: Lawrence Erlbaum Associates.

Bass, B., & Riggio, R. (2006). *Transformational leadership* (2nd ed.). Mahwah, NJ: Lawrence Erlbaum Associates.

Baumrind, D. (1971). Current patterns of parental authority. *Developmental Psychology Monograph, 4,* 1–103.

Becker, W., Madsen, C., Arnold, C., & Thomas, D. (1967). The contingent use of teacher attention and praise in reducing classroom behavior problems. *Journal of Special Education, 1,* 287–307.

Bem, D. (1972). Self-perception theory. In L. Berkowitz (Ed.), *Advances in Experimental Social Psychology* (Vol. 6, pp. 1–62). New York: Academic Press.

Benne, K. (1943). *A conception of authority.* New York: Russell and Russell.

Benne, K., & Birnbaum, M. (1960). Change does not have to be haphazard. *The School Review, 68,* 283–293.

Bennis, W. (1962). Goals and meta goals of laboratory training. *NTL Human Relations Training News, 6,* 3.

Bennis, W., Benne, K., & Chin, R. (Eds.). (1984). *The planning of change* (4th ed.). New York: Holt, Rinehart and Winston.

Berne, E. (1964). *Games people play–The basic handbook of transactional analysis.* New York: Ballantine Books.

Biddle, B. (1979). *Role theory: Expectations, identities and behaviors.* New York: Academic Press.

Biddle, B., & Thomas, E. (Eds.). (1966). *Role theory: Concepts and research.* New York: Wiley.

Blake, R., & Mouton, J. (1964). *The managerial grid: The key to leadership excellence.* Houston: Gulf Publishing Co.

Blanck, P., Rosenthal, R., & Cordell, L. (1985). The appearance of justice: Judges' verbal and nonverbal behavior in criminal jury trials. *Stanford Law Review, 38,* 89–164.

Brophy, J. (1983). Research on the self-fulfilling prophecy and teacher expectations. *Journal of Educational Psychology, 75,* 631–661.

Brophy, J. (1985). Teacher-student interaction. In J. Dusek (Ed.), *Teacher expectancies* (pp. 303–328). Hillsdale, NJ: Lawrence Erlbaum Associates.

Brophy, J. (1988). Educating teachers about managing classrooms and students. *Teachers and Teacher Education, 4*, 1–18.

Brophy, J. (1999). Perspectives of classroom management: Yesterday, today, and tomorrow. In H. J. Freiberg (Ed.), *Beyond behaviorism: Changing the classroom management paradigm* (pp. 43–56). Boston: Allyn & Bacon.

Brophy, J. (2006). History of research on classroom management. In C. Everston & C. Weinstein (Eds.), *Handbook of classroom management: Research, practice and contemporary issues* (pp. 17–43). Mahwah, NJ: Lawrence Erlbaum Associates.

Brophy, J., & Everston, C. (1981). *Student characteristics and teaching.* New York: Longman.

Brophy, J., & Putnam, J. (1979). *Classroom management in the elementary grades: A literature review.* Research series No. 32. East Lansing, MI: Institute for Research on Teaching, Michigan State University. ERIC # ED167537.

Butler, R. (2007). Teachers' achievement goal orientations and associations with teachers' help-seeking: Examination of a novel approach to teacher motivation. *Journal of Educational Psychology, 99*, 241–252.

Chavez, R. (1984). The use of high inference measures to study classroom environments: A review. *Review of Educational Research, 54*, 237–261.

Chin, R., & Benne, K. (1984). Generalized strategies for effecting change in human systems. In W. Bennis, K. Benne & R. Chin (Eds.), *The planning of change* (4th ed., pp. 22–45). New York: Holt, Rinehart & Winston.

Coie, J., Dodge, K., & Coppotelli, H. (1982). Dimensions and types of social status: A cross-age perspective. *Developmental Psychology, 18*, 557–570.

Cooper, H., & Good, T. (1983). *Pygmalion grows up.* New York: Longman.

Cooper, H., & Hazelrigg, P. (1988). Personality moderators of interpersonal expectancy effects: An integrative research review. *Journal of Personality and Social Psychology, 55*, 937–949.

Crandall, V. I., Katkovsky, W., & Crandall, V. J. (1965). Children's belief in their own control of reinforcements in intellectual-academic achievement situations. *Child Development, 36*, 91–109.

Deci, E., & Ryan, R. (1985). *Intrinsic motivation and self-determination in human behavior.* New York: Plenum.

DePaulo, B. (1992). Nonverbal behavior and self-presentation. *Psychological Bulletin, 111*, 203–243.

DePaulo, B. (1994). Spotting lies: Can humans learn to do better? *Current Directions in Psychological Science, 3*, 83–86.

DePaulo, B., & Friedman, H. (1998). Nonverbal communication. In D. Gilbert, S. Fiske & G. Lindzey (Eds.), *The handbook of social psychology* (4th ed., pp. 3–40). Boston: McGraw-Hill.

DePaulo, B., Lindsay, J., Malone, B., Muhlenbruck, L., & Cooper, H. (2003). Clues to deception. *Psychological Bulletin, 129*, 74–112.

DePaulo, B., & Rosenthal, R. (1979). Ambivalence, discrepancy and deception in nonverbal communication. In R. Rosenthal (Ed.), *Skill in nonverbal communication* (pp. 204–248). Cambridge, MA: Oelgeschlager, Gunn, & Hain.

Dion, K. (1972). Physical attractiveness and evaluations of children's transgressions. *Journal of Personality and Social Psychology, 24*, 207–213.

Dorman, J. (2002). Classroom environment research: Progress and possibilities. *Queensland Journal of Educational Research, 18*, 112–140.

Dweck, C. (1999). *Self theories: Their role in motivation, personality and development.* Philadelphia: Psychology Press.

Dweck, C., & Elliott, E. (1983). Achievement motivation. In P. Mussen (Series Ed.) and E. Hetherington (Vol. Ed.), *Handbook of child psychology, Vol. 4,*

Socialization, personality, and social development (4th ed., pp. 643–691). New York: Wiley.

Eden, D. (1990). *Pygmalion in management: Productivity as a self-fulfilling prophecy.* Lexington, MA: Lexington Books.

Eden, D. (1992). Self-fulfilling prophecy as a management tool: Harnessing Pygmalion. *Academy of Management Review, 9,* 64–73.

Ekman, P. (1984). Expression and the nature of emotion. In K. Scherer & P. Ekman (Eds.), *Approaches to emotion* (pp. 319–343). Hillsdale, NJ: Lawrence Erlbaum Associates.

Ekman, P. (1985). *Telling lies.* New York: Norton.

Ekman, P., & Friesen, W. (1969a). The repertoire of nonverbal behavior: Categories, origins and coding. *Semiotica, 1,* 49–98.

Ekman, P., & Friesen, W. (1969b). Nonverbal leakage and clues to deception. *Psychiatry, 32,* 88–106.

Ekman, P., & Friesen, W. (1971). Constants across cultures in the face and emotion. *Journal of Personality and Social Psychology, 17,* 124–129.

Ekman, P., & Friesen, W. (1978). *Facial Action Coding System: A technique for the measurement of facial movement.* Palo Alto, CA: Consulting Psychologist Press.

Elias, M., & Schwab, Y. (2006). From compliance to responsibility: Social and emotional learning and classroom management. In C. Everston & C. Weinstein (Eds.), *Handbook of classroom management: Research, practice and contemporary issues* (pp. 309–341). Mahwah, NJ: Lawrence Erlbaum Associates.

Elliott, E., & Dweck, C. (1988). Goals: An approach to motivation and achievement. *Journal of Personality and Social Psychology, 54,* 5–12.

Elliott, E., & Dweck, C. (2005). *Handbook of competence and motivation.* New York: Guilford Press.

Elliott, E., & Harackiewicz, J. (1996). Approach and avoidance achievement goals and intrinsic motivation: A mediational analysis. *Journal of Personality and Social Psychology, 70,* 461–475.

Ellis, A., & Dryden, W. (2007). *The practice of rational emotive behavior therapy* (2nd ed.). Dordrecht, the Netherlands: Springer.

Emmer, E. (1994). *Teacher emotions and classroom management.* Paper presented at the annual meeting of the American Educational Research Association. Atlanta, GA.

Emmer, E., & Gerwels, M. (2006). Classroom management in middle and high school classrooms. In C. Everston & C. Weinstein (Eds.), *Handbook of classroom management: Research, practice and contemporary issues* (pp. 407–437). Mahwah, NJ: Lawrence Erlbaum Associates.

Everston, C., Emmer, E., & Worsham, M. (2003). *Classroom management for elementary teachers* (5th ed.). Boston: Allyn & Bacon.

Everston, C., & Weinstein, C. (Eds.). (2006a). *Handbook of classroom management: Research, practice and contemporary issues.* Mahwah, NJ: Lawrence Erlbaum Associates.

Everston, C., & Weinstein, C. (2006b). Classroom management as a field of inquiry. In C. Everston & C. Weinstein (Eds.), *Handbook of classroom management: Research, practice and contemporary issues* (pp. 3–15). Mahwah, NJ: Lawrence Erlbaum Associates.

Feldman, R. (Ed.). (1992). *Applications of nonverbal behavioral theories and research.* Hillsdale, NJ: Lawrence Erlbaum Associates.

Festinger, L. (1954). A theory of social comparison processes. *Human Relations, 7,* 117–140.

Festinger, L. (1957). *A theory of cognitive dissonance.* Stanford, CA: Stanford University Press.

Fiedler, F. (1978). The contingency model and the dynamics of the leadership process. In L. Berkowitz (Ed.), *Advances in experimental social psychology* (Vol. 12, pp. 59–112). New York: Academic Press.

Fiedler, F. (1981). Leadership effectiveness. *American Behavioral Scientist, 24*, 619–632.

Flanders, N. (1970). *Analyzing teacher behavior.* Reading, MA: Addison Wesley.

Frank, M. (2005). Research methods in detecting deception research. In J. Harrigan, R. Rosenthal & K. Scherer (Eds.), *The new handbook of methods in nonverbal behavior research* (pp. 341–368). Oxford: Oxford University Press.

Fraser, B. (1991). Two decades of classroom environment research. In B. Fraser & H. Walberg (Eds.), *Educational environments: Evaluation, antecedents and consequences* (pp. 3–27). London: Pergamon Press.

Fraser, B. (1994). Research on classroom and school climate. In D. Gabel (Ed.), *Handbook of research in science teaching and learning* (pp. 493–541). New York: Macmillan.

Fraser, B. (1998). Classroom environment instruments: Development, validity and application. *Learning Environment Research, 1*, 7–34.

Fraser, B., Anderson, G., & Walberg, H. (1982). *Assessment of learning environments: Manual for Learning Environment Inventory (LEI) and My Class Inventory (MCI).* (3rd vers.). Perth, Australia: Western Australian Institute of Technology.

Fraser, B., & Fisher, D. (1983). Use of actual and preferred classroom environment scales in person-environment fit research. *Journal of Educational Psychology, 75*, 303–313.

Fraser, B., & O'Brien, P. (1985). Student and teacher perceptions of the environment of elementary-school classrooms. *Elementary School Journal, 85*, 567–580.

Freiberg, H. J. (Ed.). (1999). *Beyond behaviorism: Changing the classroom management paradigm.* Needham Heights, MA: Allyn & Bacon.

Freiberg, H. J., & Lapointe, J. (2006). Research-based programs for preventing and solving discipline problems. In C. Everston & C. Weinstein (Eds.), *Handbook of classroom management: Research, practice and contemporary issues* (pp. 735–786). Mahwah, NJ: Lawrence Erlbaum Associates.

French, J., & Raven, B. (1959). The bases of social power. In D. Cartwright (Ed.), *Studies in social power* (pp. 150–167). Ann Arbor, MI: University of Michigan Press.

Freud, A. (1946). *The ego and the mechanisms of defense.* New York: International Universities Press.

Friedman, I. (1993). Burnout in teachers: The concept and its unique core meaning. *Educational and Psychological Measurement, 53*, 1035–1044.

Friedman, I. (1995). Student behavior patterns contributing to teacher burnout. *Journal of Educational Research, 88*, 281–289.

Friedman, I. (2000). Burnout in teachers: Shattered dreams of impeccable professional performance. *Journal of Clinical Psychology, 56*, 595–606.

Friedman, I. (2006). Classroom management and teacher stress. In C. Everston & C. Weinstein (Eds.), *Handbook of classroom management: Research, practice and contemporary issues* (pp. 925–944). Mahwah, NJ: Lawrence Erlbaum Associates.

Fromm, E. (1941). *Escape from freedom.* New York: Rinehart. British version: Fromm, E. (1941). *The fear of freedom.* London: Routledge.

Gada-Jain, N. (1999). *Intentional synchrony effects on job interview evaluation,* Unpublished Master Thesis, University of Toledo.

Gewirtz, J. (1967). Deprivation and satiation of social stimuli as determinants of their reinforcing efficacy. In J. Hill (Ed.), *Minnesota Symposium on child Psychology* (Vol. I). Minneapolis: University of Minnesota Press.

Gewirtz, J. (1969). Potency of a social reinforcer as a function of satiation and recovery. *Developmental Psychology, 1,* 2–13.

Goethals, G., & Darley, J. (1987). Social comparison theory: Self-evaluation and group life. In B. Mullen & G. Goethals (Eds.), *Theories of group behavior* (pp. 21–47). New York: Springer Verlag.

Goffman, I. (1956). *The presentation of self in everyday life.* New York: Doubleday.

Goh, S., & Fraser, B. (1998). Teacher interpersonal behavior: Classroom environment and student outcomes in primary mathematics in Singapore. *Learning Environments Research, 1,* 199–229.

Good, T., & Brophy, J. (1972). Behavioral expression of teacher attitudes. *Journal of Educational Psychology, 63,* 617–624.

Good, T., & Brophy, J. (1974). Changing student and teacher behavior: An empirical examination. *Journal of Educational Psychology, 66,* 390–405.

Good, T., & Brophy, J. (1990). *Educational psychology: A realistic approach* (4th ed.). Reading, MA: Addison-Wesley.

Good, T., & Brophy, J. (2003). *Looking at classrooms* (9th ed.). Boston: Allyn & Bacon.

Good, T., & Weinstein, R. (1986). Teacher expectations: A framework for exploring classrooms. In K. Zumwalt (Ed.), *Improving teaching.* (The 1986 ASCD Yearbook). Alexandria, VA: Association for Supervision and Curriculum Development.

Hall, J. (1978). Gender effects in decoding nonverbal cues. *Psychological Bulletin, 85,* 845–857.

Hall, J. (1984). *Nonverbal sex differences: Communication accuracy and expressive style.* Baltimore: The Johns Hopkins University Press.

Hall, J. (1998). How big are nonverbal sex differences? The case of smiling and sensitivity to nonverbal cues. In D. Canary & K. Dindia (Eds.), *Sex differences and similarities in communication: Critical essays and empirical investigations of sex and gender in interaction* (pp. 155–177). Mahwah, NJ: Lawrence Erlbaum Associates.

Harackiewicz, J., Barron, K., Pintrich, P., Elliott, A., & Thrash, T. (2002). Revision of achievement goal theory: Necessary and illuminating. *Journal of Educational Psychology, 94,* 638–645.

Hargreaves, D. (1975). *Interpersonal relations and education.* London: Routledge and Kegan Paul.

Harris, M., & Rosenthal, R. (1985). Mediation of interpersonal expectancy effects: 31 meta-analyses. *Psychological Bulletin, 97,* 363–386.

Harris, M., & Rosenthal, R. (2005). No more teachers' dirty looks: Effects of teacher nonverbal behavior on student outcomes. In R. Riggio & R. Feldman (Eds), *Applications of nonverbal communication* (pp. 157–192). New York: Routledge.

Hart, A. (1995). Naturally occurring expectation effects. *Journal of Personality and Social Psychology, 68,* 109–115.

Hersey, P., & Blanchard, K. (1982). *Management of organizational behavior* (4th ed.). Englewood Cliffs, NJ: Prentice-Hall.

Hidi, S., & Harackiewicz, J. (2000). Motivating the academically unmotivated: A critical issue for the 21st century. *Review of Educational Research, 70,* 151–179.

Homans, G. (1961). *Social behaviour: It's elementary forms.* London: Routledge and Kegan Paul.

Hyman, I., Bryony, K., Tabori, A., Weber, M., Mahon, M., & Cohen, I. (2006). Bullying: Theory, research, and interventions. In C. Everston & C. Weinstein (Eds.), *Handbook of classroom management: Research, practice and contemporary issues* (pp. 855–884). Mahwah, NJ: Lawrence Erlbaum Associates.

Jack, S., & Ronan, K. (2008). Bibliotherapy practice and research. *School Psychology International, 29,* 161–182.

Jones, V. (2006). How do teachers learn to be effective classroom managers? In C. Everston & C. Weinstein (Eds.), *Handbook of classroom management: Research, practice and contemporary issues* (pp. 887–907). Mahwah, NJ: Lawrence Erlbaum Associates.

Jussim, L., & Harber, K. (2005). Teacher expectations and self-fulfilling prophecies: Knowns and unknowns, resolved and unresolved controversies. *Personality and Social Psychology Review, 9,* 131–155.

Jussim, L., Smith, A., Madon, S., & Palumbo, P. (1998). Teacher expectations. In J. Brophy (Ed.), *Advances in research on teaching: Expectations in the classroom* (Vol. 7, pp. 1–48). Greenwich, CT: JAI Press.

Kahneman, D., Slovic, P., & Tversky, A. (Eds.). (1982). *Judgment under uncertainty: Heuristics and biases.* New York and Cambridge: Cambridge University Press.

Kelman, H. (1958). Compliance, identification, and internalization: Three processes of attitude change. *Journal of Conflict Resolution, 2,* 51–60.

Koneya, M. (1976). Location and interaction in row-and-column seating arrangements. *Environment and Behavior, 8,* 265–282.

Kounin, J. (1970). *Discipline and group management in classrooms.* New York: Holt, Rinehart & Winston.

Kruglanski, A., & Mayseless, O. (1990). Classic and current social comparison research: Expanding the perspective. *Psychological Bulletin, 108,* 195–208.

Landrum, T., & Kauffman, J. (2006). Behavioral approaches to classroom management. In C. Everston & C. Weinstein (Eds.), *Handbook of classroom management: Research, practice and contemporary issues* (pp. 47–71). Mahwah, NJ: Lawrence Erlbaum Associates.

Landsberger, H. (1958). *Hawthorne revisited.* Ithaca, NY: Cornell University Press.

Lee, M., Matsumoto, D., Kobayashi, M., Krupp, D., Maniatis, E., & Roberts, W. (1992). Cultural influences on nonverbal behavior in applied settings. In R. Feldman (Ed.), *Applications of nonverbal behavioral theories and research* (pp. 239–261). Hillsdale, NJ: Lawrence Erlbaum Associates.

Lewin, K. (1951). *Field theory in social science: Selected theoretical papers.* D. Cartwright (Ed.). New York: Harper & Row.

Lewin, K., Lippitt, R., & White, R. (1939). Patterns of aggressive behavior in experimentally created social climates. *Journal of Social Psychology, 10,* 271–299.

MacAuley, D. (1990). Classroom environment: A literature review. *Educational Psychology, 10,* 239–253.

Marrow, A. (1969). *The practical theorist: The life and work of Kurt Lewin.* New York: Basic Books.

Marzano, R., & Marzano, J. (2003). The key to classroom management. *Educational Leadership, 61,* 6–18.

Maslach, C., & Leiter, M. (1999). Teacher burnout: A research agenda. In R. Vandenberghe & A. Huberman (Eds.), *Understanding and preventing teacher burnout* (pp. 295–303). Cambridge, UK: Cambridge University Press.

Maslow, A. (1943). A theory of human motivation. *Psychological Review, 50,* 370–396.

Maslow, A. (1954). *Motivation and personality.* New York: Harper & Row.

Mayo, E. (1933). *The human problems of an industrial civilization.* New York: MacMillan.

McClelland, D. (1953). *The achievement motive.* New York: Appleton-Century-Crofts.

McCroskey, P., & Richmond, J. (1992). Increasing teacher influence through immediacy. In V. Richmond & J. McCroskey (Eds.), *Power in the classroom: Communication, control and concern* (pp. 101–119). Hillsdale, NJ: Lawrence Erlbaum Associates.

Mehrabian, A. (1966). Immediacy: An indicator of attitudes in linguistic communication. *Journal of Personality, 34*, 26–34.

Mehrabian, A. (1971). *Silent messages*. Belmont, CA: Wadsworth.

Mehrabian, A. (1972). *Nonverbal communication*. Chicago: Aldine-Atherton.

Moore, D., & Glynn, T. (1984). Variation in question rate as a function of position in the classroom. *Educational Psychology, 4*, 233–248.

Moos, R. (1974). *The social climate scales: An overview*. Palo alto, CA: Consulting Psychologists Press.

Moos, R. (1978). A typology of junior and high school classrooms. *American Educational Research Journal, 15*, 53–66.

Moos, R., & Trickett, E. (1987). *Classroom Environment Scale Manual* (2nd ed.). Palo Alto, CA: Consulting Psychologists Press.

Moreno, J. (1934). *Who shall survive?* New York: Beacon House.

Moreno, J. (1943). Sociometry in the classroom. *Sociometry, 6*, 425–428.

Moreno, J. (Ed.). (1960). *The sociometry reader*. Glencoe, Il: The Free Press.

Murray, H. (1983a). Low-inference classroom teaching behaviors and students' ratings of college teaching effectiveness. *Journal of Educational Psychology, 75*, 138–149.

Murray, H. (1983b). Low- inference classroom teaching behaviors in relation to six measures of college teaching effectiveness. In J. G. Donald (Ed.), *Proceedings of the conference on the evaluation and improvement of university teaching: The Canadian experience*. Montreal: Center for Teaching and Learning Services, McGill University.

Murray, H. (1938). *Explorations in personality*. Oxford: Oxford University Press.

Nash, B. (1981). The effects of classroom spatial organization on four and five-year old children's learning. *British Journal of Educational Psychology, 51*, 144–155.

Nash, R. (1976). Pupils' expectations of their teachers. In M. Stubbs & S. Delamont (Eds.), *Explorations in classroom observation* (pp. 83–98). London: John Wiley.

Nicholls, J. (1984). Concepts of ability and achievement motivation. In R. Ames & C. Ames (Eds.), *Research on motivation in education: Vol. 1, Student motivation* (pp. 39–73). New York: Academic Press.

Nickols, F. (2003). Four change management strategies. www.nickols.us.

Nisan, M. (1991). The moral balance model: Theory and research extending our understanding of moral choice and deviation. In J. Gewirtz & W. Kutines (Eds.), *Handbook of moral behavior and development* (Vol. 3, pp. 213–250*)*. Hillsdale, NJ: Lawrence Erlbaum Associates.

O'Leary, K., & O'Leary, S. (1972). *Classroom management*. New York: Pergamon Press.

Pellegrini, A., & Blatchford, P. (2000). *The child at school: Interactions with peers and teachers*. New York: Oxford University Press.

Perry, R. (1991). Perceived control in college students: Implications for instruction in higher education. In J. Smart (Ed.), *Higher education: Handbook of theory and research* (Vol. 7, pp. 1–56). New York: Agathon Press.

Perry, R. (2003). Perceived (academic) control and causal thinking in achievement settings. *Canadian Psychologist, 44*, 312–331.

Perry, R., Hall, N., & Ruthig, J. (2007). Perceived (academic) control and scholastic attainment in higher education. In R. Perry & J. Smart (Eds.), *The scholarship of teaching and learning in higher education: An evidence-based perspective* (pp. 477–551). Dordrecht, The Netherlands: Springer Publications.

Philippot, P., Feldman, R., & McGee, G. (1992). Nonverbal behavioral skills in an educational context: Typical and atypical populations. In R. Feldman (Ed.), *Applications of nonverbal behavioral theories and research* (pp. 191–213). Hillsdale, NJ: Lawrence Erlbaum Associates.

Pianta, R. (2006). Classroom management and relationships between children and teachers: Implications for research and practice. In C. Everston & C. Weinstein (Eds.), *Handbook of classroom management: Research, practice and contemporary issues* (pp. 685–710). Mahwah, NJ: Lawrence Erlbaum Associates.

Pines, A., & Aronson, E. (1988). *Career burnout: Causes and cures*. New York: Free Press.

Riggio, R. (1992). Social interaction skills and nonverbal behavior. In R. Feldman (Ed.), *Applications of nonverbal behavioral theories and research* (pp. 3–30). Hillsdale, NJ: Lawrence Erlbaum Associates.

Riggio, R., & Feldman, R. (Eds.). (2005). *Applications of nonverbal communication*. New York: Routledge.

Rogers, C. (1951). *Client-centered therapy: Its current practice, implications and theory*. London: Constable.

Rogers, C. (1959). A theory of therapy, personality and interpersonal relationships as developed in the client-centered framework. In S. Koch (Ed.), *Psychology: A study of science. Vol. 3: Formulations of the person and the social context*. New York: McGraw-Hill.

Rogers, C. (1961). *On becoming a person: A therapist's view of psychotherapy*. London: Constable.

Rogers, C., & Freiberg, H. J. (1994). *Freedom to learn* (3rd ed.). Columbus, Ohio: Merrill.

Rokeach, M. (1954). The nature and meaning of dogmatism. *Psychological Review, 61*, 194–204.

Rokeach, M. (1960). *The open and closed mind*. New York: Basic Books.

Rosenthal, R. (1963). On the social psychology of the psychological experiment: The experimenter's hypothesis as unintended determinant of experimental results. *American Scientist, 51*, 268–283.

Rosenthal, R. (1966). *Experimenter effects in behavioral research*. New York: Appleton-Century-Crofts.

Rosenthal, R. (1973). On the mediation of Pygmalion effects: A four factor "theory". *Papua New Guinea Journal of Education, 9*, 1–12.

Rosenthal, R. (1979). *Skill in nonverbal communication*. Cambridge, MA: Oelschlager, Gunn, & Hain.

Rosenthal, R. (1989, August). *The affect/effort theory of the mediation of interpersonal expectancy effects*. Donald T. Campbell Award Address, Annual convention of the American Psychological Association, New Orleans.

Rosenthal, R., & DePaulo, B. (1979). Sex differences in eavesdropping of nonverbal cues. *Journal of Personality and Social Psychology, 37*, 273–285.

Rosenthal, R., Hall, J., DiMatteo, R., Rogers, P. & Archer, D. (1979). *Sensitivity to nonverbal communication: The PONS test*. Baltimore: The Johns Hopkins University Press.

Rosenthal, R., & Jacobson, L. (1968). *Pygmalion in the classroom*. New York: Holt, Rinehart and Winston.

Rosenthal, R., & Rosnow, R. (1991). *Essentials of behavioral research: Methods and data analysis* (2nd ed.). New York: McGraw-Hill.

Rotter, J. (1954). *Social learning and clinical psychology*. New York: Prentice-Hall.

Rotter, J. (1966). Generalized expectations of internal versus external control of reinforcements. *Psychological Monographs, 80,* (Whole No. 609).

Rubovitz, P., & Maehr, M. (1973). Pygmalion Black and White. *Journal of Personality and Social Psychology, 25,* 210–218.

Schmuck, R. (1978). Helping teachers improve classroom group processes. *Journal of Applied Behavioral Science, 4,* 401–435.

Schmuck, R., & Schmuck, P. (1975). *Group processes in the classroom* (2nd ed.). Dubuque, Iowa: Wm. C. Brown Company.

Schutz, W. (1958). *FIRO: A three-dimensional theory of interpersonal behavior.* New York: Rinehart.

Sherif, M., Harvey, O., White, B., Hood, W., & Sherif, C. (1961). *Intergroup conflict and cooperation: The Robbers' Cave experiment.* . Norman, OK: Institute of Group Relations.

Silberman, M. (1969). Behavioral expression of teacher attitudes toward elementary school students. *Journal of Educational Psychology, 60,* 402–407.

Silberman, M. (1971). Teachers' actions and attitudes toward their students. In M. Silberman (Ed.), *The experience of schooling.* New York: Holt, Rinehart and Winston.

Snyder, M. (1987). *Public appearances/private realities: The psychology of self-monitoring.* New York: Freeman.

Sommer, R. (1967). Classroom ecology. *Journal of Applied Behavioral Science, 3,* 489–503.

Steinberg, L. (1996). *Beyond the classroom: Why school reform has failed and what parents need to know.* New York: Simon and Schuster.

Stires, L. (1980). Classroom seating location, student grades and attitudes: Environment or self-selection? *Environment and Behavior, 12,* 241–254.

Superka, D., Ahrens, C., & Hedstrom, J. (Eds.). (1976). *Values education sourcebook.* Boulder, CO: Social Science Education Consortium.

Tal, Z. (1987). *Teachers' differential behavior toward their students: Investigation of the "teacher's pet phenomenon."* Doctoral dissertation, Hebrew University of Jerusalem, Israel.

Tal, Z., & Babad, E. (1989). The "teacher's pet" phenomenon as viewed by Israeli teachers and students. *Elementary School Journal, 90,* 99–110.

Tal, Z., & Babad, E. (1990). The teacher's pet phenomenon: Rate of occurrence, correlates, and psychological costs. *Journal of Educational Psychology, 82,* 637–645.

Thibaut, J., & Kelley, H. (1959). *The social psychology of groups.* New York: Wiley.

Tversky, A., & Kahneman, D. (1974). Judgment under uncertainty: Heuristics and biases. *Science, 185,* 1124–1130.

Vrij, A. (2000). *Detecting lies and deceit: The psychology of lying and its implications for professional practice.* Chichester: John Wiley and Sons.

Walberg, H. (1981). A psychological theory of educational productivity. In F. Farley & N. Gordon (Eds.), *Psychology and education: The state of the union* (pp. 81–108). Berkeley, CA: McCutchan.

Walberg, H., & Anderson, G. (1968). Classroom climate and individual learning. *Journal of Educational Psychology, 59,* 414–419.

Watzlawick, P., Weakland, J., & Fisch, R. (1974). *Change: Principles of problem formation and problem resolution.* New York: Norton.

Weiner, B. (1992). *Human motivation: Metaphors, theories and research.* Newberry Park, CA: Sage Publications.

Weinstein, C. (1979). The physical environment of the school: A review of the research. *Review of Educational Research, 49,* 577–610.

Weinstein, C. (1999). Reflections on best practices and promising programs: Beyond assertive classroom discipline. In H. J. Freiberg (Ed.), *Beyond Behaviorism* (pp. 147–163). Needham Heights, MA: Allyn & Bacon.

Weinstein, R. (2002). *Reaching higher–the power of expectations in schooling.* Cambridge, MA: Harvard University Press.

Weinstein, R., Marshall, H., Brattesani, K., & Middlestadt, S. (1982). Student perceptions of differential teacher treatment in open and traditional classrooms. *Journal of Educational Psychology, 75*, 678–692.

Weinstein, R., Marshall, H., Sharp, L., & Botkin, M. (1987). Pygmalion and the students: Age and classroom differences in children's awareness of teacher expectations. *Child Development, 58*, 1079–1093.

Weinstein, R., & McKown, C. (1998). Expectancy effects in "context": Listening to the voices of students and teachers. In J. Brophy (Ed.), *Advances in research on teaching: Expectations in the classroom* (Vol. 7, pp. 215–242). Greenwich, CT: JAI Press.

Weinstein, R., & Middlestadt, S. (1979). Student perceptions of teacher interaction with male high and low achievers. *Journal of Educational Psychology, 71*, 421–431.

Wentzel, K. (2006). A social motivation perspective for classroom management. In C. Everston & C. Weinstein (Eds.), *Handbook of classroom management: Research, practice and contemporary issues* (pp. 619–643). Mahwah, NJ: Lawrence Erlbaum Associates.

Wheldall, K., & Lam, Y. (1987). Rows versus tables. II. The effects of two classroom seating arrangements on classroom disruption rate, on-task behaviour and teacher behaviour in three special school classes. *Educational Psychology, 7*, 303–312.

White, R. (1959). Motivation reconsidered: The concept of competence. *Psychological Review, 66*, 297–333.

Wineburg, S. (1987). The self-fulfillment of the self-fulfilling prophecy. *Educational Researcher, 16*, 28–44.

Witt, P., Wheeless, L., & Allen, M. (2004). A meta-analytical review of the relationship between teacher immediacy and student learning. *Communication Monographs, 71*, 184–207.

Wood, A. (1998). The effects of teacher enthusiasm on student motivation, selective attention, and text memory. Doctoral dissertation, University of Western Ontario. *Dissertation Abstracts International, Section A: Humanities and Social Sciences.* US, 1999 March 59 (9-A): p. 3355.

Wood, T., & McCarthy, C. (2000). *Understanding and preventing teacher burnout. ERIC Digest.* Washington, DC: ERIC Clearinghouse on Teaching and Teacher Education.

Woolfolk Hoy, A., & Weinstein, C. (2006). Student and teacher perspectives on classroom management. In C. Everston & C. Weinstein (Eds.), *Handbook of classroom management: Research, practice and contemporary issues* (pp. 181–219). Mahwah, NJ: Lawrence Erlbaum Associates.

Zuckerman, M., DePaulo, B., & Rosenthal, R. (1986). Humans as deceivers and lie detectors. In P. Blanck, R. Buck & R. Rosenthal (Eds.), *Nonverbal communication in the clinical context* (pp. 13–35). University Park, PA: Pennsylvania State University Press.

Author Index

Subject Index